Northwestern University
STUDIES IN *Phenomenology & Existential Philosophy*

Reason and Evidence in Husserl's Phenomenology

David Michael Levin

Reason and Evidence in Husserl's Phenomenology

Northwestern University Press
Evanston 1970

Open access edition funded by the National Endowment for the Humanities/Andrew W. Mellon Foundation Humanities Open Book Program.

David Michael Levin. Reason and Evidence in Husserl's Phenomenology. Evanston, Ill.: Northwestern University Press, 1970.

ISBN 978-0-8101-0298-9 (cloth)
ISBN 978-0-8101-3850-6 (paper)
ISBN 978-0-8101-3851-3 (ebook)

Manufactured in the United States of America

Original edition LCCN 75-99739

To My Mother and Father

Contents

List of Abbreviations

CM	Husserl, *Cartesian Meditations,* trans. Cairns. Page references in parentheses refer to German edition, *Cartesianische Meditationen.*
EP	Husserl, *Erste Philosophie*
EU	Husserl, *Erfahrung und Urteil*
FHCC	Sokolowski, *The Formation of Husserl's Concept of Constitution*
Ideas	Husserl, *Ideas: General Introduction to Pure Phenomenology,* trans. Gibson. Page references in parentheses refer to German edition, *Ideen.*
Ideen	Husserl, *Ideen zu einer reinen Phänomenologie und phänomenologische Philosophie,* ed. Biemel
Idées	Husserl, *Idées directrices pour une phénoménologie,* trans. Ricoeur
Krisis	Husserl, *Die Krisis der europäischen Wissenschaften und die transzendentale Phänomenologie,* ed. Biemel
Logik	Husserl, *Formale und transzendentale Logik*
LU	Husserl, *Logische Untersuchungen*
PP	Merleau-Ponty, *Phenomenology of Perception*
SH	Bachelard, *A Study of Husserl's* Formal and Transcendental Logic, trans. Embree
VPZ	Husserl, *Vorlesung zur Phänomenologie des inneren Zeitbewusstseins,* ed. Heidegger
WIZ	Brand, *Welt, Ich und Zeit*

Acknowledgments

My deepest gratitude goes to Mr. Allen Merrill, rare *philosophe,* for without his constant guidance and his searching, profoundly lucid mind this book certainly would never have come into being. And to his wife, Elizabeth Merrill, I likewise owe many thanks: her patience, her encouragement, and above all her faith in my project were helpful beyond measure. I also wish to thank Professors Robert Cumming and Charles Parsons, whose valuable criticisms of earlier drafts of this work have contributed significantly to its clarity as well as its philosophical merit. Finally, I would like to recall more than a decade of conversations with Michael Slote. Out of our interminable dialogue many of the fundamental positions behind the arguments in this book first emerged and took shape. Ultimately, of course, the views which I have developed rest squarely on my shoulders, and I willingly take responsibility for both their meaning and their soundness.

D. M. L.

Preface

The Greeks of antiquity believed that philosophy begins with a sense of wonder. And, just as firmly, they thought that, while it should also eventuate in wonder, the principal aim and consummatory value of philosophical reflection must be the decisive reign of reason. Thus, their world, or rather their knowledge of the world, whose inherent but concealed rationality it was the unquestioned task of philosophy to decipher, became for them the source of a profound challenge: through purely philosophical method, to disclose the evidence of reason in the foundation of all knowledge.

From its inception to the contemporary moment, systematic thought in philosophy has been pervasively shaped by the endeavor to provide knowledge with an unbreachable and enduring foundation. As a matter of fact, the intransigent search for absolute certainty has often defined theories of knowledge which, in other respects, were significantly dissimilar. For the common assumption was that nothing short of an indubitable form of knowledge could serve as such a foundation.

Philosophers have differed as to what the best candidate for certain knowledge is, or should be. They have proposed, for example, mathematical axioms (Pythagoras), revelation (St. Augustine), faith (the medieval German mystics), the proposition expressed in a special mental act (Descartes), logic (Leibniz), "protocol statements" (Carnap), "sense data" (Russell and Ayer), and "terminating judgments" (C. I. Lewis). But, for the most part, they have been in agreement that knowledge must have a foundation of some sort if skepticism is to be refuted; and it would seem that, with the exception of theist philosophers who wish to ground knowledge in faith or revelation, they were committed to the view that the foundation is altogether "of a piece" with the fund of knowledge to be given a foundation, even though it must be a very special kind of knowledge. In other words, they assumed, one and all, that the foundation is something that must, ultimately, be articulated in the form of propositions capable, in principle, of clear location *within* the structure of our knowledge.

With phenomenology, Edmund Husserl undoubtedly inaugurated a novel way of philosophizing. But how are we to understand his firm claim to radicality? Here we must consider what that meaning of "radicality" is which Husserlian phenomenology exhibits, either explicitly or implicitly. For example, Husserlian phenomenology is not, after all, radical in the sense that, abandoning the traditional ideal of reason, it denies the very endeavor to give knowledge some kind of absolute and indubitable foundation; nor is it radical in the sense that it *unerringly* sought for a foundation "outside" the proper category of knowledge itself. The subsequent phenomenologies of Sartre and Merleau-Ponty are, in these respects, more radical enterprises, inasmuch as knowledge is shown to be grounded "outside" itself, in the (philosophically prior) *lived* (simply experienced) acts of intentional meaning, whence our knowledge is constituted.

Husserl conceived phenomenology to be the first and the only genuine philosophy, the first and only rigorous science, and this precisely because it can actually bring to evidence the absolute foundation for which philosophers, over the centuries, have been searching. It is in this context that Husserl announced the authentically radical meaning of phenomenology as he construed it: he took the Cartesian method of doubt to its extreme limit, namely, beyond the merely psychological and empirical *ego cogitans* with which Descartes is satisfied, and he performed the very different operation of doubt which he designates the "phenomenological reduction." It is this process of reduction which ultimately "recovers" the transcendental ego as the only absolutely certain, indubitable evidence—suitable as the foundation for knowledge.

The ensuing study proposes, therefore, to examine Husserl's concept of necessary, a priori, and absolutely certain, indubitable evidence (which he calls "apodictic"), and, as fundamentally related to it, his concept of complete, or perfect, evidence (which he terms "adequate"). Thus, in effect, we are going to investigate the nature and merits, in Husserl's phenomenology, of the *ideal of the evidence of reason.*

In the Introduction, we shall consider some of the more general relevant features of his phenomenology, in the hope that the central significance of our specially delimited investigations for phenomenology as a whole may be better understood. The larger perspective, within which Husserl's special theory of adequate and apodictic evidence takes shape and to which it is always of necessity committed, helps to disclose whatever consistency and tenability his theory, as such, exhibits. Furthermore, if we hope to discern the genesis of this theory, as well as provide an explanation for such development, then we must ultimately establish its meaning *in relation to* the rest of his phenomenological system.

The exposition of this larger perspective, to which the Introduction is devoted, concerns the broad significance of phenomenological philosophy, as "first science," for an understanding of the common man's conceptions about the world and of the way in which the diverse special (empirical) sciences have developed; the general goals and norms of this philosophy; the meaning of Husserl's particular idea of rationality as a genuine philosophic norm; and finally, the theoretically central concepts of intentionality, immanence, transcendence, objectivity, and constitution.

Following the introductory exposition, then, we shall proceed to an examination in detail of Husserl's theory of evidence, focusing on the "rational" concepts of adequacy and apodicticity. Our examination will advance chronologically through the relevant primary works of Husserl. Thus, a separate chapter will be devoted to each of these works: *Logische Untersuchungen; Ideas regarding a Pure Phenomenology and Phenomenological Philosophy; Erste Philosophie; Formale und transzendentale Logik;* and *Cartesian Meditations.*

In a final chapter, we shall analyze Husserl's very important theory of ideation (eidetic reduction and intuition). This separate treatment would seem justified not only because it raises special problems, but also for the two fundamental reasons that phenomenology, as he defines it, is and must be eidetic research; and he contends that it is in the domain of phenomenological "essence" that adequate and apodictic evidence is chiefly to be found.

Let us distinguish, now, (1) a criticism of the "internal" logic of Husserl's concepts of adequacy and apodicticity, and (2) a criticism of the logic of their relations to his phenomenology as a whole. Then, under the designation of internal criticism, we submit that our investigations are intended to provide a satisfactory defense for the view that Husserl's theory of adequate and apodictic evidence, in itself and quite apart from its function in and consistency with his phenomenology as a whole, is plagued by confusions, incongruities, and other difficulties which, at the very least, seriously limit its scope and imperil its plausibility.

To be precise, we shall demonstrate that the most serious internal problem is that he does not have just one, clearly defined, simple concept of apodicticity (and, correlatively, of perfect adequation). Sometimes, when apodictic evidence is viewed more as the consummated act of insight, it is dignified with the property of finality and associated with the perfect satisfaction of inquiry; but at other times, when it is viewed more as the guiding focus or goal of a process of inquiry, the finality and irrevocability of its achievement is subordinated—without, however, being entirely forsaken—to its functioning in an infinite, interminable, continuous system of evidence.

In this regard, it is contended that it is just the *first* version of the principle of apodicticity which Husserl advocates most consistently, although the second, which appears only in the work of Husserl's philosophical maturity, assumes greater weight than the first, when judged in the context of his growing concern with, for example, the historicity of consciousness, the infinite horizons of evidence, and critique through genetic constitution. *Our criticisms of adequacy and apodicticity are directed only against the "strong" first version.*

Furthermore, we should like to discover whether these concepts went through a genuine evolution (as Husserl seems to have thought); and if such is the case, to establish the exact nature and degree of this evolution, insofar as this is feasible.

If we adopt a straightforwardly chronological approach to Husserl's theory of evidence, it should be possible to exhibit, in the clearest and simplest way, whatever degree of evolution there may be and to suggest some underlying reasons for those changes. We must recognize, here, that Husserl himself never submitted these two concepts to any comprehensive analysis of their genesis and development. One can at best only surmise, then, how he came by them, and to what extent their centrality in his phenomenology reveals their significance for his pre-phenomenological thinking, primarily determined, one may judge, by models of systems in mathematics and geometry. However, it does seem reasonable to assume that, in his mind, these concepts did evolve through several clearly discernible stages. More precisely, he seems to recognize a pre-phenomenological stage (found in the naive theory of the *Logische Untersuchungen*); the first truly phenomenological stage (elaborated in the *Ideas*); a stage of greater clarity and conceptual determination (found in *Erste Philosophie*); and finally, the most mature stage (established in the *Cartesian Meditations*), according to which the conceptual explication advanced in *Erste Philosophie* is denied, explicitly and beyond question. Husserl gives no indication that he recognizes any evolution beyond that in the *Meditations*. And it does indeed seem that, however innovating and significant the *Krisis* and his other very late works may be, they do not suggest any new conceptual approaches to the concept of apodictic evidence.

Our studies attempt to trace and clarify, in a manner at once more explicit and more intensive than that which characterizes Husserl's own statements, the pattern of this evolution in theory. It is submitted that we have discovered, first, a considerably less significant transition from the pre-phenomenological to the genuinely phenomenological stage than Husserl is wont to suppose; and second, an erroneous belief that the conceptual formulations of the *Meditations* constitute a fundamental revision of the earlier formulations belonging to *Erste Philosophie*. On the other hand, there would seem to be a significant reformulation in the *Formale und transzendentale Logik*, to which, most curiously, Husserl gives no special attention. So we shall propose an explanation for his treatment.

At the same time that we evaluate the purported evolution of the concepts of adequacy and apodicticity themselves, we shall also exhibit and measure the development of these concepts in relation to Husserl's phenomenology as a whole (our second kind of criticism). It should be observed that our criticism in this regard is advanced *within* the framework of Husserlian phenomenology, as we interpret it. But, to anticipate some possible confusion, we want now to observe that the point of departure for our analysis is Husserl's most mature phenomenology; and, too, that we want to comprehend directions of thought, intimations, which in fact were not clearly established by Husserl, even in his last published works. Naturally, though, our criticisms are intended to satisfy the minimum condition that they should at least be consistent with some important tendency in Husserl's own investigations.

The limits which define the project of this study make it necessary for our critique of adequacy and apodicticity, in their relation to his phenomenology as a whole, to *presuppose*, without demonstration, some sense of the way in which his philosophy developed. That is to say, we shall not attempt to argue conclusively that "apodicticity" evolved at a slower and more ambiguous pace than did other aspects of his phenomenology—for example, the concepts of constitution and objectivity (i.e., transcendence). However, we want to provide some corroboration for this hypothesis, inasmuch as we can suggest respects in which his concept of apodictic evidence, even at its most developed stage of evolution, is more subversive to what we take to be his mature phenomenology than it is to the earlier.

In other words, it should become apparent that, however much the concept of apodicticity (and, correlatively, therefore, adequate evidence) may have evolved in the course of Husserl's philosophical labors, it really suffered but a fragmentary and abortive development in relation to the rest of his phenomenology. Consequently, even the most prominent version of apodicticity defended and utilized in his most mature works not only is fraught with perplexing internal irregularities and problems, but seriously conflicts with the full-fledged phenomenological theory of genetic constitution, as well as with the associated historical and teleological dimensions which he eventually discovered in the life of consciousness—dimensions absolutely essential to the norm of rationality (that is, the evidence of Reason) professed in his late writings (for example, in the *Krisis*).

Therefore, we shall attempt to show that, *if* one should want to accept as both significant and valuable certain other very compelling and fundamental phenomenological doctrines, especially those comprising his most advanced philosophical thought, and centered around his theory of the genetic constitution of transcendent objectivity, *then* one ultimately must concede that apodicticity, even in its most mature formulation, is still in contradiction to the more "evolved" concepts of his phenomenology, for example, the historicity of the phenomenological ego and the genetic, teleological legitimation of phenomenological experience (evidence) in general. And it is a concept hostile to the general spirit of his more mature writings, in which he gives free reign to his phenomenological dreams and aspirations, his motivating *Weltanschauung*. Such contradiction, we affirm, would constitute a fundamental criticism of apodicticity and adequacy as *plausible and legitimate* norms for Husserlian phenomenology.

Husserl originally believed that it was the special office of philosophy to provide an absolute foundation for all knowledge. To this end, he sought an indubitable first principle of rational evidence, awaiting possession once and for all as our eternal property. Levinas quite appropriately observed that "philosophy appears to be, in this conception, as independent of the historical situation of man as the theory attempting to consider everything *sub specie aeternitatis*."[1] It could be said, therefore, that this absolutized norm of rationality, Husserl's commitment to this conception of philosophy, logically entails commitment to something like the principle of apodicticity. Thus, his original convictions about the function of philosophy, and the necessity for an absolute evidence of reason, explain his ambition to discover apodicticity, whatever the sacrifice. Indeed, they go far to explain the unstable prominence of apodicticity at the very heart of his phenomenological programme.

It should become clear that his theory of rational evidence, bringing him much closer than he would ever have suspected to the idealistic rationalism of Descartes and the curiously empiricistic rationalism of David Hume, encounters the very same and regrettably familiar objections which these latter two philosophers, as well as all those of like persuasion, have had to face. And one might immediately think, here, of the logical, atomistic "constructionism" which so tempted the young Russell, Carnap, Goodman, Ayer, and the Wittgenstein who composed the *Tractatus Logico-Philosophicus*. For a devoted phenomenologist, such affinities should indeed bring great dismay.

On the other hand, there is also a very different philosophical norm, toward which Husserl's mature thinking was gradually evolving. But this norm is most consistent with the overthrow of his principle of apodicticity in favor of a norm that encourages an open process of evidential discovery and critique (genuinely phenomenological grounding). Rationality, with its roots deep in the *Lebenswelt*, came to mean, for Husserl, an unflagging devo-

1. Emmanual Levinas, *La Théorie de l'intuition dans la phénoménologie de Husserl* (Paris: Alcan, 1930), p. 220.

tion to the "absolute" of endless inquiry itself. In the philosophic life whose vocation is the cause of Reason, the telic and the historical, recognized to be further dimensions of rationality, gradually assumed more importance than the establishment of absolute truth. Husserl's view of philosophy as the guardian of a devotion to truth and knowledge, can be said with justice really to have evolved: no longer outside history, outside the determination of time and situation, as if it were an absolute and total vision, philosophy was finally understood to be preserved and maturing through the difficult dialogue of the inheritance, verification, and transmission of knowledge which takes place within the infinite community of thinkers. In the context of such a philosophy, expressed, for example, in the *Formale und transzendentale Logik* and the *Krisis,* the affirmation of an apodictic and adequate, thus totally "rational" evidence, is clearly out of place.

In the Preface to the second edition of the *Critique of Pure Reason*, Immanuel Kant observes that the method of critique

> is opposed only to *dogmatism,* that is, to the presumption that it is possible to make progress with pure knowledge, according to principles, from concepts alone . . . as reason has long been in the habit of doing; and that it is possible to do this without having first investigated in what way and by what right reason has come into possession of these concepts. Dogmatism is thus the dogmatic procedure of pure reason, *without previous criticism of its own powers.*[2]

Kant is anxious to provide a genuinely rational foundation for the sublime aspirations of *metaphysics*, the flower and essence of reason. For too long, he believes, metaphysics has been without such a foundation; thus, it has been illegitimate, dogmatic, and merely speculative. So the endeavor to justify metaphysics

> is a call to reason to undertake anew the most difficult of all its tasks, namely, that of self-knowledge, and to institute a tribunal which will assure to reason its lawful claims, and dismiss all groundless pretensions. . . . This tribunal is no other than the *critique of pure reason.*[3]

2. Immanuel Kant, *Critique of Pure Reason* (New York: St. Martin's Press, 1956).

3. *Ibid.*, preface to the first edition.

Kant, of course, sought to assure the authority of reason "in accordance with its own eternal and unalterable laws"; he firmly believed that the critique of reason could be deemed successful only if it were to achieve an "*apodictic* (philosophical) certainty," [4] that is, both necessity and completeness, or universality.

It is just such a critique that we consider absolutely essential, with regard to Husserl's commitment to apodicticity. Apodictic evidence is at once a guiding methodological presupposition and an evidential (and thus ontological) outcome of his investigations. Despite his efforts at methodological rigor, his many scruples, and his systematic asceticism, Husserl in fact molds his phenomenology around the ideal of an apodictic, purely rational evidence, without ever submitting it to sufficiently rigorous examination. It therefore functions, within the structure of his phenomenological researches, in a speculative and dogmatic way. Accordingly, whereas both Kant and Husserl presuppose without critique a certain evidential paradigm of reason, we are concerned precisely with the question of critique. The radical nature of Husserlian phenomenology will not be established until there has been a thoroughgoing critique of phenomenological reason. The conclusion of our critique is that the ideal of apodicticity can never be anything but an illegitimate and, indeed, subversive pretension for the phenomenological enterprise.

4. *Ibid.*, italics added.

Reason and Evidence in Husserl's Phenomenology

1 / Introduction

[1] The Three Stages of Understanding: The Naive, the Scientific, and the Phenomenological

Phenomenology asserts itself to be the first of the sciences or, more generally speaking, the first in the order of knowledge, in that it is the ground for all the particular sciences, for all the individual domains of knowledge. Moreover, it provides a foundation for those correct everyday beliefs which the "man in the street" is wont to accept. These beliefs are held, as Husserl expresses it, in the "naive" or "natural attitude."

Phenomenology shows us how it is that, just as the natural and the exact, mathematical sciences systematize and, in their own way, provide a rational basis for correct but naive commonsense beliefs, so phenomenology in turn discloses the rational insufficiency and incompleteness which characterize even the most satisfying of sciences; and it accordingly uncovers the genuine foundation for these sciences which heretofore were regarded as ultimate. The phenomenological world is discovered to be the ground for the everyday world and the world of science in that it is epistemically prior and absolute, both in the sense of being nonrelative and in the sense of being indubitable.

Originally, we who philosophize are, like the ordinary man, simply immersed in the world. We have activities we are anxious to pursue, duties and tasks to perform, projects we are engaged in actualizing. We *live* our belief in the reality of the (natural) world and other persons in every mode of action and utterance, without making this belief the special theme of philosophical reflection. If one regards doubt, strictly speaking, as either a stage in or the outcome of a reflective, thematic posture (what Husserl describes as the process of "modalization"), then one should say that this simple, lived belief in the existence of the world is prior to doubt, and in that unique sense, absolutely certain, that is, neither dubitable nor indubitable. This is what Husserl calls the "primordial and unmodified original mode of certain validity." [1]

The lived world, lived in an awareness of its givenness prior to all thematization (i.e., positing, predicative activity), *can* of course be "rendered thematic in a rational fashion, as the ground of all our concerns and life-projects, among which the theoretical interests of the objective sciences form only a small, special group." [2] The ordinary man, we know, has occasion to reflect upon his experience only when he has reason to doubt, correct or modify his previous perceptions and beliefs in the light of subsequent ones and, in general, whenever perplexity and wonder inspire him to interrogate the world in which he otherwise dwells. It is in some such way that the sciences are born.

The serious endeavor to investigate nature in terms of a satisfying conceptual structure capable of both universal description and universal explanatory power, calls for the explicit adoption of a new perspective, that of the "positive" or "scientific attitude." In the natural attitude one lives with pragmatically justified standards of precision, confirmation, organization and clarity. But in the scientific climb from mere *doxa* to secure *epistēmē*, in other words, to a stage of greater theoretical objectivity, determinateness, and intelligibility, new and very different standards must be fixed and then given a systematic, critical, and reflective function. Man's natural propensity to understand, explain and evaluate his given world motivates him to transcend his naive and magical beliefs and find a scientific knowledge more conformable to his ideal of a rational universe.[3]

But there is, Husserl contends, a "movement" from within natural science itself (by which he means to include geometry, mathematics, *and psychology*) toward its transcendence, its fulfillment in a radically different *founding* science. For the propo-

1. *EU*, p. 110.
2. *Ibid.*, p. 64. Note further *Logik*, pp. 110–11; and *Krisis*, pp. 145, 157, and 459.
3. *Krisis*, Appendix II, pp. 357–59.

sitions of science, no matter how "concrete" and "particularized," are of necessity idealities and abstractions. In their employment, the exact methods of the natural sciences and mathematics suppose the world to be such that it is intrinsically capable of exact determination, articulation in precise and universal propositions, and exhaustive explication in terms of the conceptualizations of reflective consciousness.[4] What Husserl wishes to uncover, beneath this world illumined by natural science, is the primordial experience of the life-world, prior to these ideal scientific abstractions, and able therefore to serve as their foundation. Such experience admits no exact space, no exact objective time, and no objective causality; consequently, the methodic instruments of the natural sciences are altogether unsuitable for the explication of the genuine foundation of all knowledge.

Not until we understand that natural science covers the world with "a cloak of ideas," to introduce Husserl's felicitous expression,[5] can we recognize the necessity for phenomenological inquiry into the primordial origins in experience of the abstract, objectified world interpreted by science.[6] Ultimately, we are to see that, in traditional science, "the transcendental life and activity of experiencing, thinking, querying, and grounding consciousness remain subtly anonymous, unseen, unthematized, and hence even incomprehensible." [7]

Phenomenology does not intend to undermine the exact sciences; rather it grounds and illuminates them, exposing their presuppositions and settling the scope of their concepts. The scientific, objective world, fixed in its sedimented meanings, can only be grasped in its full "intelligibility" as that which emerges from the lived, original *meaning*-endowing performances of transcendental subjectivity.[8] It is this special dimension of sub-

4. *EU*, pp. 40–41.
5. *Ibid.*, p. 46.
6. This explains why Husserl refers to Galileo as "both a discovering and a concealing genius." Galileo discovered laws of nature which do indeed make the natural world comprehensible, to a certain degree; but at the same time these laws themselves, just because they satisfy so well our primary and immediate (practical) concerns, tend to conceal the meaning of consciousness, the systematic exploration of which can alone, he thinks, make the scientific explanation fully "rational." See *Krisis*, p. 53.
7. *EP*, II, 26–27.
8. Consider the *Krisis*, pp. 49, 70, 130–33.

jectivity, disclosed through phenomenological method, that functions as intentional source of our diverse structures of meaning, the most abstract of which is the world of science.

Paradoxically, then, the very success and advancement of natural science reveals its inadequacy, when we subject it to radical reflection; but also, at the same time, it happily indicates the way to overcome this insufficiency. For there is, so to speak, a *conatus*,[9] an underlying *telos* within science which inclines it toward fulfillment (i.e., legitimation and clarification) in a science of still higher dignity: this science is phenomenology.

Even the natural sciences, we discover, are naive insofar as they have not been grounded phenomenologically, insofar as they have not been subject to a rigorous critique. At first we must see that the scientific, positive attitude surpasses the common man's attitude: it constructs a fruitful descriptive-explanatory theory and accepts its propositions in a strictly hypothetical way, always engaged in systematic criticism of its "possessions" in knowledge. But then we learn that this critique in science must itself in turn become the object of a critique, more radical in its aim. In fine, unless we assent to an infinite regress, we recognize that "the scientist himself is brought to the idea of a perfect evidence, or of an evidence one can make perfect gradually and systematically." [10]

If natural science may be deemed a secondary critique—a thematic sphere in which everyday beliefs are put to the test and developed into verifiable codifications—then phenomenology may be called the critique of natural science. Its special theme is "the constituting subjectivity 'behind' every domain and every scientific treatment of these domains." [11] We have here advanced from a merely "positive" critique of knowledge to the authentic critique of reason, in other words, to the transcendental critique of knowledge. The demand for a critique of this kind is implicit, Husserl argues, in the very attempt to shape science into a rationally satisfying system.[12] And the scientific goal of system is not to be won without a transcendental grounding, otherwise our acquired knowledge is left to hang in mid air.[13] Whereas:

9. In *EP*, II, p. 336, Husserl even uses the phrase "researching Eros," thus stressing the affective, voluntaristic dimension.
10. *Logik*, pp. 110–11.
11. *Ibid.*, p. 152.
12. See *EP*, II, 337.
13. *Ibid.*, p. 472.

> Having reached the transcendental ego, one becomes aware that one is in a sphere of evidence behind which it is nonsense to want to question. By contrast, each usual appeal to evidence, insofar as further questioning back must be cut off arbitrarily, is theoretically no better than an appeal to an oracle in which God revealed himself. All natural evidences, those of the objective sciences, . . . belong to the realm of the self-evident, and have in fact their background of opacity (*Unverständlichkeit*). Every evidence has a problematic title, except for phenomenological evidence, which has clarified itself and demonstrated its ultimacy.[14]

Thus, by a methodic inner dialectic, the very aims as well as the achievements of positive natural science prepare the way for their "abandonment," only to be appropriated again, by a sort of delicate "archaeology," as the grounded outcome of the meaning-performances of consciousness.[15] Such appropriation is for the first time a truly legitimated possession, representing knowledge not in its "naive clarity," but instead in the "higher-level evidence of transcendental and primordial clarity."[16] As Husserl maintains in his introductory remarks to the *Logik:*

> In that way, modern science has abandoned the ideal of authentic science which influenced in such a lively manner all sciences since Plato's time; and in the practical attitude it has assumed, it has wholly abandoned the radicalism of its scientific self-responsibility. Its internal impulsive force is thus no longer constituted by this radicalism which, in itself, constantly poses the demand that no knowledge be admitted for which it is not possible to give an account in terms of primordially given first principles that are perfectly evident, principles of such a nature that it would make no sense to try to discover something behind them. The science which would actually be realized in this regard could only be very imperfect. But the essential point is that this radical obligation should direct a practical effort toward a corresponding perfection and that, as a result, logic would remain, but changed, now bearing an important function, namely, to investigate with an essential generality the possible roads which lead back to ultimate principles. . . . Nothing could be farther from this demand than a sort of purely technical achievement whose naïveté is in sharp contrast to the accomplishment of a radical self-imposition of norms derived from truly ultimate principles.[17]

14. *Krisis*, p. 192.
15. See *EP*, II, 29.
16. *Ibid.*, p. 30.
17. *Logik*, pp. 3–4.

Man's essential desire to understand his life and his world, the desire which first motivated him to engage in scientific inquiry, finally encounters frustration. The demands of reason, calling, Husserl believes, for a genuinely absolute, universal, and systematic science, cannot be fulfilled within the framework of natural science, although they are there efficacious and at least of germinal import. Science, it turns out, gives an illusory intelligibility and clarity when measured against the radical demands of reason. What, more precisely, is this norm of rationality which directs his phenomenology? And what is the nature of his commitment to it? The answers to these questions should contribute to the elucidation of the question: Why is a phenomenological science, grounded in apodicticity, *necessary* as the foundation for our knowledge?

Husserl's original commitment to rationality meant striving towards the most perfect conceivable self-consciousness: that epistemic state wherein consciousness comes to see that what it had accepted as being "other-than-consciousness" is not truly other: "Only if spirit returns to itself out of its naive outward-direction and remains with itself in its purity, can it suffice unto itself." [18] Such self-containedness is the height of rationality; no irrational surd remains as a disquieting reminder of the finitude and fallibility of reason. The process by which the "other being" is assimilated, totally enclosed within the evidential circle of consciousness, can be further defined as a process through which the reality of that other is authenticated (justified in evidence). Whatever is, is there to be grasped, ultimately, not only as an intentional theme of consciousness, but as an absolute, adequate, and apodictic evidence.

Reason, the essence of philosophical responsibility, is the mode of consciousness which "necessitates" (that is, uncovers the evidential necessity or apodicticity of) its objects. It is the faculty of supreme evidence and therefore, equivalently, the faculty wherein a critique of evidence is executed. Critique and self-understanding imply, moreover, a rigorous, never-ending questioning of all premises and presuppositions (including the axioms of logic) in our knowledge. The outcome of such endeavor is the disclosure of an "immediate knowledge," an "apodictic knowledge" of being.[19] The apodictic ground which phe-

18. *Krisis,* p. 345. Cf. further *Logik,* p. 241.
19. See *EP,* II, 472.

nomenological critique finally reaches is epistemically first, and expressed in terms of first principles, though it is last in being discovered, the outcome of radical reflection. It is epistemically primary because:

> If every experience were to presuppose others, and if none were apodictic, then it would seem that each experience would hang in the air. Thus there are experiences and therewith varieties of knowledge at the lowest level, called upon to bear the weight of the edifice of knowledge. Thus it appears as the first task to thematize this level and its corresponding reality: a first science of the first being.[20]

Husserl's point is that, if there were no such thing as apodicticity, then "all talk of a truth valid in itself and all striving for truth would have lost its sense."[21] Underlying the movement from natural science to phenomenology is the deliberate, explicit abandonment of "positive rationality," and a firm commitment to the norm of a radical "transcendental rationality."[22] To adopt such a norm is to recognize the possibility of winning apodictic, absolute, and adequate knowledge; it is furthermore to believe that such knowledge is a legitimate ideal or norm for philosophy, and that it is and must be capable of realization. Husserl's argument here is neither original in theory of knowledge nor especially satisfying.[23] Is it the case that there would be no knowledge at all unless some knowledge were apodictic? The foundation must indeed be rationally compelling. But must it be apodictic?

In Husserl's later writings, reason assumes, as he expresses it, a self-imposed responsibility to come to full consciousness, in other words, to ground itself. According to its essence, it confronts its own task of disclosing the meaning (rationality) of the universe, and thereby insuring that the world will be more conformable to the spiritual aspirations and well-being of the

20. *Ibid.*, p. 408.
21. *Ibid.*, p. 366.
22. *Ibid.*, p. 358.
23. Cf., for example, C. I. Lewis' argument for an absolutely certain evidence in *An Analysis of Knowledge and Valuation* (La Salle, Ill.: Open Court, 1958), p. 333. And see the counterposition of William James, in his preface to *The Meaning of Truth*, in *Pragmatism and Four Essays from The Meaning of Truth* (New York: Meridian Books, 1958), p. 199.

human community.[24] Phenomenology, the only rigorous (apodictic) science, offers itself as the one and only road to freedom, to spiritual and even social autonomy. For autonomy is at once the necessary consequence of and the reward for willingness to bear ultimate philosophical responsibility. Rational man, as Husserl interprets him, bears "a responsibility for full and absolute truth," an essential motivation to live a life of optimum auto-critique.[25] It is this incessant will to exemplify Socrates' "examined life" that is to free man for a blessed life of self-fulfillment. This kind of existence is inconceivable so long as man is under the sway of prejudice and presuppositions, and does not understand the fundamental nature of his surrounding world from the standpoint of absolute consciousness. Inasmuch as this responsibility is a demand for all time, and inasmuch as it pertains to the human community as a whole, the philosopher's achievements belong to this infinite historical community of rational beings. The philosopher neither meditates *de novo*, spurning the wisdom of the ages, nor bequeathes to posterity an impregnable, unimpeachable corpus of knowledge that will not tolerate endless examination. The truth acquired by the philosopher "is for him not just an inherited possession, but in fact a stage for the attainment of new truth." [26] Knowledge is essentially, we might say, in perpetual "becoming" (*ein wesenhaftes Werden*).[27] The impossibility of omniscience accords man the opportunity to exhibit, with as much eloquence as he is capable of, his undying dedication to the community-*forming* ideals of *philosophia* and of a *sapientia universalis*.

[2] The Evidence of Intentional Objects Transcendent to Consciousness, and the Constitution of these Objects

Husserl declares in the *Krisis:*

> *It is not a question of assuring objectivity, but of understanding it.* One must finally see that no objective science, however exact it

24. See *EP*, I, pp. 9–10 and 34; II, 216 and 249; *Logik*, pp. 4–5; and finally, the *K*, pp. 275 and 429.
25. *EP*, II, 197.
26. *Ibid.*, p. 204.
27. W. Biemel, "Die entscheidenden Phasen der Entfaltung von Husserls Philosophie," *Zeitschrift für philosophische Forschung*, XIII (1959), 200.

may be, seriously clarifies anything or ever could clarify anything. To deduce is not to elucidate. . . . Everything objective stands under the demand of full intelligibility. Knowledge about nature, of a scientific sort, thus gives no genuinely clarifying or ultimate knowledge, for in general, it does not investigate nature in its absolute connection. . . . thus it never arrives thematically at its being.[28]

In what, then, does this understanding consist? Husserl's phenomenology begins with the insight that whatever there is, is only as accessible to consciousness.[29] He proclaims the *primacy* of consciousness over the "things" which populate that world (our familiar world!) which *is* for consciousness: a primacy of *being* and a primacy of *meaning*.[30] It is this primacy which gives consciousness title to claim it must be the starting point and the ground of all real understanding. Whatever there is, is only as noematic correlate of intentional acts of consciousness. Objectivity can be understood only in terms of the subjectivity of consciousness. But equally, subjectivity can be clarified only in terms of objectivity; for in a sense, consciousness is primarily what it is by virtue of its involvement with objectivity (that is, either the so-called "real" objects of the natural world or the "ideal" objects of our mental activity, for example, mathematical entities, pains, and concepts in general). Consciousness is always, as the phenomenologist never wearies of incanting, a "consciousness of. . . ."

It is only necessary now to unpack and explore these propositions, to discern in them all the rudimentary phenomenological concepts. Let us begin with the fact that consciousness is involved with objects. The life, the experience, and hence, too, the history of consciousness is consumed in a streaming intentional activity, wherein objects are "given" to and "grasped" by consciousness. "Intentionality" describes consciousness in its active grasp of its objectivations. These acts of intentionality are acts of "meaning." The directed, positing experience of objectivations is what Husserl defines as "evidence":

Evidence signifies . . . the intentional achievement (*Leistung*) *of the giving of things themselves.* To speak more precisely, evidence

28. *Ibid.*, p. 193.
29. This is properly called the principle of intentionality.
30. See *Ideas*, § 55.

> is the general form par excellence of "intentionality," of the 'consciousness of something.'[31]

Again:

> . . . *a life of consciousness . . . cannot exist without evidence;* and moreover, this life . . . [is] a consciousness related to objectivity.[32]

Of course, it is only after a phenomenological and, eventually, an eidetic analysis of consciousness that the interweaving of the concepts of intentionality, evidence, and objectivity is comprehensible. To begin with:

> *Intentionality in general,* the lived consciousness of anything whatever, and *evidence, the intentionality of the giving of things (Sachverhalte) themselves,* are *concepts which,* by their very essence, are intimately related.[33]

A study of the life of consciousness must be a phenomenological study of the diverse modes of evidence through which consciousness (as "noesis") constitutes intentions with an *objectivated* sense (the "noema"), and strives toward the most perfect articulation of this activity through intensified intuitive reflection. Evidence, then, as Husserl recognized, is the central problem of phenomenology.[34]

Thus far we have derived the concept of evidence from the concept of intentionality. But what exactly is evidence, aside from its intentional character? In its most fundamental (primordial) sense—that is to say, as distinguished from other, more refined senses which satisfy the fully developed theoretical structure of phenomenology, such as pertain, for example, to apodictic insight—it can be said that evidence is intuition, or the giving of the state-of-affairs (the "fact," the "thing") itself. It is that form of consciousness

> in which the object of consciousness is present to it in the mode of "the grasped itself," "seen itself"; and consciousness is related to the object in the mode of being-present-to-this object-itself.[35]

31. *Logik,* p. 141.
32. *Ibid.,* p. 255.
33. *Ibid.,* p. 143.
34. *Ibid.,* p. 145. Cf. also *Ideas* I, §§ 19, 24, and 136.
35. *Logik,* pp. 185–86, also 141.

This notion defines primordial consciousness, the lowest stage in a hierarchy of evidences, at which there is a living fulfillment in intuitive presence of the intentional act, a genuine *seeing* of an "agreement between the actual sense of the expression and the self-given content." [36]

The cornerstone of Husserlian phenomenology is his principle of pure evidence: nothing will be recognized, whatever its mode of being, unless it is grasped exactly as it was meant, and "is itself directly before our eyes as being thus and so." [37] Husserl announces the guiding norm for phenomenological science when he states that "self-giving should be our measure, and its absolute maximum that according to which we test all our judgments, all our existential meanings (*Seinsmeinungen*)." [38]

That the phenomenological reduction—describable in a most general way as "reducing" objects to the pure evidence consciousness has (or can have) of them—is not only possible but in fact requisite, becomes clear, according to Husserl, once it is recognized that:

> *The category of objectivity and the category of evidence are coordinates. For each fundamental species of objectivity*—as intentional unities which must be maintained in an intentional synthesis, and finally for each fundamental species of possible *"experiential"* unity—*there is a suitable fundamental species of experience, or evidence.*[39]

In other words, every kind of object will have its own appropriate kind of evidence, or self-giving. Objects in general, as meanings, cannot be understood or justified as knowledge without an analysis of their evidence in and for consciousness.

The phenomenological connection between objectivity and evidence is completed by the concepts of "reality" and "transcendence," and their respective correlative pairings, "ideality" and "immanence."

In the natural attitude (the starting point for philosophical analysis and clarification), and prior to the execution of phenomenological reduction, "reality" simply designates whatever is typically regarded as belonging to the spatio-temporal world

36. *LU*, I, 190–91.
37. *EP*, II, 32; cf. also *Ideas* I, § 24.
38. *EP*, II, 33; cf. further *CM*, p. 13 (pp. 53–54).
39. *Logik*, p. 144. Cf. Eugen Fink, "Das Problem der Phänomenologie Edmund Husserls," *Revue internationale de philosophie*, I (1939), 252.

"outside" and "independent" of consciousness. But through the reduction, which is the first significant step in phenomenology, "reality" comes to designate *whatever is given the phenomenological meaning* (that is, a meaning *for* consciousness), "existent in spatio-temporal dimensions." [40] The separation of reality (in the sense of the natural attitude) from consciousness makes the phenomenological reduction possible; and this process of reduction, in turn, makes it possible to consider reality purely as meaning, purely as phenomenon. Correlatively, the concept of "ideality," originally used, in the sense of the natural attitude, simply to designate whatever is conceptual in its ontological status,[41] denotes in its new philosophical employment *whatever is given the phenomenological meaning*, "existent and enduring, as an identity, through a temporal unity only." [42]

However, in the *Ideas* and later works, Husserl developed another and more profoundly phenomenological employment for these two correlative concepts. Indeed, the increasing prominence of these other senses is a valuable clue to the step-by-step refinement and maturation of Husserl's phenomenological method in general. Consider, on the one hand, his argument for the existence (reality) of essences (which, of course, are not spatio-temporal objects),[43] and, on the other hand, his remarks about the ideality even of "worldly" (i.e., spatio-temporal) things, once they are considered from the phenomenological standpoint.[44] Thus, Husserl says:

> Accordingly there is a certain *ideality* implied in the sense of any object whatsoever grasped by experience, even a physical object . . . as opposed to the multiple "psychic" processes, *separated* by an individuation whose temporality is immanent. . . . *It is the general ideality of all types* of objectivities, *intentional unities* as opposed to the *multiplicities* which constitute them.[45]

Here, at this deeper stage of analysis, it would seem that Husserl has made "reality" and "ideality" equivalent in respect of their

40. See Husserl's Preface to the English edition of *Ideas* I for the pre-phenomenological sense, and § 3 for the genuine phenomenological sense.
41. See § 22 of Husserl's *Ideas* I.
42. Consider § 28 of *Ideas* I.
43. *Ibid.*, §§ 22, 55, and 135.
44. *Ibid.*, Introduction.
45. *Logik*, p. 148. Also see pp. 36 and 119.

extension. They are *intensionally* different, however, in that they serve to introduce two altogether distinct phenomenological points. "Reality" in this sense calls attention to the *ontological status* of *whatever* has become the objectivated and securely evidenced concern of consciousness, regardless of whether it be an ideality or a reality in the original phenomenological sense. To be sure, spatio-temporal dimensions belong to and define a special favored class of reality (objectivity), namely, that class of objects to which consciousness has accorded the sense, "existent out there in the 'external' world." Nevertheless, it is not spatio-temporality as such which defines the domain of reality, but rather the fact of being an intentional *objectivation* with an identity through time, abidingly available for a multiplicity of noetic postures. And "ideality," in this context, designates the *same* class of realities (i.e., not only the objectivations with a merely temporal identity and unity, but also those with a spatio-temporal identity and unity), though it attends instead to the crucial fact that they are, one and all, *constituted in a temporal synthesis* as objectivities for a living, streaming consciousness. "Reality" emphasizes *securely evidenced objective availability,* whereas "ideality" points out the fact of *temporal constitution,* and thus sheds light on the conditions for the possibility of such objective availability. In this manner, then, "reality" and "ideality" become concepts which guide us into the very heart of transcendental phenomenology.

In the phenomenological reduction, Husserl also introduces the concepts of "transcendence" and "immanence." These, of course, are strictly phenomenological concepts. Because Husserl introduces them within the framework of phenomenological method, he is able to give them more precision and greater methodological efficacy, greater explanatory power, than the concepts of "reality" and "ideality." Indeed, at a certain stage of analysis, they tend to take over the burden of the reality/ideality schema, and they carry his phenomenological investigations into the deepest regions of transcendental clarification.

At first, however, "transcendence" and "immanence" merely serve to capture the rudimentary, though essential, distinction between consciousness and reality, mapping it onto the domain recovered through phenomenological reduction. "Transcendence" describes the spatio-temporal world, the "real" world of persons and things, from the standpoint of their being *other than and "outside"* the stream of consciousness.[46] The fact of spatial profiles, at this stage of clarification, is taken to be the essential characteristic of that which is transcendent. But the effectuation of the phenomenological reduction altogether *modifies* this fact by considering it as a *meaning*, or *sense*, deposited through the functioning of consciousness. The actual execution of the reduction *shows* that "between consciousness and reality there yawns a true abyss of sense." [47]

"Immanence," in its corresponding phenomenological employment, signifies the nature of whatever objects have been reduced, in respect of their sense, to the transcendental sphere uncovered through phenomenological reduction. Consciousness and its deposited meanings are immanent. Intentional acts directed towards objects *intended* with the *sense* that they belong to the *same* stream of consciousness as the acts which know them are acts of "immanent perception." [48] The objects of such acts—for example, pains and the essences of fear and volition—are "immanent objects." The field of immanence is essentially nonspatial. Immanent objects do not exhibit spatial profiles.[49] In fact, such objects are distinguished from transcendent objects in that they are not at all adumbrational; they are given in an absolute unity with their correlative intentional acts.

The depth of phenomenological clarification which Husserl achieves through the concepts of "transcendence" and "immanence," construed in the sense we have just explicated, is unfortunately far from satisfactory. Unquestionably, it guides us right into the field of phenomenological investigation; at the same time, however, it engenders some haunting and troubling problems. For example, if we suppose that the absence of spatial profiles could be a sufficient condition for immanence, then it would seem that we should have to consider mathematical entities and axioms as immanent objects, and in this respect no different from pains, fears, violitions, and acts of perception. Furthermore, since essences, as such, cannot be spatio-temporal in nature, it should seem puzzling to find that Husserl could have framed the notion of "transcendent essences," [50] unless this is to be construed simply as *an abbreviated description* of the

46. *Ideas* I, 121 (p. 96).
47. *Ibid.*, p. 138 (p. 117).
48. *Ibid.*, § 38.
49. *Ibid.*, §§ 42–44.
50. Consider *Ideas* I, § 60.

transcendent *reference* of certain essences (e.g., the essences "house," "book," and "garden"). If, on the other hand, the absence of such profiles could not be a sufficient condition for immanence, then we might plausibly wonder why it is that Husserl should consider even pains, fears, volitions, acts of perception, and the essences of these states of consciousness to be truly immanent, insofar as they are to be treated as objectivated through diverse intentional acts of consciousness. In sum, these and other important questions testify to the need for a deeper level of phenomenological clarification.

Now it turns out that Husserl did, in fact, push his investigations into the nature of transcendence and immanence much farther. The proof for this contention is that it is possible to discover another sense of "transcendence," which we shall hereafter call (in keeping with what we understand to be the spirit and orientation of Husserl's late phenomenology) the *broad and truly fundamental sense*. Husserl actually laid the groundwork for this sense, and thus for the extremely fruitful dimension of transcendental clarification which it allowed to appear, in works as early as the *Philosophie der Arithmetik* and the *Logische Untersuchungen;* [51] but he really began to work with (and in

51. Robert Sokolowski observes that, in the *Philosophie der Arithmetik,* Husserl argues that the objectivity of logical categories lies in the abiding possibility that "we can identify a given logical (or mathematical) form or entity as identically the same individual in a series of different occurrences" (*FHCC,* p. 19). Sokolowski continues: "If logical entities are dissolved into a stream of psychological events, there is nothing left to be constituted. The concept of constitution . . . does suppose that a subjective process produces a form or category which is no longer subjective, but in some way transcends the subjectivity which produces it." In other words: "Categorical objects do not have the same ontic status as things in the world, but they do have an objectivity that we must recognize and account for" (*ibid.,* p. 66).

In the *Logische Untersuchungen,* Husserl says that a meaning, "as identical, . . . is itself in turn an object in reference to various new meanings—all this exactly like other objects that are not meanings, such as horses, stones, psychic acts, etc. Only because the meaning is something identical, can it be treated as something identical" (II, pt. 1, 111–12. Cf. also *ibid.,* p. 77).

And in his *Vorlesungen zur Phänomenologie des inneren Zeitbewusstseins,* Husserl writes: "Immanent units are not known in their constitution in the same way as that which appears in transcendent appearance, or that which is perceived in transcendent perception" (p. 444). "On the other hand," he notes, "they still must have

terms of) it only in his later work, the *Formale und transzendentale Logik*.[52] The importance of this sense for our critique of Husserl's ideal of rational evidence lies in the fact that apodicticity is *not compatible* with a phenomenological framework in which this broad and fundamental sense of "transcendence" is fully and explicitly worked out.

To be sure, it is both feasible and important to differentiate and describe the *various types* (ontological "regions") of intentional objectivation. But the transcendental purport of this truly fundamental sense of "transcendence" is to show that all possible distinctions between types of objects must be *subordinate* to the phenomenologically crucial fact that they are, one and all, intentional objectivations, posited with an accessible identity through time.[53] An objectivation, as a pole of identity, unifies and supports a harmonious set of intentional experiences, and in that manner *transcends* (stands over against) the *multiplicity* of intentional acts through which it is given. In the *Logik*, therefore, we find Husserl admonishing: "If, however, we *separate immanent from transcendent objects*, that can only signify a *separation within* this larger concept of transcendence."[54] It

---

something in common." The fundamental similarity, of course, is that immanent objects are also constituted as identities through a manifold of intentional acts. In the constitution of immanent objects, there is a manifold of temporal profiles (phases); in our knowledge of material objects, there is a manifold of spatio-temporal appearances. Temporal extension gives immanent objects their individuality and unity; it also gives them objectivity and transcendence.

52. Consider the remark of Suzanne Bachelard, that "paradoxically, only when one fails to see the logical formations *detach themselves* from subjectivity with the sense of objects, does one fail to raise the truly subjective problems regarding them, the problems of their 'constitution' by a transcendental subjectivity" (*SH*, p. 202).

53. Robert Sokolowski implicitly acknowledges the fundamental transcendence even of Husserl's so-called "immanent objects," when he observes that "immanent objects *are constituted* in temporal phases which flow from the immediate present. On the other hand . . . the immediate present is not constituted in any way" (*FHCC*, p. 200, italics added). Constitution is the source of objective sense, and therefore of transcendence, in the broad and fundamental sense. Sokolowski makes it perfectly clear that he associates objective sense and the sense of "independence" with the characteristic of transcendence, and moreover, that he intends these descriptions to obtain for "logical" and "imaginary" objects as well as for "real" objects. See, for example, p. 203.

54. *Logik*, p. 148; cf. further *FHCC*, p. 170.

will be found that this sense of "transcendence" captures in full the purport of Husserl's final explication of the concepts of "reality" and "ideality," and thereby gives to them a fundamental *transcendental* function.

The transcendence disclosed at this deepest level of phenomenological explication is, therefore, a *transcendence in immanence,* a transcendence characteristic of all intentional objectivations explicated *within* the sphere of consciousness uncovered through the phenomenological reduction.[55] It is, in fact, altogether reasonable that Husserl should not have come to this understanding of transcendence until the time he worked intensely on the problems in the *Formale und transzendentale Logik.* For *the broad and fundamental sense of "transcendence" is really a cornerstone of his transcendental logic.* The thesis that objectivation, as such, entails transcendence is, in other words, a fundamental doctrine of transcendental logic.[56]

The transcendent nature of all intentional objects does not at all mean, however, that we cannot continue to speak, as Husserl certainly does, of "immanent objects." That is to say, there is still room for a meaningful distinction between immanent and transcendent objects (in the *less* fundamental sense of these concepts which we explicated earlier). The genetic constitution of the *former* is through acts of reflection which have focused on some temporal phase(s) of the *same* mental life (*Erlebnisstrom*) as the acts themselves; these "immanent objects" are states (phases) of consciousness intended (and experienced) as truly inherent, truly "present" components, belonging to the same mental life through whose intentive performances of discernment, identification, reiteration, and synthesis they first emerged. Yet, insofar as they are objectivated, they possess a "life" of their own; they are intended as transcendent-to-consciousness, as *unities* standing opposite the *manifold* of acts of reflection, abidingly available through the flow of time. Whereas the *latter* are constituted through acts of objectivation which

55. Not only are there different *stages* of reduction, as Lauer (among others) has pointed out; but there are also (at least three) different "ways" to reduction. See Iso Kern, "Die drei Wege zur transzendental-phänomenologischen Reduktion in der Philosophie Edmund Husserls," *Tijdschrift voor Philosophie,* XXIV (1962), 303–49.

56. Therefore, it may fairly be said that our refutation of apodicticity derives purely from a working out of the deepest implications of Husserl's *transcendental logic.*

have given them the sense of spatio-temporal existence; and they are meant as *not* truly belonging to the stream of consciousness which knows them. Pains, for example, are born in consciousness; flowers and stones are not. This fundamental sense of "transcendence" thus does not in any way abrogate the possibility of differentiating intentional objects *in respect of the nature of their genetic constitution.*[57] *Within* this framework of transcendence it still remains feasible to distinguish between immanent and transcendent objects; indeed, the significance of this distinction becomes truly clear for the first time.

It must also be observed, here, that the fundamental transcendence of immanent objects does *not* entail the existence of a *second stream* of consciousness, a curious "spectator" stream observing its objects *ab extra.* Rather, it merely indicates the *same* stream *in a different temporal phase* and *in a different modality* (namely, intentive and objectivating). To speak of the transcendence of immanent objects is to attend to the fact of a *passage* of time, the fact that consciousness is a streaming life of primordial temporal phases, a multiplicity opposite the unity of immanent objects. To note that even immanent objects are transcendent is to take account of the essential *temporality* of consciousness, and to begin a full account of the genetic constitution of such objects within the temporal flow of conscious life.

Corresponding to the concept of "transcendence" developed in the *Logik,* there is, as we should expect, a vital sense of "immanence" which is operative at the same depth of transcendental clarification and description. It serves both to uncover and describe the most primordial dimension of consciousness (the authentically radical foundation for knowledge that Husserl sought) and also, of course, to clarify further the nature of transcendence. Even in the *Ideas* of 1913 and in the *Vorlesungen zur Phänomenologie des inneren Zeitbewusstseins* of 1928, it is possible to see Husserl wrestling with the problem of articu-

57. On the other hand, this sense of "transcendence" *does* mean that, strictly speaking, there can be no truly immanent *objects.* To speak of such objects, then, is to make an *abbreviated* reference to their genetic constitution, i.e., to describe their genesis in the immanence of the stream of consciousness itself. But the objectivations themselves, strictly speaking, will not be immanent. The *genesis* of an *objectivated* pain, for example, is completely different from that of an objectivated house or stone; pain originates in consciousness, as a lived state of conscious life, and differs altogether, in this respect, from houses or stones.

lating this dimension of pure immanence.[58] One can just detect, in the writings of Husserl's late years (notably, *Erfahrung und Urteil* and some of his as yet unpublished late manuscripts), an awakening, but still dim appreciation of this immanence.[59]

If objects must be constituted as objective and transcendent, then, correlatively, it is the intentionality of consciousness which must constitute objects.[60] But the haunting question is, how are we to describe this consciousness through whose intentional acts these objects are originally given and constituted? If, now, we unerringly follow this path of inquiry into the darkest transcendental regions, we will ultimately recover a simply lived, pre-thetic, totally non-objectivated experience, consciousness as "lived awareness," "which precedes the presence of objects." [61] We are confronted with the pure stream of experience in its immediate, primordial, sensuous temporality. Itself non-constituted, this experience is the *ground* of all genetic constitution.

Husserl struggled for many years with the problem of immanence and transcendence, recognizing that here was indeed the secret to a truly "radical" transcendental phenomenology.

58. See Rudolf Boehm, "Zijn en tijd in de filosofie van Husserl," *Tijdschrift voor Philosophie,* XXI (1959), 243–76; and also Theodor Celms, *Der phänomenologische Idealismus Husserls,* Acta Universitatus Latviensus, vol. XIX (Riga: Walters and Rapa, 1928), pp. 418–19. Robert Sokolowski suggests that even the structures of immanence, the so-called "real components of subjectivity," are "relative" to the living consciousness which constitutes them, and "depend for their possibility of phenomenological existence on a still deeper absolute" (*FHCC,* p. 161; consider also pp. 160, 162, and 199–200). Thus, he implies that even immanent objects are transcendent in respect of the immediate temporal phases of lived consciousness.

59. See *Ideas,* I, 216 (p. 198). Husserl writes, rather cryptically: "The transcendental 'absolute' which we have set up through the reductions is in truth not the ultimate; it is something which constitutes itself in a certain profound and wholly unique sense, and which has its primal source in the ultimate and true absolute." Later, in the *Logik,* he shows a firmer grip on the problem: "But in the immanent 'internality' of the ego, there are no objects given in advance . . ." (p. 253).

60. Insofar as Husserl continued to speak of "immanent objects," and overlooked their fundamental transcendence, it is fair to say that he has pictured consciousness as nothing but a stream of objects. This picture of the mind is disturbingly reminiscent of David Hume's description of the mind as a kind of private inner theatre, with objects continually flitting across an inner stage.

61. *FHCC,* p. 193.

Nevertheless, he failed to understand the full significance of these concepts. This is, as we shall make clear in our following chapter analyses, one of the principal sources of his overweening intellectualism, with its concomitant doctrine of apodictic evidence; and it represents the crucial point at which the existential phenomenologies of Jean-Paul Sartre and Merleau-Ponty diverge, thus taking the decisively "radical" turn.

In subsequent chapters, we shall examine the far-reaching consequences of Husserl's failure to grasp the radical meaning in the disclosure of pure immanence. These consequences bear directly on Husserl's belief that it is possible to ascribe adequacy and apodicticity to immanent objects (in particular, to his "immanent essences").[62]

Once we recognize that the intentional object is a *transcendent* formation of consciousness (a *Leistungsgebilde*), then we can fruitfully investigate the *genesis* of its evidence. This means that one is led "back" (genetically) from the object to the motivated performances of consciousness, through whose functioning the object could emerge.[63]

Intentional objects, as we may surmise from the fact of their transcendence, are not all given with a uniformly luminous self-evidence, not to mention adequacy. There are, Husserl finds, various stages of evidence and, what is more, degrees of evidence within those stages. Such objects can be given, or beheld, in greater or lesser clarity, and with greater or lesser certainty. Consciousness seems disposed to alembicate the confused into the distinct, the less clear into the more clear, and the dubitable into the less dubitable. Consciousness, in its most "authentic" and essential moment, attempts the perfection of its evidences. Ultimately, too, it must achieve a satisfactory *justification* of its evidential holdings. Only then are the labors of reason—the "universal teleological structure" of consciousness in general—fully consummated.[64]

62. In the *Ideas,* for example, Husserl claims that immanent objects *can* be apodictic and absolute, not only because there are no spatial profiles, but because the acts of immanent perception form an *indivisible whole* with the immanent object they intend. The *essence and structure,* as well as the *existence* of these objects, can, he thinks, be indubitably given. See § § 42–44 and 46.

63. *EP,* II, 247.

64. *Logik,* p. 143. Also note *ibid.,* pp. 253–55, and *EP,* II, 33, 169–71, and 491.

There are several different, yet converging ways to characterize this process of justification or critique. Of primary importance is the condition that there can be no reference to any norms or criteria outside of consciousness, outside intentional evidence, nor does one have privileged access to another, special "faculty" of legitimation. Husserl is adamant in maintaining that it is only in seeing that I can make evident and explicate what is truly involved in an act of seeing.[65]

Critique is, besides, a posture of *seeing.* It can therefore also be interpreted, at any level whatsoever, as simply the achievement of evidence endowed with a certain superior title and authority. The maximally authoritative posture is accorded the special name of "apodictic evidence." From this point of view, Husserl elaborates two levels of evidence: (1) The foundational level, at which it is primordial possession of the state-of-affairs in its "bodily presence"; and (2) that higher level, at which it is the propriety which an evidenced *judgment* has by virtue of its conformity (adequation) to the evidence, in its first aspect. Here, evidence means a primordial consciousness of justification (*Richtigkeitsbewusstsein*). It represents consciousness at the stage of critique, where the fulfillment in intuition of the intentional judgment in question is for the first time recognized and asserted.[66]

When we are confronted with the propositions of the ordinary man in the street, or equally, of the man in positive natural science, the critique assumes the form of a motivated return from these propositions ("predicative" evidences, or judgments) to the "evidences of experience" (the "ante-predicative" stage of evidence). To fully achieve a critique entails a return to the transcendental subjectivity which constitutes this pregiven world. Husserl indicates the necessary steps: (1) the return from the already given world, with all its sedimentations of meaning, its sciences and scientific determinations, to the primordial life-world, and (2) the return from the life-world to the subjective performances out of which this life-world arises. For the latter, too, is not "simply a pregiven; it too is a formation, about whose modes of constitutive formation we can inquire." [67] In fact, corresponding to the steps in the analysis of transcend-

65. *Logik*, p. 142.
66. *Ibid.*, pp. 113–14 and 130.
67. *EU*, pp. 38 and 49.

ence and immanence which we have already noted, there is a third and final step in phenomenologico-transcendental critique, wherein the radical philosopher "withdraws" from the transcendental ego (inasmuch as it is a transcendent structuration for and by consciousness), in order to recover the living, streaming now-present (*lebendig-strömende Gegenwart*), that is truly and purely immanent.[68] It is to this stage of critique that Husserl refers in the pronouncement: "A critique of *transcendence* requires, if it is to be radical, a prior critique of *immanence*."[69] The final stage in this critique of immanence, namely, going "behind" the transcendental ego to the momentary, streaming, living (and simply lived) present, is taken only in Husserl's very late research, and then but hesitantly. Total acceptance of this step would mean, in fact, the end of his commitment to a *foundation* in an apodictic evidence.

The method which consciousness follows, in its striving for ever more perfect (i.e., clear, distinct, and rationally compelling) evidence, is defined by the *epochē*. *Epochē* is the first of the phenomenological reductions,[70] whereby consciousness abstains from judging (positing) or assuming the existent status (*Dasein*) of the objects with which it is involved, and furthermore effects explicit recognition of the "revelatory" insight that its objects are intentional. The real external world is thereby treated merely as phenomenon, as correlate of (immanent) conscious activity. The several stages of reduction are stages in which objects (and, in general, the world) abandoned through the methodic *epochē* are finally repossessed—or rather, legitimately and rationally possessed for the first time—according to the manner of their evidence.

Two distinct but intimately associated aims motivate rational consciousness in its transcendental critique. How are these aims operative?

1. Let us consider the first aim, the establishment of a ra-

68. See *EP*, II, 175.

69. *Ibid.*, p. 378. Cf. further pp. 222, 247, and 489–91.

70. Quentin Lauer discerns "at least six" levels of reduction, "on each of which we have a subject of greater purity" (*Phenomenology: Its Genesis and Prospect* [New York: Harper and Row, 1958], pp. 51–57). It seems, however, that there are *also*, if Iso Kern is right, (at least three) different "ways" to reduction. See his "Die drei Wege zur transzendental-phänomenologischen Reduktion in der Philosophie Edmund Husserls."

tionally satisfactory foundation. Our commerce in and with the "real" world is, at first, merely lived in the naive, natural attitude, and, moreover, lived with a certainty that is as yet unquestioned. For example, we simply perceive the fountain in the garden splashing and playing, as we are wont to say, "directly, before our very eyes." Husserl styles such perception "unmodalized," "prethematic," and "ante-predicative."

But even the slightest reflection on the course of one's perceptual encounters with the world inevitably conducts one to the abstractive, or, if you like, the methodic recognition that encounters can be errant and sometimes even hallucinatory, however compelling they may be at the time of their occurrence, and however well-justified according to the natural attitude; and hence we are always more or less limited in our demand for truth to the active, pragmatic mode of being-in-the-world.

Consequently, the leap from lived encounter to the first stage of reflection heralds a modalization of the encounter—purely as method, and usually altogether unmotivated by any particular concrete grounds for doubt or perplexity [71]—according to which the perceptions are assigned a merely presumptive status, regardless of their overwhelming harmony and coherence.[72] The objective world suffers *epochē;* the fundamental and essential contingency of the world and of all the "things" which are en-

71. This qualification is of the utmost significance. Note Husserl's remark: "No, I have no special ground for doubting that the world may not be. But I ask myself whether it is then so fully certain . . . and if I reflect on, say, *mathematical evidence,* then I realize that here we must distinguish between empirical and apodictic indubitability" (*EP*, II, 311). Elsewhere, he says that every sensible experience admits the possibility that it might be overthrown by subsequent experiences (p. 126). Perhaps one of his most explicit statements is: "Nothing at all speaks for the world's not being, whereas everything speaks for its being. . . . But we must recognize that this completely empirical assurance, this empirical indubitability, still allows the possibility that this world may not be; and that this possibility arises, even though absolutely nothing speaks for the empirical realization of this possibility . . . our empirically indubitable perceptual certainty about the existence of the world is perfectly *compatible* with the proposition that the world is a pure nothing, a mere transcendental illusion" (*EP*, II, 54).

72. Such status is not equivalent, then, to their being at all dubious or even just probable or hypothetical (in the customary usage of the natural sciences). See the *Krisis*, p. 265.

countered in the world, is brought to expression.[73] It is thus possible for a proposition about this world to be indubitable, but only in an *empirical* sense, by which it is meant that there are no concrete, empirical grounds for calling the given proposition into question.[74] Objective encounter may well provide a continuous, harmonious articulation of it, such that there could be every (empirically justified) reason for believing that the further experiences that it has intentionally predelineated, according to a certain style, will actually be fulfilled in intuition.[75]

Yet, Husserl argues, the objective world of encounter still would be altogether *dubitable,* from the transcendental standpoint of absolute consciousness. For the objective world *could conceivably* be a very special kind of "illusion": namely, a *transcendental* illusion. The radical philosopher must confront this pure possibility, disclosed through a kind of "thought experiment" (in truth, Husserl's method of eidetic variation) which establishes dependent and independent "contents": the world's annihilation is thinkable, despite the overwhelming confirmation for our empirical, existential certainty (*Daseinsgewissheit*) that the world truly exists.[76] Doubtless, Husserl's choice of the word "illusion" is misleading and infelicitous. Novelty of vision often compels a distortion of perspective, giving an air of paradox to some important philosophic statement. What I think he really wanted to say is, that the method of reduction has yielded two momentous insights: (a) The objective world is relative to (is a "dependent" correlate of) consciousness; (b) Consciousness, as the *source of meaning,* can be the only absolute, and is, in this special sense, both philosophically *prior* to (as the necessary condition for the possibility of) its meanings and rationally

73. The objective world must be definitively distinguished from the universal, non-thematic, lived world which is horizon, or field of the reduced consciousness. See the *Krisis,* pp. 146 and 408. The latter "world" is the source and ground of all judgment, hence for all correction and revision, too.

74. Husserl is not, as one might suppose, in any way loathe to introduce in this context the phrase "relative apodicticity." But it is plain that this is a "degenerate" usage, although justified within its proper domain of definition. See *EP,* II, 387, 398, 400, and 406.

75. Husserl is willing to call this presumptive but livingly believed anticipation an "apodictic style of form" (*Formstil*) (*ibid.,* p. 386; cf. also pp. 52, 125, and 484).

76. *Ibid.,* pp. 53 and 304.

indubitable.[77] The object of which I am conscious may be an illusion; but my consciousness itself, the consciousness I have of something, the fact *that* I am having an object-giving experience, whether veridical or illusory, cannot be doubted. This Cartesian style of reasoning leads us back to transcendental subjectivity, the rational source of evidence.[78] The idea of a "transcendental illusion" should perhaps be taken, then, as a dramatic way of introducing the standpoint of transcendental rationality.[79]

77. Sokolowski argues (correctly, I think) that "Husserl does not set before himself the task of showing the relativity of reality; this is not a thesis he tries to justify. He assumes, as something plainly given, that reality receives its sense from subjectivity, and that it is therefore relative to consciousness and constituted by it. If we were to analyze his argument logically, we would have to say that the relative, constituted nature of reality is an axiom, and not the conclusion of an argument." (*FHCC*, p. 133). But it is one thing for Husserl to recognize the fact that consciousness is what gives sense, even to reality; and it is quite a different thing for him to assert that not only the *sense,* but the *existence* of the world is dependent on consciousness, in a way that should make it truly *thinkable* that the world could cease to be while consciousness would survive. *Can* we, in fact, conceive of consciousness *apart from* reality? It does not seem at all unreasonable to think that we *cannot* conceive of this real world being annihilated, while consciousness somehow survives, *unless* we have already conceded the view of the Cartesian dualist and solipsist philosopher, that "real worlds" are just the creations of one's mind. But Husserl insists he is not a solipsist. Sokolowski valiantly attempts to defend Husserl in this regard, but he fails to dispel our uneasiness. He argues that transcendental constitution of the world does not mean "creation" of the world, but only a dependency of the *sense* of the world on the intentionality of consciousness. But then, it does *not* follow, as Husserl would have it, that the world, as such, can be conceived not to exist.

78. Consider the *Logik,* p. 147.

79. However, in subsequent argumentation we shall see that, inasmuch as (1) we likewise have no special concrete reasons for doubting the evidence of what Husserl calls "immanent objects" (e.g., the "immanent essences"); (2) the fundamental *transcendence* of immanent objects constitutes *them, too,* as relative to the consciousness which has posited them; and (3) it is, in fact, possible to conceive the evidence for the ontological status of such immanent objects as somehow annulled, or at least *essentially* different, parity of reason should oblige us to declare immanent objects to be as vulnerable to this special kind of transcendental dubitability as Husserl's "real world" is.

2. Let us now examine the second of the motives inspiring rational consciousness. A radical critique, a full explication of evidence, executed within the *epochē,* is just begun with the self-conscious, reflexive turn back to the transcendental ego. A rationally satisfying clarification of knowledge demands much more: nothing less than *a constitutional analysis*, to show us the intentional genesis and development of our structures of meaning (heretofore naively opined to be detached from consciousness) in their emergence from consciousness. They will henceforth be regained by consciousness, no longer sundered in their existence from the multiplicity of subjective acts.[80] Here, finally, we come to the most profound, the most intense, and the most compelling stage of evidence.[81] Meanings do not become fully evident until they are possessed as the outcome of *genetic constitution.* Since it is ultimately the transcendental ego which bestows meaning and desiderates a full presentation of the putatively evidential, the source of constitution is uncovered in this very ego.

Why is constitutional analysis called for? Husserl's own explanatory remarks are worthy of recall:

> . . . one must guard against the error which consists in believing that the *datum* as object is already *fully constituted when it makes its real appearance* in the lived experience. We would argue that evidences are functions which operate only in their intentional contexts.[82]

Objects are not "already there," formed independently of conscious identification and synthesis. Consequently, "one must always come back to the question: What constitutes the existent

80. "*Each and every existent* . . . is, finally, relative, and . . . *relative to transcendental subjectivity.* But only transcendental subjectivity is in itself and for itself, and that, in a hierarchy corresponding to the constitution which leads to different levels of such subjectivity" (*Logik,* p. 241).

81. This stage is identified as the "overcoming" of contingency, of facticity. The fact is alembicated into essential necessity, which is alone held intelligible in the "truest" sense. For the most sublime stage of self-consciousness, i.e., rationality, is the faculty of necessity. See the *Logik,* p. 241; and *Ideas,* I, 160–61 (p. 140), 166 (pp. 147–48), and 191 (p. 171).

82. *Logik,* p. 251; cf. further the *Krisis,* p. 157, wherein Husserl resoundingly casts out the Humean sense-datum as an epistemically first being.

as something existing *identically* for an identical ego?"[83] All intentional objects,

> *as finished products of a "constitution," of a "genesis," can and must be queried relative to their constitution, their genesis.* It is the very essence of such products that they are *meanings* which, as implicated products of their respective geneses, bear in them a *sort of historicity;* and that within them, in a gradual way, the sense points back to the *original sense* and the corresponding *noetic intentionality.*[84]

The term "constitution" has a double focus—a fact which has caused some commentators to argue that it is an ambiguous concept with Husserl.[85] On the one hand, it designates process and achievement (both contained in the meaning of the German *Leistung*), whereby consciousness uncovers and presents in evidence the legitimation which the history of the sense of its judgments discloses. In the *Krisis* Husserl remarks that "all constitution, of every kind and stratum of existent, is a temporalizing, which ascribes to every unique sense of existent in the constitutive system its own temporal form.[86] Consciousness thus comes to "possess" its posited meanings for what they are essentially and, as it were, "at bottom": intentional objects-of consciousness. Constitutive activity appears, from this vantage point, as a founding, right-giving process (a critique) which, as Bachelard puts it, "brings something, not into existence, but into genuine existence, i.e., into an existence which can be accounted for."[87] On similar grounds, Walter Biemel, wanting a descriptive synonym for "constitution," opts for the German *Restitution.*[88]

83. *Logik,* p. 251.
84. *Ibid.,* pp. 184–85; cf. *Ideas,* I, 390 (pp. 374–75).
85. Consider Paul Ricoeur's criticism that "constitution" hides a real ambivalence in its recesses. "Étude sur les *Méditations Cartésiennes* de Husserl," *Revue philosophique de Louvain,* LII (1954), 75–109.
86. *Krisis,* p. 172.
87. *SH,* p. 118.
88. "Die entscheidenden Phasen der Entfaltung von Husserl's Philosophie," *Zeitschrift für philosophische Forschung,* XIII (1959), 200. He substantiates his preference with a quote from Husserl's letter to Hocking, dated 25 January, 1903, wherein Husserl writes: "The expression which comes up again and again, that 'objects are constituted' in an act, always means the property of the act by which it *presents the object (den Gegenstand vorstellig zu machen)*: not 'constitution' in the ordinary sense!"

On the other hand, constitution is also and essentially a *seeing;* the process of critique (clarification) must be consummated, to whatever extent feasible, and this will be in an act of seeing. But there is an unhappy tendency for Husserl to maintain here that to constitute an object is to see it, to present it in a luminous intuition, absolute, adequate, and apodictic, *without* regard to the way in which it emerged as meaning of and for consciousness.[89] This tendency, in other words, *detaches* the operation of constitution (the critique of evidence) from its moorings in the historicity of evidential acts of consciousness; and it awards primacy to the perfection and finality of evidence, rather than to the depth and intensity of *genetic* clarification, reaching back through the opacity of an historical, living consciousness. It is, quite clearly, more favorable to the ideal of apodicticity than is the former focus.

We shall find that these two aspects of constitution—the *process* of genetic clarification and the *moment* of evidence—must be accorded equivalent weight. To acknowledge the decisive value of the *act* of seeing should not purport a denial of its function as integral to and pervading the whole laboriously generated constitutive process. It is not as if there were a "blind" constitution consummated, finally, in a moment of genuine evidence. Rather, the task of constitution, grounding the objectivity under question in the temporality of conscious performances, is through and through, and at each moment, a "making evident." And conversely, a genuine and full seeing, in respect of an objectivity, will emerge only through a *process* of genetic "return" to the primordial, lived acts of intentional consciousness. So that a philosopher, motivated by his commitment to the radical norm of transcendental rationality, shall have retreated, in his reflections, far from the exigencies of the mundane world, and even from the abstract, algebraicized world of the natural sciences; and he shall have discovered, to be sure, a vast realm of anterior "knowledge."

But the asceticism of his method cannot destroy, or hope to conceal, the very conditions which have made such reflection possible in the first place. These conditions, among which temporality is dominant, will forever retard man's striving to disclose the fully rational ground of his naive worlds through a

89. See G. Berger, *Le Cogito dans la philosophie de Husserl,* (Paris: Aubier, 1941), pp. 97–100.

sovereign vision that is somehow defiantly outside his historicity and immediately present to an absolute, eternal truth.

In fact, history has surely proven all too keenly that the perennial vision of the reign of reason can both inspire and betray many otherwise quite divergent philosophical enterprises. For this vision can be conceived, on the one hand, as the demonstration that there truly exists a special privileged *kind* of evidence (knowledge), a truly "rational" evidence, as the support and measure for all other kinds of evidence (knowledge); [90] or, on the other hand, it can be conceived as affirming the primacy of a methodological value, animating a process of evidential clarification and justification which is, from a logical point of view, always incomplete and tentative. According to the first interpretation, we might say, reason is thoroughly *substantival,* a finished product, and truth is consequently treated as a peculiar kind of *property* (attribute), presumably qualifying either a privileged kind of insight, or else a somehow specially "marked" kind of proposition.[91] While according to the second, reason is instead *procedural,* essentially creative, always, as some philosophers are fond of saying, in a state of perpetual "becoming" (phenomenological anticipation), and located, as it were, in the interstices, the evidential interconnections and interdependencies of the structure of knowledge.[92] And here, then, truth is simply a matter of the contextual evaluation of the conditions which justify knowledge.

We shall discover that, in the *Logische Untersuchungen,* and especially in the *Cartesian Meditations,* Husserl has plainly favored the former conception of reason; whereas in the *Ideas,* and even more explicitly in the *Formale und transzendentale Logik,*

90. It might be rewarding to attack Husserl's theory of apodictic evidence from an angle somewhat like John Austin's assault on sense-data and certainty theories. See his book, *Sense and Sensibilia* (London: Oxford University Press, 1968).

91. See Alfred Tarski's renowned paper, "The Semantic Conception of Truth," reprinted in *Readings in Philosophical Analysis,* ed. Feigl and Sellars (New York: Appleton-Century-Crofts, 1949). Tarski surely intends to refute just such an approach to truth and the evidence of reason, but only from the formal and linguistic standpoint. Husserl's investigations in the *Ideas* would seem to yield the counterpart of this refutation from the phenomenological standpoint.

92. See John Dewey, *Experience and Nature* (New York: W. W. Norton, 1949), and A. N. Whitehead, *The Function of Reason* (Boston: Beacon Press, 1958), for illustrations of this latter conception of reason in philosophical systems very different from Husserl's.

he has worked, in effect, with the latter conception.[93] In the *Krisis* (one of Husserl's last works), however, we encounter a profound tension between these two contradictory conceptions: for, just as in the works strongly committed to the Cartesian (rationalistic) spirit, the ideal of reason is still thought to be embodied in the apodictic evidence of the transcendental ego; yet at the same time, this work *as a whole* attempts to delineate, in a novel and adventuresome manner that exhibits strong affinities to C. S. Pierce's pragmaticist theory of evidence, a conception of reason which inserts it totally into the infinite, interlocking stretches of evidence, and gives the evidence of truth not to a privileged moment or kind of philosophical insight, but rather to the ceaseless inquiries engaging the actual and potential community of philosophers. But it would seem that Husserl, insufficiently cognizant of this conceptual strife, could not himself resolve it in a decisive way, even at the period of his greatest philosophical maturity.

93. It will be noticed that each of the two conceptions has polarized an early and a late work. Apodicticity does not exhibit, in other words, a simple *linear* development. The explanation, very simply, is this: throughout his lifetime, Husserl failed to examine what his commitment to apodicticity really amounted to, in terms of his phenomenological program as a whole. Consequently, one or another feature of apodicticity will stand out, depending on the larger orientation of the work involved.

2 / The *Logische Untersuchungen*

[1] Introduction

One can discover in the *Logische Untersuchungen* [1] both a destructive and a constructive intention. On the one hand, Husserl wants to refute psychologism in theories about the foundation of logic and mathematics; while on the other hand, he hopes to elucidate "the relationship between the subjectivity of knowing and the objectivity of the content of knowledge." [2] The latter concern involves Husserl in the general problem of evidence and intentional meaning.

It would be desirable to avoid an examination of his arguments against psychologism in general, as well as his arguments in defense of the objective and immutable nature of mathematical and logical truths. These issues, important though they be, are too vast for the compass of our study; nor are they in any way central. The examination in this chapter will treat of psychologism only in so far as it bears directly on the concept of apodicticity. And it will recognize a concern with logical and mathematical truths only insofar as these truths are asserted to exhibit an apodictic evidence.

Perhaps what most strikes the reader already well-versed in phenomenology about Husserl's *Logische Untersuchungen*, especially those portions which did not undergo extensive revision in the second edition of 1913 (i.e., after *Ideas* I was completed), is its relatively non-phenomenological, "naive" method and point of

1. Citations referring to the *Logische Untersuchungen* will be from the revised second edition because of greater accessibility.

2. *LU*, I, Preface, p. vii.

view. It is not until the introduction to Part I of Volume II, in the revised second edition, that a truly phenomenological standpoint is noticeably adopted. The *Prolegomena* was also, of course, reworked and cast into a form more acceptable to the Husserl who had composed the *Ideas*.

In the present chapter, we propose to exhibit the problems which attend Husserl's early formulations and use of the concepts "adequate evidence" and "apodicticity." As following chapters will disclose, Husserl was not insensitive to certain fundamental inadequacies in the theory of evidence presented in the *Logische Untersuchungen;* in subsequent work, he sets out expressly to rectify the weaknesses. One finds that he submits the concept of evidence in general to further differentiation, structured according to the process of genetic constitution, and attempts to understand apodicticity specifically within the framework of phenomenological method (i.e., within the phenomenological and eidetic reductions) and the effectuation of phenomenological critique. It remains for later chapters to show, then, whether and to what extent Husserl recognized the nature of the problems in the *Logische Untersuchungen* and is able, in his more mature works, successfully to address himself to their resolution.

[2] Adequate Evidence

Husserl deems knowledge in the strict and full sense to entail "possession" of an objectivity through evidence exhibiting a "luminous certainty": it must recommend itself to us in an immediate experience (*Innewerden*) of the "truth." [3] Science, in the genuine philosophic sense, is not something that reaches beyond evidence; rather, it is coextensive with it, and the sole "material" it structures is evidence. As one should expect, only a certain kind of evidence deserves elevation to the position of scientific ideal. Science (i.e., knowledge), as the norm for the *perfection* of evidence, therefore creates a primary task for Husserl: the differentiation of evidence by stages and degrees, according to criteria generated within the phenomenological method. The total *perfection* of evidence, designated "truth" or "true being," is conceived in a quite general way to be an abso-

3. See further, *LU*, I, chap. 1, p. 13, and the conclusion, chap. 11, p. 229.

lute "agreement" (conformity) between an empty intention and its fulfilled meaning (the evidence); there is achieved a complete and perfect *"adequatio rei et intellectus,"* an adequate experience (*Erlebnis*) or perception (the concept "perception" hereby being enlarged to include non-sensible intentionalities).

However, in the intuitive fulfillment of intentions pregnant with meaning, there often will be a *progression* of intuitive fullness, as the representative "content" is brought ever more adequately to giving the "whole" object as it itself is. To be sure, all genuine presentations (*Vorstellungen*) truly give the object itself; but either they may give the object completely (in perfect and absolute adequation) or they may truly give the object only by means of incomplete adumbrations (i.e., inadequate or adequate to a less than perfect degree). These adumbrations are aspects of the object itself, but not of the object in its possible (potential) phenomenal totality.[4] There is, in short, a scale of adequation, wherein purely signitive (empty) contents belong at one end, and pure, full intuitive contents belong at the other.[5] There can even be "chains" of increasing fulfillments of what was once implicit, signitive meaning merely, as for example when one clarifies the symbol $(5^3)^4$ by going back to the "simplest" definitional presentations. Eventually, in this particular case, one would arrive at a fully articulated formula, giving, first of all, the number 5 in its intuitive clarity: $5 = 4 + 1, 4 = 3 + 1, 3 = 2 + 1, 2 = 1 + 1$.[6]

If now, there is no residue of signitive meaning, the presentation is called "pure." It follows that all pure intuitions must be complete; although completeness does not, in turn, entail purity. For the intention may be completed, but only as the outcome of a *process* whereby a manifold of acts, each of which is a *partial* fulfillment (perhaps in itself quite pure), *cumulatively* completes the giving of the object. The ideal of adequacy is thus the having of evidence which is complete and pure. It is "the complete self-appearance of the object in so far as it was meant in the intention to be fulfilled."[7]

It should be observed that there are diverse *modes* (kinds) of evidential presentation, as well as diverse stages. For instance, the linguistic expression "a green house" can be envisaged (*ver-*

4. *LU*, II, Sixth Study, chap. 3, pp. 97–98.
5. *Ibid.*, pp. 80–81.
6. *Ibid.*, pp. 69–70.
7. *Ibid.*, chap. 5, p. 121; cf. also p. 118.

anschaulicht) by an act of intuitive imagination or, instead, let us say, by an act of recollection—both of which may be "complete" in their own right; but, so it is argued, a greater completeness would be achieved if there were an adequate presentation in visual-tactile perception.[8]

Since, Husserl contends, meaning must be analysed into two components, namely, the "thought" (noesis), on the one hand, and the state-of-affairs (noema), on the other, there are two corresponding aspects inherent in the perfect adequation of the pregnant intention to the intended: (1) on the noematic side: the *conformity to* the intuition is complete, inasmuch as the thought does not mean anything which the fulfilling intuition does not present as belonging to it;[9] (2) on the noetic side: there is a perfection in the complete intuition itself. Husserl writes:

> Every true and pure description of an intuitive object or occurrence provides an illustration of the first completeness; and if the objectivity is immanently experienced (*erlebt*) and is grasped in reflective perception, just as it is, then the second completeness is joined with it.[10]

Evidence, if truly adequate, will thus have the following properties: (1) an intuitively complete, or perfect noetic-noematic coincidence (*Deckung*), in which the intuitive presentation fully coincides with the empty intention; (2) a nonthematic act of

8. *Ibid.*, chap. 3, p. 100. One might with justice argue, in this regard, that Husserl's conception of completeness is unduly oriented toward spatio-temporal objects, which give themselves through incomplete spatial profiles. Nonspatial objects (comprising a class larger than that of so-called immanent objects, if, for example, mathematical entities are construed as transcendent) are *not* given and completed in intuition in the *same* way. In a sense, however, it would seem reasonable to maintain that the intentional meaning of certain non-spatial objects (e.g., mathematical and logical propositions) *is* actually fulfilled in the very operation through which the meaning was originally acquired in the first place, as "something understood." Adequacy of fulfillment here involves very different criteria, quite unlike those implicit in the fulfillment of meanings having a spatio-temporal reference. See below chap. 5, § 6; and chap. 6, § 6.

9. Husserl refers to this aspect as "objective completeness," i.e., completeness on the object-side of the intentionality.

10. *LU*, II, Sixth Study, chap. 5, p. 119.

identification, bringing intention and its fulfillment together; and (3) an objectivating act (i.e., a judgment).[11] These are not stages or separate processes, but rather components or aspects of the one unified adequation.

Husserl examines the act of adequation in relation to the traditional inner-outer dualism in epistemology. He argues that this dualism should be replaced by the phenomenologically primary and more fruitful concepts of adequacy and inadequacy.[12] The inner-outer classification is secondary because, for one thing, even so-called "inner" experiences (that is, the "psychic" events proper to the science of psychology) can be inadequate. But a phenomenological reduction (based on the distinction between transcendence and immanence) is a requisite condition for the disclosure of the inadequacy of "inner" (but transcendent) mental processes.[13] The adequate, on the other hand, exactly corresponds to the immanent, phenomenologically reduced realm of experience:

> To doubt that which *is* immanent, and is meant merely thus, would be unreasonable. I may doubt whether an outer object ever exists, and whether any perception referring to such objects is correct: but I cannot doubt the *experienced sensuous content* of the perception—naturally, only when I 'reflect' upon it and simply intuit it, *just as it is*.[14]

11. *Ibid.*, chap. 13, pp. 77; chap. 5, p. 121; and chap. 6, p. 148. It should be noted that, as Husserl himself stresses, the identity relevant to (2) must be distinguished from the thematic grasp of this identity as an identity, in an act of reflection.

12. *Ibid.*, Fifth Study, chap. 1, pp. 354–55.

13. This is an important point. Husserl writes: "Only the perception of one's own actual experiences is indubitable or evident. Not every perception is evident, however. Thus, in the perception of a toothache, the pain may appear as boring in a healthy tooth. The perceived object in this case is not the pain as it is experienced, but is the pain which has been transcendently interpreted and ascribed to the tooth. . . . We obviously only have evident (i.e., adequate) perception of our experiences insofar as we take them purely and do not go beyond them apperceptively" (*ibid.*, Sixth Study, p. 240). Cf. further the warning against psychologism in *ibid.*, Fifth Study, chap. 3, p. 440. These passages, added in the second edition of 1913, are crucial in defining immanence, and establishing the concept of adequacy in terms of this immanence, instead of in terms of the non-phenomenological inner-outer categories.

14. *Ibid.*, Sixth Study, Appendix, p. 238, cf. also pp. 237 and 239–40; and Fifth Study, chap. 1, pp. 354–55.

Immanent experience (*Erlebnis*) can be adequate and, what is more, indubitable, because, Husserl maintains, "the sensed *content* is the same as the *object* of the perception. The content does not mean anything else; it stands for itself." [15] Here, there is not any problem of an "intentional residue" still in need of fulfillment.[16] Outer, or transcendentally directed, experience cannot give the object "in one fell swoop" (*in Einem Schlage*), but must give it in and through a synthesized manifold of partial and continuing adumbrations intentionally predelineated in the meaning of the object in question.[17] The phenomenologically "real" natural object can be truly presented (*gegenwärtigt*) as it itself, and not merely presentified (*vergegenwärtigt*), as it would be if recollected, imagined, or simply articulated symbolically; but nevertheless it is not a genuinely *present* being in its completeness (*ein Gegenwärtigsein*).[18] Completeness of evidence, the norm of adequate evidence, is, by contrast, only feasible where the intentional object perceived is altogether immanent, and fully bracketed according to the method of reduction.[19]

[3] Apodicticity

The completeness achieved in the process of immanentization, which matches the norm of adequation, is, in a quite general manner, a kind of certainty, a form of "compulsion" in the evidence. But, Husserl's research into the foundations of logic and mathematics guided him to another, more profound kind of certainty, to which he refers as apodicticity or

15. *Ibid.*, Sixth Study, Appendix, p. 239.
16. *Ibid.*, Sixth Study, chap. 3, p. 67.
17. *Ibid.*
18. *Ibid.*, Sixth Study, chap. 5, p. 116.
19. At this stage in his thinking, Husserl has no appreciation of the problem inherent in treating an *object* as immanent. Despite the repudiation of psychologism, he seems inclined, in the *Logische Untersuchungen*, to think of mathematical entities, once subjected to the *epochē*, as truly immanent. But this confuses them with other, very different objects, also designated immanent, like pains and emotions, and more seriously, with the radical immanence of nonthematized, merely lived present experience. Consequently, he could slip very easily into speaking about winning adequacy and apodicticity for the thetic and transcendent domains of mathematics and logic—trading, thus, on their alleged immanence. In the *Ideas*, Husserl seems rather disinclined to favor mathematics and logic with an apodictic title.

insight (in the strictest sense of this word). Such insight has the following principal attributes: (1) adequacy, (2) primordiality, (3) the highest possible certainty (indubitability, or necessity) and (4) genuine a priori status, or, in other words, confinement to an eidetic employment.

Since we have already examined Husserl's concept of adequate evidence, let us consider the second aspect of apodictic insight. Primordiality characterizes apodictic insight in the sense that the evidence is an "immediate" (non-inferential and present) experienced seeing of the state-of-affairs in question, given as it itself. When there is a primordial and adequate evidence that has the further distinction of being certain beyond all conceivable doubt, and hence authentically necessary, one is entitled to claim apodicticity.

A certain given proposition, Husserl observes, may give rise to a feeling that it is invulnerable, but this does not amount to the *logical* necessity of an insight.[20] Psychological analysis could indicate the presence of such a feeling, even when the relevant proposition is false. Insight, on the other hand, is so related to truth that one cannot have an authentic insight into something which could, in any sense, prove to be false. Truths are what they are, he maintains, whether or not we have insight into them; but an insight that deserves its title, a genuine apodictic insight into some state-of-affairs, expressed, let us say, in the form of a proposition, '*p*,' is possible if and only if '*p*' is in fact a true proposition.[21] Apodictic insight is an experienced (*erlebt*) apprehension of an unshakeable, hence eternal, validity.[22] The various intentional *acts* of judgment in which a truth—"outside" temporality by virtue of its being an ideal unity—is grasped *can*, of course, be described in psychological terms; and these *acts* are "causally determined" and subject to change in their (*subjective*) necessity.[23] But the validity (*Gültigkeit*) of the judgment itself is otherwise, so that it is possible for us to have an apodic-

20. See *LU*, I, chap. 8, § 51, pp. 188–90.
21. *Ibid.*, chap. 11, p. 238.
22. *Ibid.*, chap. 7, pp. 128–29.
23. *Ibid.*, chap. 8, p. 191: "The ideality of truth constitutes (*ausmacht*) its objectivity. In other words, it is the case that " 'validity' or 'objectivity' . . . do not belong to the assertion (*Aussage*) as this temporal experience, but rather to the assertion *in specie*, the (pure and identical) assertion 2 × 2 is 4, and the like." Cf. further, chap. 7, pp. 119 and 129.

tic insight into the nature of truths.[24] To see with apodictic insight that a certain state-of-affairs obtains is "to have knowledge of the ground of this state-of-affairs, or of its truth." [25] And "truth is an idea; we experience it like any other idea in an act of ideation grounded in intuition (clearly this is what is called an act of insight). . . ." [26] Insight, unlike feelings of certainty, is legitimated in reference to the truth; this is the case, even though one's only access to the truth is through insight. Mere feelings of certainty, by contrast, exist without reference to the truth, and their legitimation consists simply in the existence of intentional acts expressive of such feelings.

Husserl admits that "I cannot compel anyone to see (*einsehen*) what *I* see." But he also asserts that

> I myself cannot doubt; indeed, I see that in this case, where I possess an insight, i.e., grasp the truth itself, every doubt would be perverse (*verkehrt*); and thus I find myself in general at the point which I must either acknowledge as the Archimedean point, in order to delimit from here out the world of unreason and doubt, or on the contrary, abandon and therewith surrender all reason and knowledge. I see that matters are thus, and that if one could still speak of reason and unreason in the latter case, I should then have to cease all rational search for truth, all assertion and grounding.[27]

Knowledge begins with and ends in apodictic insight.[28]

Evidence, the judging, that is, with insight, if construed as the experience of a coincidence between meaning and the meant, rather than as a peculiar psychological *feeling* contingently attached to the act of judgment, does not permit that relativism commonly associated with insight theories. Husserl thinks he has a doctrine of insight free from traditional objections: "If someone experiences the evidence *A*, then it is evident that no other person can experience the absurdity of the same *A;* for if *A* is evident, that means that *A* is not merely meant, but is moreover truly given; it is in the strictest sense itself present." [29]

24. *Ibid.*, chap. 11, p. 240: "To the manifold of individually distinct acts of knowledge of the same content corresponds the *one* truth, as the truth of precisely this ideally identical content."
25. *Ibid.*, p. 231.
26. *Ibid.*, chap. 7, p. 129.
27. *Ibid.*, chap. 7, p. 143.
28. *Ibid.*, p. 152.
29. *Ibid.*, II, Sixth Study, chap. 5, p. 127.

According to Husserl, a judgment *J*, executed with insight, is equivalent to the insight *that the truth* J *obtains*. And truths, naturally, are either eternally truths, or else they never were and never could be truths. Hence, if there is a full evidence of the truth at all, of an insight, it will be apodictic, or indubitable and necessary. And thus:

> we also have the insight that no one's insight can conflict with ours—insofar as the one and the other are truly insight. For this only means, in fact, that what we have experienced as true also simply is true.[30]

In fine, if there is a judgment *J* which is executed with insight, and is therefore putatively apodictic, then there can be no judgment *not-J* such that it is likewise an apodicticity, or insight.[31]

Apodictic insight has the characteristic, therefore, of being what Husserl calls "necessity," a very special compulsion of thinking, intuitional in nature through and through, and consequently bound in an especially intimate way with the *being* (state-of-affairs) evidenced: "What we cannot think cannot be, and what cannot be we cannot think." [32] This thinking to which Husserl refers is not a formal, merely symbolic, conceptual manipulation of being; nor is it, on the other hand, a subjective, relative, psychological affection of the mind. It is not "a subjective incapacity of not-being-able-to-conceive(*vorstellen*)-otherwise, but rather an ideal-objective necessity of something's not-being-able-to-*be*-otherwise," [33] disclosed as the result of a kind of imaginative variation of possibilities. It is Husserl's contention that, if I have an insight into the state-of-affairs S, and cannot *conceive* it as other than it is, then I am entitled to assert that it is *impossible* for S to *be* otherwise, that it is necessary for S to *be* as I (must) conceive it, or again, that my insight regarding S is apodictic (indubitable).

Moreover, apodictic necessity is a stance of consciousness in respect of *essential* (i.e., nonfactual and noncontingent) *a priori* laws.[34] It is that "unique consciousness in which the insightful

30. *Ibid.*, I, chap. 8, p. 191.
31. *Ibid.*
32. *Ibid.*, II, Third Study, chap. 1, p. 239.
33. *Ibid.* To be sure, Husserl does have the rudiments of a theory of eidetic variation in the *Logische Untersuchungen*. But he has not integrated such variation into the whole of phenomenological method.
34. *Ibid.*, p. 240.

grasp of a *law* or of something lawful is constituted." [35] In this early work, Husserl seems to believe that it is possible for one to have an apodictic insight into purely logical laws (e.g., the proposition which expresses the law of contradiction) and even into pure mathematical propositions (e.g., that $2 + 2 = 4$).[36] For such propositions treat exclusively of universal laws, assumed to be genuinely a priori in nature. It is not a question here of the existence (*Dasein*) of any individual experiences (*Erlebnisse*). Evidence for the existence (facticity) of particulars is always, as Husserl calls it, "assertoric," and never truly apodictic.[37] In other words, judgments intending particulars will, according to their very nature, serve merely to assert the existence (or something about the existence) of the particulars involved; whereas universal, a priori and necessary judgments, capable of apodicticity, serve instead to enunciate *essential* truths quite independent of any particularities, any existential facts, be they psychic or "real." [38] Apodictic evidence cannot be announced in experiential judgments (*Erfahrungsurteile*), whatever their empirical persuasiveness, and however "vivid" they may present themselves in intuition. Hume's psychologistic criteria for the evidential status of logical and mathematical judgments are thus not at all satisfactory, or even relevant, for the issue of apodicticity.

Husserl presumably wants to formulate, in the *Logische Untersuchungen*, completely non-psychologistic, non-relativist, and non-subjective criteria for ascribing apodicticity to a priori propositions in the exact and formal sciences. And consequently, it is primarily in relation to propositions in *these* very sciences, rather than to the propositions of Husserl's fully developed phenomenology, that he introduces and employs the concept of apodictic evidence.

[4] A Critique of the Concept of Apodicticity Proposed in the *Logische Untersuchungen*

The several criticisms which follow either represent guideposts to problems for which, as we shall discover, Husserl's own later critical research is intended to provide sufficient resolution; or they constitute directions for phenomenolo-

35. *Ibid.*, I, chap. 7, p. 134; cf. also chap. 11, p. 238.
36. *Ibid.*, chap. 7, pp. 62–63.
37. *Ibid.*, chap. 5, p. 91.
38. *Ibid.*, II, Third Study, chap. 1, p. 240.

gical analysis which, though not, indeed, explicitly recognized in Husserl's thinking, nevertheless can, for the most part, be summoned forth from the deepest resources of his *mature* phenomenology.

1. Apodicticity is introduced, we know, as a special style of evidence. Yet, from the standpoint of Husserl's later works, we can appreciate that, in the *Logische Untersuchungen,* it is introduced neither clearly nor with any great determinacy, as belonging exclusively within the enunciation of the phenomenological method. One cannot establish with any great certainty whether Husserl supposes that apodicticity is possible only in respect of those intentional objects which have eventuated from the various reductions. The relation between apodictic evidence and the *epochē is not clearly recognized, much less examined and defended.*[39]

Apodicticity, it is asserted, depends on freedom from existential positionality, hence from every element of facticity. In his later works, the a priori method of ideation is asserted to be the source of authority for apodictic insight. But in the *Logische Untersuchungen,* Husserl does not yet have a well-developed phenomenological theory of eidetic reduction and variation. Therefore, he could not defend apodicticity on the basis of its function in the consummatory insight of the eidetic reduction.[40]

Husserl describes the a priori in respect of "all that belongs to the ideal essence of the understanding in general . . . and hence that which cannot be suspended so long as the understanding, or the acts defining it, are what they are." [41] He insists that his a priori, as a phenomenological concept and thus neither psychological nor logical, is thoroughly satisfactory, whereas previous traditional concepts are not.[42] But if the a priori rests on (and is even, perhaps, reducible to) an analysis of the *eidos,* "consciousness in general," we may expect that the same prob-

39. There is no definite point at which we may say with assurance that the *epochē* is adopted and carried out, as there is, by contrast, in the *Ideas.* Consider chap. 3, §§ 30–32.

40. Consider Husserl's self-criticism in § 61 of *Ideas* I. In the *Logische Untersuchungen,* it is true, Husserl describes and explicates a priori laws that obtain *between eide;* but he does not present a theory of the apprehension and phenomenological constitution of the *eide* themselves. Hence, the function of apodicticity remains unclarified and ungrounded. Note *LU,* II, Third Study, chap. 1.

41. *Ibid.*, Sixth Study, chap. 8, p. 198.

42. *Ibid.*, p. 203.

lems which confront the theory of eidetic judgment also confront the doctrine of the a priori. And furthermore, insofar as the method of eidetic variation is not sufficiently developed, just so far is Husserl unable to legitimate apodictic insight on the grounds of its a priority. This means, in turn, that he cannot sustain the title of apodicticity on the presumed evidence of its independence from facticity, or contingency. The first step in authenticating the pretensions of apodicticity must be the formulation of *phenomenological* criteria for a priori and eidetic judgment. The critical question, at this point, exposes a certain *petitio principii* at the very heart of Husserl's concept of apodicticity: Given Husserl's special claims for an apodictic evidence, to what extent is he free to justify the genuine apodictic title of some evidence on the ground of an appeal to the essential nature of consciousness when, antecedent to such justification, he cannot guarantee the apodicticity of his purported insight into the essentiality of consciousness? If our insight into the *eidos* of consciousness is in any way (however slight) erroneous or incomplete, then specific insights cannot pretend to be more than hypothetical.

These are no trivial shortcomings. For he introduces and employs apodicticity without any criteria for achieving, recognizing, or guaranteeing it. Without the specification of phenomenological, and more especially of eidetic, method, he can give no rules for winning apodictic insights; and, more seriously, he has no rules for testing or judging them. Most important in this regard is his subsequent avowal, in the *Cartesian Meditations*, that (putative) apodictic evidences which have not been submitted to a rigorous critique (itself carried out in apodictic insight) are inherently "naive," phenomenologically "abortive." From the standpoint of the later phenomenology, the doctrine of apodicticity in the *Untersuchungen* is not just naive, for want of the effectuation of a critique, but is not yet integrated into the enormous web of interlocking and forever advancing styles and stages of evidence; although it is, indeed, the case that Husserl does undertake to differentiate evidences (and apodicticity among them). The *Logik* and the *Meditations*, written almost three decades later, really assume the burden of such a task for the first time.

2. A second criticism, intimately related to the first, is that Husserl makes no attempt to understand apodictic insight as a process, exhibiting a genesis, a history. It must be owned that

apodicticity is conceived to be an active, "living" seeing-into; but this seeing is still described in relatively static terms of perfection, as if it could occur in a miraculous isolation, without a genesis, without any method or strategy to achieve it, and without any eventuality in further evidence, any evidential "becoming" that is accessible to renewed exploration. Once again, the later works of Husserl, wherein the concepts of genetic constitution and a history of the judging consciousness are fully elaborated, suggest vast improvements in the general theory of evidence, even if they should prove unable to legitimate apodicticity.

In the *Logische Untersuchungen,* the concept of apodictic insight is simply, and with considerable naivete (as Husserl himself came to realize), employed to describe the evidence for those propositions, especially in mathematics and logic, whose truth is traditionally taken for granted in the theory of a priori and necessary knowledge.[43] But, one wants to know, what does the affirmation of insight in these cases amount to? Whence the legitimacy of their pretensions—these ancient and familiar propositions? And finally, if these truths are expressed in what we are to construe, according to phenomenological theory, as "formations" of consciousness, and if these formations can be (and must be) queried as to their history in consciousness, what are we to say about any insights concerning them? Can we not regard the legitimation or grounding of these insights as born in

43. Whereas in the *Logische Untersuchungen* (e.g., *Prolegomena,* chap. 8, pp. 157 ff.) he does not hesitate to speak of apodicticity in reference to insights into mathematical or geometrical axioms (a priori laws), without so much as signaling the execution of the *epochē,* in his late work, the *Krisis,* he concludes an historical examination of apodicticity, from Plato through Galileo, Descartes, and Kant, with the announcement of a new and radical meaning for it, and importunes: "It would naturally be fundamentally wrong-headed (*grundverkehrt*) to foist upon (*unterschieben*) the foremost sense of apodicticity here indicated the usual sense which derives from traditional mathematics" (p. 74). And he now insists that "What heretofore appeared as apodictic, e.g., the mathematical axioms, indeed permit the possibility of doubt, thus also the conceivability of falsehood—this is first precluded and the claim to apodicticity justified when a mediate and *absolute grounding* is won" (p. 80). This grounding is, of course, the process of genetic constitution, showing such axioms in the constitutive performances of transcendental subjectivity. But prior to genuine phenomenological grounding, one is indeed justified in querying how Husserl can differentiate, for instance, his "apodictic" insights into the *eidos* of consciousness from Galileo's insights into the gravitational laws of falling bodies.

the very process whereby these formations are interrogated in regard to their historicity? If this should make sense, from a phenomenological point of view, then Husserl's ascription of apodicticity, in the *Untersuchungen,* to propositions of the exact and formal sciences must be considered premature, at the very least, and perhaps illegitimate, prior to the genetic constitution of their intentional (i.e., meaning-) objectivations. In fact, it will be argued that phenomenological constitution, fully and radically conceived, entails the *impossibility* of apodicticity, in Husserl's strong sense. Thus the naivete and illegitimacy of apodicticity in the *Logische Untersuchungen* is overcome in later phenomenological theory, only to be replaced, however, by other and quite insurmountable problems.

3. Husserl's distinction between the *act* of meaning (with its corresponding psychological conditions) and the *object* meant (that is, the "ideal unity of meaning," the "content" of the act) is a powerful weapon in the assault on psychologistic theories intended to explicate objectivity. But it is difficult to comprehend what exactly he is substituting in their stead, when the issue is not that of meaning as such, but is precisely the determination and defense of meanings purporting to be apodictically necessary, true and immutable for all eternity. A meaning, simply as an objectivated communicable being, will endure as such forever, over against the manifold historically determined and passing *acts* through which it is grasped; but it need not endure forever as having the specific doxic sense of a "true" meaning, or a "confirmed" meaning, or an "indubitable" meaning, etc. Husserl's general argument against psychologism thus has *no relevancy* to the doctrine that there can be meanings about which it is possible to assert that they will and must (i.e., cannot be conceived not to) retain their epistemic status of validity forever. *Other* arguments must be brought forth to defend this latter doctrine, entailed by the concept of apodicticity. The most that a repudiation of psychologism can establish is that, *if* a meaning is in fact valid (whether or not we *know* it to be so), it is always valid.

4. Necessity of evidence, of which Husserl speaks, is not, we have been told, a merely psychological state of mind, a mere feeling of compulsion which just happens to overwhelm one at the moment. It is a necessity that characterizes consciousness on those occasions when there is an evidential seeing, to which it intrinsically belongs that one sees the state of affairs could not

be otherwise. But what assures me that I have seen the matter as it truly is? What establishes the objectivity (the veridical nature) of my seeing? Husserl does not want to prove that we encounter objectivity; he believes one must accept this as plain fact. But even if his concern be just to explain or clarify *how* subjectivity can encounter objectivity, he is obliged to provide some criteria for distinguishing veracious from deceptive claims, once he has affirmed the possibility of apodictic insight and, at the same time, discerned gradations in the perfection of seeing (intuition). At least, he should provide a general method for insight and a methodic critique; otherwise, the correlation of conceivability (or inconceivability) and being (i.e., the evidenced objectivity) remains programmatic, rather than fully grounded in the framework of phenomenological science.

Husserl does allow that conflicts in seeing-claims are possible, even for the life of a single consciousness. This suffices to make it incumbent upon him to delineate procedures for the adjudication of such conflicts, if the possibility of apodicticity or necessity is to be established. However, the most Husserl can do in the *Untersuchungen* is formulate the necessity in hypothetical fashion: If *J* is "in fact" a truth, then if *J* is *seen* in its apodictic necessity, the claim that *J* is apodictic will be grounded and justified. Obviously, though, the apodicticity in question could be verified only through (further) evidential acts of consciousness. For a phenomenologist, in other words, our only access to whatever there is is through our consciousness of it; so it makes no sense to suppose an escape from the subjectivity of one's own consciousness that would give a privileged "direct" access (as to a "*Ding an sich*") to that which is given in this putatively apodictic evidence. Consequently, in the absence of any plausible *phenomenological* procedures for establishing the apodicticity of an evidence, *we cannot dispense with the hypothetical form.*[44] And this, in turn, really means that Husserl has not shown that the claim regarding *J* is capable of any justification at all.

While this concession to a hypothetical form does *not* prove deleterious for a complete theory of phenomenological evidences, it certainly plagues the quest for apodicticity and, at the very least, demands that the concept of apodicticity be introduced as an integral part of a network of evidences and eviden-

44. Cf. in this regard, H. Spiegelberg, "Phenomenology of Direct Evidence," *Philosophy and Phenomenological Research,* II (1942), 427–56.

tial critique; and because of the interdependence and horizontal cross-references of evidential judgments (i.e., protensions and retensions), it means that apodicticity must be introduced by *derivation* from the more pervasive concepts of genetic constitution and the historicity of consciousness. Furthermore, if the claim to apodicticity must be expressed in hypothetical form, Husserl cannot maintain that he has actually won a specific instance of apodicticity; what he has achieved is a mere formal definition of apodicticity in general (of what it would be like to have an apodictic evidence).[45] But it is precisely such formalism that it is the purpose of phenomenology to bring to evidence.[46] In other words, before the phenomenological authority and fruitfulness of apodicticity can properly be appraised, Husserl must first explicate the relevance of constitution for the theory of evidence as a whole. Here, if anywhere, lies the arsenal of weapons to combat the threat of psychologism.

The upshot of our criticism is that, however sound Husserl's refutation of psychologism in the *Logische Untersuchungen* may be (in some respects), he has not been able to formulate the concept of apodicticity *exclusively* and *sufficiently within* phenomenological theory, that is, in terms of distinctively phenomenological (and not psychological) methods and criteria; hence he has not succeeded in sheltering apodicticity from the objections which can be raised against psychologism, as he himself has defined it. Nor is he able to advance the concept of apodicticity beyond a formal, hypothetical position even if one should concede the general efficacy of his refutation of psychologism. In the *Cartesian Meditations*, Husserl affirms that an apodictic *critique* is requisite to overcome the naivete (and thus, too, the provisional nature) of apodictic evidence. The *Untersuchungen,* however, are far from accomplishing, or even recognizing the task of radical phenomenological critique.

45. Here we find the justice of Quentin Lauer's objections to Husserl's theory. See *La Phénoménologie de Husserl* (Paris: Presses Universitaires de France, 1955), pp. 413–14 and 429.

46. It is questionable whether anything is left of apodicticity once this has been accomplished. A merely hypothetical apodicticity is not an apodicticity at all.

3 / The *Ideas* of 1913

[1] "The Principle of All Principles"

When Husserl wrote the *Ideas*,[1] he declared his persuasion that the problem of intentionality, the nature of evidence, must be the very heart of phenomenological theory.

He stated the "principle of all principles," to define both the task and the subject of phenomenology:

> that the most primordial giving intuition is the source of authority for knowledge, that whatever presents itself in "intuition" in primordial form (as it were in its "bodily" reality), is simply to be accepted as it gives itself out to be, though only within the limits in which it then presents itself.[2]

A *principle* is simply what gives expression to such immediate and primordial data as can provide a foundation for all other forms of experience; as *principium*, as fundament, it designates "especially, essential judgments that are general in form." [3]

Continuing the arguments in the *Logische Untersuchungen*, Husserl repudiates all psychological theories of evidence. Theories based on "feelings of self-evidence," or on some merely "mystical *Index veri*," are self-contradictory (for feelings are

1. Citations give the pagination in W. R. Boyce Gibson's translation (Collier Books edition, 1962), followed by the German pagination in parentheses. In using quotations from the *Ideas*, the author has availed himself of Boyce Gibson's work, but the translations are his own.
2. *Ideas* I, § 24, p. 83 (p. 52).
3. *Ibid.*, § 24, p. 84 (p. 52).

completely indifferent to the question of objectivity), circular (since the only way to differentiate feelings is by reference to the objectivities they presume to establish), and in general quite unable to discern and explore systematically the styles and degrees of evidence. What is required, Husserl proposes, is a thorough examination of the various *types* of *consciousness*, according to their *essential* differences. The theory of evidence must be both transcendental (i.e., concerned with what has been phenomenologically "bracketed") and eidetic.[4]

It is equally unreasonable to leap from the extreme of completely subjective psychic states to the other extreme of absolute apodicticity. Not all evidence, Husserl justly maintains, need be apodictic.[5] It would be absurd, he thinks, to demand a uniform perfection of self-evidence, namely, that of apodictic necessity. Such perfection is attainable for eidetic judgments, but not for other very different evidential contents.[6] Still, he believes that the *foundation* of knowledge must be apodictic, otherwise the gigantic structure of knowledge rests, as it were, on quicksand.[7]

Doubts and error cannot be excluded a priori from all modes of evidence. Thus, while the first basic form of "rational consciousness" is primordial object-giving "vision," i.e., positional experiences in which what is posited is truly "perceived," it must be recognized that there are diverse types of experience. For example, the once primordial perception "is this no longer, *after* the living fulfillment of the insight (*Einsicht*), for the latter passes off at once into the obscurity of a retentional modification."[8] It will, of course, still bear a greater rational weight than "any other dim or confused consciousness of the

4. *Ibid.*, § 21, p. 79 (p. 47).
5. The same idea is also expressed in *EP*, I, 324.
6. *Ideas* I, § 138, p. 357 (p. 340).
7. See *EP*, II, 365–66 and 408. Even in the present century Husserl is not alone in advancing this somewhat dubious argument. C. I. Lewis sustains a similar view in *An Analysis of Knowledge and Valuation* (La Salle, Ill.: Open Court, 1946), p. 186. On the other side, William James stoutly argued that experiences lean upon and support one another, without requiring any transcendent system for support and order. Cf. *Essays in Radical Empiricism* (New York: Longmans Green, 1958), chap. 2, p. 42; and *A Pluralistic Universe*, chap. 2, p. 73. Briefly, our rejoinder to Husserl is that, for the establishment of the objectivity of an evidence, further evidence is indeed requisite; but there is no *prima facie* reason to suppose that this evidence would have to be apodictic.
8. *Ideas* I, § 136, pp. 350–51 (pp. 333–36).

same meaning," or than any contradicted or totally unfulfilled (empty) intentional meaning.[9] What is no longer primordial permits subsequently of ramification, possible doubt, and even cancellation, unless the evidence may be supposed apodictic. In this regard, as in scientific endeavor generally, the proper attitude is neither skepticism nor absolutism, but careful criticism and improvement through further investigations.[10] Precisely this attitude should hold even for that evidence which Husserl designates "self-evidence" ("primordial intuition"). Husserl does not provide any criterion to define the scope of the self-given and self-evident; nor, if phenomenological definition be impossible, has he shown why this must be so.[11]

What are the criteria for judging that one has accepted the given in intuition only within the limits prescribed by the presented thing itself? What constitutes going "beyond" evidential givenness? If one not only *describes* a piece of self-evidence, but claims that this self-evidence cannot mislead, is he not perhaps going *beyond* what is strictly self-given? The most one is phenomenologically warranted in saying is that the experienced object gives the appearance (the provisional character) of being self-given (self-evident). One can, and indeed must follow up any intentional references implied by the present evidence. But these evidential references and cross-references may well be unlimited in extent; and in this sense, even the most evident object is not given in an absolutely complete evidence.[12] These are important questions *in any case;* but they are especially urgent and *cannot* be postponed (as Husserl has done) *if* one wishes to maintain a principle of absolute incorrigibility.[13] Otherwise, one can simply admit a certain presumptiveness into the experience of evidence,

9. *Ibid.*

10. *Ibid.*, § 87, pp. 216–17 (pp. 235–36).

11. See Herbert Spiegelberg, "The Phenomenology of Direct Evidence," *Philosophy and Phenomenological Research,* II (1942), 427–56. He proposes some fundamental modifications to Husserl's formulations regarding the self-evident. But ultimately, Spiegelberg's modified position is open to the very same objections that one may raise about Husserl's. In fine, their theories fail to take fully into account the interdependency of evidential judgments.

12. See Aron Gurwitsch, "Contribution to the Phenomenological Theory of Perception," in *Studies in Phenomenology and Psychology* (Evanston, Ill.: Northwestern University Press, 1966).

13. We shall see that, even as late as the *Meditations,* Husserl poses the question of evidential scope, without providing any answer.

and look to *subsequent* intuitions for specific decrees in answering questions about evidential scope and about judgments which transcend their evidential ground. But a doctrine of incorrigibility cannot have recourse to such a solution.

These remarks are not intended in any *general* attitude of skepticism; rather, they are forwarded in accordance with the conviction that, whereas one *can* with impunity hold a thesis about the existence and primacy of genuine self-evidence ("originary intuition"), one *cannot* sustain it *in conjunction with* a second thesis about incorrigibility, without admitting to an egregious naivete. To some extent, then, Husserl shows, in his discussion of the self-given and its scope, that he has not overcome the problems which we discovered in his presentation of apodictic insight in the *Logische Untersuchungen.* But, once having recognized these insufficiencies, he will attempt, in later writings, to cast off his naivete, first with the effectuation of a *transcendental critique,* and second with eidetic analyses of the manifold types of evidential consciousness. It should become clear, however, that he was not altogether successful.

[2] Adequate Evidence, the Ideal of Perfection

1. *Transcendent Perception of "Things" in the World*

Husserl makes the most fundamental of distinctions for his phenomenology by differentiating the being of consciousness ("experience") from the being of "things" and of the world in general ("reality"). The former is the domain of pure immanence; the latter is the domain of transcendence. Corresponding to these *ontological* modalities, there are the two basic modalities of *evidence.*

The "real" object is necessarily given perspectivally ("one-sidedly," as it were, though not necessarily deceptively), as a meaningful, patterned pole of identity enduring through time, which brings together and orders a harmonious, continuing series of experienced "adumbrations." In other words, the "real" object is an *ideal* unity because, as *object,* it bears the sense of being more and other than the *acts* of consciousness that relate to it; and because it is a *synthesis,* constituted with certain perceptually *fulfilled* intentions and also, on essential grounds, with certain other predelineated and horizonally anticipated, but as yet *unfulfilled* intentional acts. The phenomenological object is an intentionally synthesized *system* of profiles, of genuine perceptual *motivations*. And since these motivations, though they are never merely empty logical possibilities, yet extend into the infinity of the object's history (i.e., both its sedimented past and its motivationally projected future), it is necessary to affirm the partial indeterminacy which defines such "real" objects. Transcendent perception (perception of things in the world) is always imperfect, incomplete, inadequate. No rational positing in such cases could be definitive or final, "invincible." The positing may indeed be rational, inasmuch as it is experientially motivated; but it is nonetheless merely presumptive.[14] What is given in adequate evidence, by contrast, is "incapable in principle of being either 'strengthened' or 'weakened,' " just because it is complete and bears no unfulfilled components.[15]

Phenomenological reflection on my consciousness of objects endowed with the sense "really existing out there in the spatiotemporal world" leads me to appreciate that this sense is inherently presumptive—justified, to be sure, because of the continuous and harmonious past course of my perceptions, each of which provides a perspective on the object in question. There is a nucleus of what is "really presented," along with an outlying zone of apprehension, of "marginal co-data," and a more or less vague indeterminacy in the field of the object.

But even this vague indeterminacy is structured according to a "style." This is what, in more precise language, Husserl defines as a "rule": Every imperfect givenness bears a rule for the possibility of its perfecting.[16] This means that "to every object 'which truly is' there intrinsically corresponds . . . the idea of a possible consciousness in which the object itself can be grasped in a primordial and also perfectly adequate way." [17]

Though no transcendent objects, no "realities," can be given with complete determination in any finite consciousness, still the "Kantian Idea" of the object (that is, of the object in its completed givenness) *is* accessible a priori: the object is an infinite field continuum, motivated both essentially and through con-

14. See *Ideas* I, § 27, pp. 91–92 (pp. 57–59) and § 41, pp. 117–20 (pp. 91–95). Also relevant are § 44, pp. 124–28 (pp. 100–104); § 47, pp. 134–35 (p. 112); and § 138, p. 355 (pp. 338–39).

15. See *Ibid.*, § 138.

16. *Ibid.*, § 149, p. 381 (p. 366).

17. *Ibid.*, § 142, p. 365 (p. 349).

crete experience in accordance with the "Idea" of it as a totality.[18] The rule, or "Idea" is, in fact, the "essence" of the thing; unlike the thing itself, it is supposed *capable* of being apprehended with "self-evidence" and "adequacy." [19]

Thus, while the general style of my experience so far entitles me to posit further anticipated perceptual adumbrations of the object, and moreover to posit them, as well as live them, with an immediate certainty, still I must recognize—in my capacity as phenomenologist reflecting on my perceptions, taking them as thematic and as subject to the various reductions—that I may be wrong, that I may not be warranted, on the ground of evidence accepted at some time in the future, in continuing to posit the object as existent in the world, or existent thus. The real object, we find, is never completely, finally, and for all eternity given; rather it is a posited meaning which grasps and structures my perceptions, and, as such, it necessarily transcends both the past and the present, however compelling they may be, toward a relevant future which is never a closed story. In fact, it is precisely because the focus of meaning of an objectivation of outer experience resides in the future, that an object can possess some sort of "objectivity" and genuine "reality" at all.[20]

In summary, the examination of transcendent perception and the nature of the transcendent "real" object helps us to understand Husserl's concept of "inadequate evidence" and, derivatively, his concept of "adequate evidence." It is the latter, of course, which carries the dignity of an evidential norm, or ideal. In subsection 3, pages 56–68 below, it will be seen to what extent this ideal of perfect evidence can be achieved.

2. *This Particular Existent World, as such*

The concept of adequacy, as well as that of apodicticity, can be explicated further through consideration of Husserl's thesis that knowledge of the world's existence is contingent (non-apodictic) and inadequate.

18. *Ibid.*, § 143, p. 366 (p. 351).
19. *Ibid.*, § 149, p. 382 (p. 366).
20. See *Ibid.*, §§ 46 and 55; and Ms. B I 15/IV, p. 3, cited on p. 188 in Alwin Diemer, *Edmund Husserl: Versuch einer systematischen Darstellung seiner Phänomenologie*, Monographien zur philosophische Forschung, vol. 15. (Neisenheim am Glan: Anton Hain, 1956).

The world (that is to say, just *this* world here, as it is, existent for us as an "out there") must be understood phenomenologically, as a correlate of consciousness. Consciousness alone is not *relative* to or dependent upon anything else and is, in this sense, an "absolute." Husserl argues that, because of their spatial profiles, particular "things" in the world are evidenced inadequately, and that we should therefore describe them as "dubitable." The world, understood, so to speak, as the "collection" of these objects, and in itself a thematic object, must in consequence also be dubitable. It is, in fact, dubitable in a profoundly transcendental sense: in contrast to the being of consciousness, whose very method (act) of doubt presupposes its being, the being of the world *can* be doubted without contradiction. This does not mean that its evidence is inadequate and dubitable in the sense that there are any *specific, concrete, empirically motivated* grounds which conflict with the normal "tremendous force of unanimous experiences," but *simply* "in the sense that a doubt is *thinkable* (*denkbar*)." [21]

There is also a second, radically different sense of "world"—a sense which Husserl only rather dimly perceives in the *Ideas*,[22] but which he develops explicitly and in detail in later writings—with respect to which this dubitability is "overcome." According to this conception, the world does not consist of a sum, or "a pile of things" (*"ein Haufen von Dingen"*); [23] it is, rather, the forever presupposed (but not thereby thematized) ground and horizon for all objectivating acts. Acts with an objectivating function belong *already* to this world; and the intentional object intended by such acts will always be an advent within it.[24]

In his very late phenomenology, Husserl inclines to conceive "world" in this more radical way: "To experience a world signifies the capacity to have systematic encounter and to be able to confirm, in the course of encounter, an identical existent sense

21. *Ideas* I, § 46, p. 132 (p. 109).

22. As in § 49, and especially § 55, where he states that "reality" and "world" are simply "certain valid *unities* of *meaning*."

23. See Ms. A VII 20, p. 97, cited in Diemer, *Versuch*, p. 195.

24. See Husserl's Mss. K III 6, pp. 386–87 (cited in *WIZ*, p. 40) and K III 6, p. 111 (cited in *WIZ*, p. 15); *Krisis*, pp. 145 and 459; and *EU*, pp. 26–27. Also relevant are Jean Wahl's "Notes sur la première partie d'*Erfahrung und Urteil* de Husserl," *Rmm*, LVI (1951), 6–34; and H. Asemissen, *Strukturanalytische Probleme der Wahrnehmung in der Phänomenologie Husserls, Kantstudien:* Ergänzungshefte, no. 73 (1957).

(*Seinssinn*), thereby excluding the discordant and introducing instead the correct." [25] *This* world is also transcendent to consciousness, but in a way very different from the naive, natural world, or from the things in that natural world. For, radically conceived, it is equivalent to the very activity of consciousness itself (that is, to the "immanence" of the transcendental ego in the fullness of its streaming life). Nevertheless, it too is necessarily transcendent *in relation to* some temporal moment, taken as the lived now-present.[26] This transcendence, because it is, for Husserl, through and through an immanence (a "transcendental"), can be indubitable (apodictic) and absolute, even if it cannot be adequate. For, on the one hand, it is prior to all doubt as the ground of all doubt, and all certainty; but on the other hand, in its unity and totality, it is never *completely* apprehended. Precisely for this reason, the several reductions *must be carried out*.[27]

3. *Immanent Perception and the Transcendental Ego*

Husserl's position is that, in marked contrast to our perception of "things," which is always both perspectival and dubitable, immanent perception is absolute, and in principle can give its objects with adequacy and even apodicticity. It does not present its intentional objects through an incomplete series of profiles. "An experience," he asserts, "has no profiles." [28] The reason Husserl gives for this is that it makes no sense to speak of perceiving from different standpoints and with a changing orientation when the intentional objects are not spatial. Spatial objects are intentional unities, necessarily involving spatio-temporal syn-

25. Husserl's Ms., AV 3, p. 13 (cited in *WIZ*, p. 17).

26. This sense of transcendence is the *broad and fundamental* sense, not that which merely describes what has not yet been phenomenologically bracketed and reduced to the transcendental sphere.

27. Husserl's Ms., B I 5 IX, p. 31 (cited in *WIZ*, p. 35).

28. *Ideas* I, § 42, p. 121 (p. 97). "Experience," here, is a translation of "*Erlebnis*." Following Sokolowski's convention in *The Formation of Husserl's Concept of Constitution*, this German concept will be uniformly translated as "experience," and the German "*Erfahrung*" will be signaled by the word "encounter," wherever there would otherwise be room for confusion. Wherever, on the other hand, no distinction is to be drawn, no confusion would arise, and when the meaning of Husserl's thought suggests a concept generically inclusive of both inner and outer perception, the term "experience" will be used.

theses.[29] Where the spatial dimension is absent, Husserl argues, such synthesis is simply not requisite to the unity of the intentional objects: "In this absolute sphere, conflict, illusion, and being otherwise have no place. It is a sphere of absolute positionality." [30] In fine, "where the data-giving (*gebende*) intuition is adequate and immanent, the sense (when primordially *filled out,* that is, and not the sense *simpliciter*) coalesces with the object meant. The object is then just what is grasped (*erfasst*) and posited in adequate intuition as a primordial self (*originäres Selbst*)." [31] But where the intuition is directed towards a transcendent reality, the objective factor, solely by virtue of its being objective, and thus "outside" the stream of consciousness, cannot be given adequately. Only the "*Idea*" of this kind of object can be adequately presented; that is, its *meaning* (in specified terms of an a priori rule) can alone be adequate. The "contents" of this meaning, the richness of implicated experience, are infinite, and thus never completed in an intuitive grasp.

In perception of transcendent "reality," the want of completeness means, as we saw, that it is always contingent and dubitable—according to the norm of transcendental rationality, the "starting point" of which is always the intentional performances of consciousness. Later empirical positions can have a bearing on past ones, and may even motivate a reconstruction of previous encounter. But an experience as such (*ein Erlebnis*), for example, a feeling altogether without any "transcendent" existent reference, has no hidden profiles. Immanent objects do admit, nonetheless, of differentiation in their evidenced presentations: differences in relative clearness or dimness, differences in fullness, and so forth.[32] But Husserl insists that *these* differences in perfection do not obtain for those conditions in which *things* are given through incomplete *perspectives.* Modifications in clarity and fullness are not, in his view, genuine *perspectival* modifications, and belong to a fundamentally different "dimension." [33] "Perspective" is accorded a strictly spatial interpretation. Naturally, in view of such a definition, the difference in perfection which Husserl is willing to acknowledge with re-

29. *Ideas* I, § 42.
30. *Ibid.,* § 46. p. 131 (p. 108).
31. *Ibid.,* § 144, p. 367 (p. 352).
32. *Ibid.,* § 44, p. 127 (p. 100).
33. ***Ibid.***

gard to immanent perception could not be called "perspectival." Consequently, Husserl is committed to the view that perception of "immanent" *objects* can be adequately evidenced, whereas this is impossible in principle for outer or "transcendent" perception.

One may well wonder, though, why the nature of spatial objects should be esteemed paradigmatic of incompleteness. The respects in which even nonspatial (and so-called "immanent") objects (pain, for example) can remain indeterminate—that is to say, vague, wanting in true intuitive fullness, and partially undifferentiated—would seem to justify one in describing them as likewise given in profiles and therefore inadequately evidenced.[34] The argument for describing even nonspatial objects as given *inadequately* assumes even greater weight, once we bear in mind Husserl's notion of an object in general and his most fundamental logical sense of transcendence, according to which all objectivations, as such, must be understood as transcendent to our consciousness of them; and once, moreover, we appreciate that nonspatiality cannot be a sufficient condition for immanence.[35] In keeping with the spirit of Husserl's mature phenomenology, we wish to contend that only, for example, a feeling of anger which is merely *lived in awareness* [36] can be

34. Yet we find a significant remark to suggest Husserl *partly* could appreciate our point: "In thought I can truly think or falsely think about it [the immanent object], but that which is there at the focus of mental vision is there absolutely with its qualities, its intensities, and so forth" (*Ibid.*, § 44, p. 126 [p. 102]). He bypasses our objections with the precarious and unelucidated distinction between thinking (articulating in propositions) and perceiving. For the real phenomenological issue concerns the nature of the relationship between the thought and the perceptual experience upon which it is based. In this regard, Husserl sustains a form-matter schema which bifurcates the total experience, and denies, in effect, the genetic approach which grounds predicative judgments in antepredicative evidence.

35. See *Ideas* I, § 135, pp. 348–49 (p. 356), and *Logik*, p. 148.

36. By "a feeling of anger which is merely lived in awareness," we mean to indicate states of consciousness as they are altogether prior to any act(s) of attentiveness directed towards them, and prior, also, to all doxic or memorial acts. Pain and anger, as intentional *objects*, however, are not *only* lived in awareness; they have *also* been identified, discriminated, noticed and described, given an identifiable nature through the passage of time, and made available to reflective and doxic acts of all sorts. In the genetic constitution of such intentional objects, we are conducted along the filaments of

truly immanent; but this anger, as an intentional object (posited, and made available, through let us say, some memorial, reflective, or doxic acts), belongs to the sphere of transcendence.[37] And it is for *this* reason, having nothing whatsoever to do with nonspatiality, that it cannot be *guaranteed* adequacy in evidence by a phenomenological demonstration.[38]

One must recognize, furthermore, that there are many different kinds of nonspatial objects (what Husserl unfortunately is wont to designate "immanent objects" *simpliciter*)—objects, that is, which do not present themselves to an explorative consciousness by means of spatial profiles. There are, for example, mathematical entities, propositions in arithmetic, geometrical figures, essences and meanings in general, inner feelings of anxiety and chill, love and resentment, this act of perceiving or

---

experience, back to the primordial stratum of consciousness: pure immanence, experiences simply as lived in awareness. For Husserl's discussion of "doxic," see *Ideas* I, §§ 103–5, 113–15, and 117.

37. To call an object "immanent," therefore, is incorrect, *strictly speaking*. It is meaningful only as a kind of *abbreviated* reference to the kind of genetic constitution proper to such objects, in contrast to the very different kind of constitution peculiar to "transcendent objects" such as horses and stones.

38. Thus, for example, even *if* we should be willing to concede to Husserl that, e.g., if I experience a pain, I can't be mistaken about it (i.e., about its existence), we could surely argue that it is not at all inconceivable that I might be mistaken about its exact *nature* (features), as well as (among other things) its transcendent cause and body location. And is it really inconceivable that I could be mistaken about its nature in such a way or to such a degree that it would be audacious for me to persist in claiming immunity from doubt as to its very existence? Husserl gives a clear and concise definition of "immanence" in the *Ideas* (§ 38): "intentional acts immanently related" are "those acts which are essentially so constituted that their intentional objects, when these exist at all, belong to the same stream of experience as themselves." But we really must argue, *without denying* that immanence is the condition in which act and object belong to the *same* stream of experience, that the fundamental and essential temporality of immanence, its pure temporal flow, as the necessary condition for the possibility of all such immanent intentionality, *entails the transcendence* of temporally determined and profiled objectivations, within the immanence of a single, unified stream of consciousness. If we overlook this transcendence, and if we fail to distinguish between experience as lived in awareness and this experience as an intentional objectivation, we turn consciousness into a Humean vaudeville show—a series of discrete entities (Husserl's "immanent objects") parading across the stage of one's mind.

of recollecting my desk, and so forth. Are we to say that none of these diverse kinds of nonspatial objects are in *any* sense transcendent to consciousness, and thus that it is possible to demonstrate that they are in no way evidenced inadequately? Is it the case that my feeling of anxiety, for example, is objectivated for me in an absolute presence, and, so to speak, as a "clear and distinct idea"? Why should we think a feeling of anxiety to be adequately evidenced and free from all *possible* "doubts," while the tables and scissors we are staring at are open to doubt and always given with inadequacy? Can propositions in arithmetic (which are not really immanent in consciousness, although bearing a nonspatial sense) be grouped with perceptions of pain in respect of their title to adequacy; or should they rather be aligned with the spatial objects of outer perception? When we wish to determine the possibility of their adequacy, the answer will depend on whether we assign primacy to the fact of their fundamental transcendence or to the mere fact of their non-spatiality. If the former is taken as the significant fact, one confronts the possibility of their inadequacy; whereas if the latter is taken as significant, one will perhaps be tempted to assert their adequacy.[39]

To be sure, Husserl seems at first to *withhold* perfection from (some) immanent objects, as well; for he observes:

> Even an experience is not, and never can be, perceived in its completeness; it cannot be grasped adequately in its full unity. It is essentially something which flows, and starting from the present moment we can swim after it, our gaze reflectively turned towards it, while it stretches out beyond us, leaving a wake that is lost to our perception.[40]

But a confusion of great moment is to be discerned, haunting this remark among others: the confusion, namely, between simply lived experience (which is truly immanent) and the imma-

39. We should grant that, in the *Ideas*, Husserl does indeed distinguish essences of "truly immanent" objects from those of transcendent objects (see § 61), and does distinguish what is only *"ideally* immanent in consciousness (after the reductions) from what is *"really"* immanent (see § 90 and § 97, for instance). However, these distinctions must be treated as *subordinate* to the fundamental phenomenological concepts of objectivity and transcendence—just the issues at stake in regard to the adequacy or inadequacy of immanent *objects* in general.

40. *Ideas* I, § 44, p. 127 (p. 105).

nent experience (perception) of so-called "immanent objects." [41] The "experience" to which Husserl refers in this remark *must* be construed as a thematic concern (an objectivation) of consciousness, and not as the sphere of immanence, pure and simple. So what Husserl should really be denying, in the first place, is the adequacy of immanent experience that has been *objectivated.*

In sections 37 and 38, he calls attention to the phenomenological fact that *intentional* consciousness is not identical with *apprehending* consciousness. If we think about an object and say something about it, we are apprehending it; but there is, as both distinct from and antecedent to this, a mere immanent "glancing towards" the object. One can, for instance, be absorbed in appreciating, valuing, or hating an object without apprehending it in a special objectifying act. Furthermore, he states, "living in the *cogito* we have not got the *cogitatio* consciously before us as intentional object; but it can at any time become so: to its essence belongs in principle the possibility of a 'reflexive' directing of the mental glance towards itself." [42]

However, these last remarks cannot be construed as exonerating Husserl from the confusion. For, in the first place, he does not differentiate apprehension from intentional direction (objectivation) in order to go "beneath" the dimension where consciousness is viewed as related to its intentional *objects*, to the dimension where it is simply living, streaming forward in awareness, and has not yet fully constituted the sense of its intentional objectivations. And in the second place, he defines acts which are "immanently directed" (for example, an act directed at a headache) as "essentially so constituted that their intentional objects . . . belong to the same stream of experience as themselves." [43] Such a definition, we have pointed out, amounts to calling the immanent stream of experience nothing more, nothing other than a "flow" of *objects*. His definition is not an innocent affirmation of the principle of intentionality; rather, it congeals simply lived experience into objects whose phenome-

41. In Husserl's later works, especially *Erfahrung und Urteil* and the as yet unpublished late manuscripts (some of which are cited in *WIZ*), this distinction between the object (objectivated experience) and the primordial immanence of merely lived experience becomes clearer and more prominent.

42. *Ideas* I, § 38, p. 111 (p. 84).

43. *Ibid.*, p. 112 (p. 85).

nological genesis will always elude the grasp of constitutional analysis.

Necessarily, even immanent objects, as objects, are transcendent to consciousness, transcendent to the originally lived experiences which have objectivated them and given them a presumptive temporal unity and endurance, though not any sense of spatial dimension. Immanent experience is simply a streaming of temporal phases. But when these phases are *constituted* as immanent *objects,* as intentional objectivations (and, too, as of a certain *kind*), they assume an identifiableness through temporal change which expresses their insertion in a field of retentional and protentional horizons. This feature, however, is precisely their transcendence, their adumbrational and "relative" ("dependent") nature.[44] An act of consciousness directed toward such objects does indeed belong to the "same" stream of consciousness as these immanent objects themselves. And if we consider this to be a significant fact, at some particular stage of investigation, we may want to distinguish such objects, as "immanent," from objectivations with a spatio-temporal sense (the sense that they are "outside" consciousness). But these "immanent objects" are not immanent in the more fundamental sense that, as objectivations, they too are at a "temporal distance" from their immanent noeses. This is the point of saying that the noetic-noematic structure is a correlation of many-to-one. A temporal phase, as such, is absolute; it is what it is, lived in awareness. But a temporal phase is not an object. Of course, when it is *brought into* the process of objectivation, it loses its absoluteness and gains an identity and a meaning-transcendence.

If Husserl wants to argue that we require *no* "special reasons" (concretely motivated evidence) for "doubting" spatio-temporal ("real") objects, then, *a fortiori,* he cannot maintain that we *do* require (but *cannot find*) such reasons in order to "doubt" immanent objects. All we should consider is the condition of transcendence, which implies (at the very least) the possibility of a non-adequate evidential givenness. Just as the non-adequacy of "real" objects, and their objectivated dependence on the acts of consciousness which posit them, entail, for Husserl, that their

44. By "relative" and "dependent" I mean that, if x is relative to (dependent on) y, then y is a necessary condition for the possibility of x. Husserl's remarks in *Ideas* I, §§ 47–51, are important here. Also consider *FHCC,* pp. 126–33 and 161.

not existing is "thinkable," so these properties of "immanent" objects should *likewise* entail that their not existing is thinkable, and therefore, that their ontological status cannot be demonstrably apodictic. I certainly can conceive of my consciousness still existing, for example, even though it should turn out that my present pain, which I locate in a tooth, is somehow not what I have objectivated it as. Consequently, it seems most perplexing that Husserl could ever have believed that the *essence and structure,* as well as the *existence* of immanent objects can be apodictically evidenced.[45] Surely, no structurations, even those constituted in respect of a lived experience (e.g., pain), are temporal phases, absolute and without profile. From the standpoint of a transcendental logic, objectivated pains are no more indubitable and "independent" than objectivated forests.

Actually, then, Husserl does *not* withhold any evidential perfection from immanent experience (i.e., experience objectivating an "immanent object") on account of its fundamental transcendence. For he still wants to argue that, in the primordiality of its being fully present, an immanent experience really is "complete," though it loses its title to such adequacy as soon as it loses primordiality. The experienced object retreats into the past, of course, and then can be preserved only in a retentional consciousness.[46] The phrase "in its full unity" signals that Husserl is no longer describing some particular, absolutely primordial immanent perception, but rather the history of a whole conscious life (the life, in fact, of the transcendental ego). In other words, it is *only* an adequate grasp of the transcendental ego, in the unity of its full concrete life, that Husserl is willing to deny. But on his view, he may *continue* to assert: "Every immanent perception necessarily guarantees the existence (*Existenz*) of its object." [47] Perception of immanent objects can be, therefore, absolute, adequate, and apodictic.[48]

45. See *Ideas* I, § 46, pp. 130–32 (pp. 107–8).

46. The notion is expressed explicitly in *Ideas* I, § 136, p. 351 (p. 334).

47. *Ibid.*, § 46, p. 130 (p. 106).

48. Obviously, on the basis of the distinction between simply lived experience, prior to objectivational involvement, and experience intentionally related to objectivations, what Husserl needs is a concept which will function as the *non*-reflective analogue of the reflective and doxic (and hence *immanently irrelevant*) concept of apodicticity. See Husserl's discussion of the concepts "thetic" and "doxic" in *Ideas* I, §§ 103–5, 113–15, and 117.

Turning, now, from Husserl's views about the immanent object (the "immanent experience"), we must consider what he thinks about the unified totality of experience which is my "life." The whole stream of experience is, clearly, lived and grasped as a unity; only, this unity, in its fullness of "content," is not to be perceived at one glance and as a *single* experience: "And in the last resort, the whole stream of my experience is a unity of which it is impossible, 'swimming after it,' to obtain a complete perceptual grasp." [49] The point is, though, that this incompleteness is not allowed to resemble the incompleteness of transcendent "realities," for here there are no spatial perspectives. Nevertheless, Husserl's analysis of the stream of consciousness will appeal to the notion of "horizons"; that is permissible, he explains, just because "the stream of experience can never consist wholly of actualities." [50] Its unity is apprehended adequately, but only in the guise of the Kantian "*Idea.*" In this one respect like the transcendent realities, it is such that there can be no adequate determination of its *content.*[51] In *Erste Philosophie*, written about a decade later, Husserl expresses his position in terms of the form-content schema: the form of transcendental subjectivity, but not its content, is both adequate and apodictic.[52]

The life of consciousness, as total flowing unity, may not be apprehended with adequacy, but it is nevertheless said to be absolute and indubitable. On the other hand, Husserl also sought to capture in "Cartesian" apodicticity something very different from the transcendental ego as a whole, and even, to some degree, different from the thetic propositions which reflective consciousness may utter as it structures and differentiates its lived experiences:

> If reflection is directed to my experience, I grasp it as an absolute being whose existence (*Dasein*) is, in principle, undeniable; that is, the insight (*Einsicht*) that it does not exist is, in principle, impossible; it would be nonsense to maintain the possibility of an experience given in such a way not truly existing. The stream of

49. *Ibid.*, § 44, p. 127 (p. 103).
50. *Ibid.*, § 35, p. 105 (p. 79).
51. *Ibid.*, § 83, p. 220 (p. 202).
52. As we shall see, this schema, unfortunately central to Husserl's formal and static structural analyses, is decidedly too rationalistic. Like the concept of apodicticity, it thwarts the maturation of Husserl's genetic-constitutional phenomenology.

> experience which is mine, of the one who is thinking, may be largely uncomprehended, unknown in its past or future reaches; yet as soon as I glance towards the flowing life and into the real present through which it flows . . . I say forthwith and because I must: I *am,* this life is, I live: *cogito.*[53]

Even if my whole life were a dream, it would be truly a dreaming *life,* all the same, and indubitably so:

> That which floats before the mind may be a mere fiction; the floating itself, the fiction-producing consciousness, still is not itself imagined, and the possibility of a perceiving reflection which lays hold on absolute existence belongs to its essence as it does to every experience.[54]

The existence of an immanent experience is assured by the very fact *that* it is experienced.

A sensitive reading of the remarks contained in the last two quotations should disclose intimations of a much deeper dimension of analysis than that heretofore made the subject for query. We have seen that Husserl found the total conscious life, the transcendental ego, to be incapable of adequacy or apodicticity in its concrete content. On the other hand, he did think that it could present itself in adequate and apodictic evidence, but only as an *eidos,* an essential structure.

Here, however, we discover Husserl beginning to move in a direction quite different from that which takes him, in his quest for a perfectly rational evidence, to essential structures; but this direction remained more or less implicit, and adopted only with hesitancy and equivocation, until a much later stage in his thinking. So Husserl writes: "But *my* empathy and *my* consciousness in general are given originally and absolutely, not only according

53. *Ideas* I, § 46, p. 130 (p. 106).

54. *Ibid.* This passage comes close to advocating the "existentialist" reworking of the Cartesian thesis. Descartes, as even Husserl saw (in spite of his residual rationalism), sought an apodictic *proposition (axiom)*; this goal was a logical consequence of his method. It is the indubitability of the *res cogitans* which, for Descartes, assures one's existence. The existential objection is that it is not the reflective *thought* which guarantees my existence, but the *act* (the *being*) of thought (or, it could be, the act of doubt, will, etc.) which is *lived* as indubitable.

to essence (*nach Essenz*), but also according to existence (*nach Existenz*)." [55] This other, more radical direction was both encouraged and obstructed by his claim that the *existence*, too, of pure subjectivity is adequate and apodictic. Husserl ventures no further determination of *what* it is whose existence is apodictic and adequate. Is it the *whole* sphere of immanence, pure transcendental subjectivity, as such? If so, what about its "irretrievable" past and its "open" future? Or is it just the immediate, primordial, lived present? Of course, even where he recognizes this primordial, existential dimension, Husserl clearly presumes the *primacy of essence* as candidate for the absolute, indubitable evidence which phenomenology "must" discover if it is to be the science of the evidence of reason. It is simply *assumed* that, in its essence, subjectivity is capable of such evidence.

We must also bear in mind, as something of fundamental significance, that, even in respect of existence, Husserl remains under the rationalist spell which motivated him to accord primacy to essences. For he thinks that what is adequate and apodictic is *not* "mere" existence (i.e., the stream of consciousness, as lived in awareness, antecedent to any thematizations); it is, rather, the outcome of a *reflection* upon my immediate existence. He states unequivocally that the transcendental ego, "which is plainly 'necessary' and indubitable," is capable of being grasped in a "self-evident unshakeable *existential thesis*." [56] We must conclude that such a statement reinforces the interpretation we want to propose, namely, that apodicticity, as Husserl conceives it, belongs to a thesis (indeed, a doxic positionality) in the domain of *reflective knowledge*. The "existence" about which he is speaking is thus a transmuted existence, belonging just as much as essences to the domain we call "knowledge." And, like other objective formations of reflective and doxic consciousness, this "existence" bears the fault of "dubitability," from the radical

55. *Ibid.*

56. *Ibid.*, § 46, p. 131 (p. 109). The word "unshakeable," of course, can only be construed as a synonym for "apodictic." It is beyond question that what Husserl here finds apodictic is not existence in the sense of the lived present, but rather in the sense of a *thesis of existence* (*Daseinsthesis*). The thetic aspect is, as we shall see, unfortunate; the existential aspect is much more promising. However, the existentialist argument in this regard would be that the "I am" (the living present) is not a doxic thesis at all, but is a lived, pre-thetic certitude. This means, moreover, that its evidence cannot be described through the concept of "apodictic evidence."

standpoint of transcendental reason.[57] For it is according to this *same* point of view, let us remember, that Husserl refuted the certainty, or purported indubitability, of the real world. The heart of his argument for the dubitability of the world, after all, was precisely its fundamental *transcendence* (exhibited through the many-to-one correlation between diverse actual and possible *noetic acts,* and the *one identical noema*), and its relativity to (dependence on) the consciousness who posits it.

There is really but one passage in the *Ideas* to serve as a good clue to the new direction his thinking began to explore, gradually taking him away from the rationalist preoccupation with certainty, essences and reflection:

> Time is, furthermore . . . a title for a completely self-contained problem-sphere, and one of exceptional difficulty. It will be seen that, in a certain sense, our previous exposition has been silent, and necessarily so, concerning a whole dimension, so as to keep free of confusion what first becomes accessible from the phenomenological standpoint alone, and quite apart from the new dimension constitutes a self-contained field of inquiry. The transcendental "absolute" which we have uncovered through the reductions is in truth not ultimate; it is something which in a certain profound and wholly unique sense constitutes itself, and has its primal source in what is *truly* ultimate and absolute.[58]

That deeper dimension, the "absolute," which he can as yet articulate only cryptically and with great difficulty, is, in fact, the *immediate, living actual (now-) present,* the "source" of the flow characterizing the inner temporality of pure subjectivity. Later works clarify and develop this nascent dimension, until, at last, the living streaming present will be recovered as the truly apodictic and adequate "starting point," the authentic fundament, for a rigorous phenomenological science.[59] We shall find

57. It is precisely on this issue that Jean-Paul Sartre and Merleau-Ponty opposed their radical existentialism to Husserl's untenable rationalism. See Sartre's *Being and Nothingness* (New York: Philosophical Library, 1956), §§ 3–4; and "Conscience de soi et connaissance de soi," paper read on June 2, 1947 before the Société Française de Philosophie; and *PP,* Introduction and chaps. 1–4.

58. *Ideas* I, § 81, p. 216 (p. 198).

59. On the one hand, we wish to commend Husserl's recovery of the primordial, lived present, and agree that this can be the authentic foundation for knowledge. On the other hand, we must attempt to refute his view that this lived present can be apodictic. Our refutation is presented below, in Chapter Three, § VI.

that, in relation to this flowing, momentary, lived present, transcendental subjectivity (that is, the transcendental ego) must be considered an objective transcendent. But Husserl never reached the point where he could deny to this ego, on the grounds of such transcendence, either its apodictic evidence *as an existent* or its adequacy *as form* (as *eidos*).

4. *Criticism of Husserl's Concept of Adequate Evidence*

In the *Logische Untersuchungen,* adequacy is introduced without a close or explicit discussion of the phenomenological reduction. By contrast, it has been possible for us to elicit from an examination of the immanent and transcendent types of perception presented in the *Ideas* a rather precise concept of adequate evidence, operative *within* the phenomenologically reduced sphere of consciousness. It is, in simple terms, a completeness of intuitive evidence. It does not seem to imply, however, completeness in every *conceivable* dimension of evidential presentation; for, even evidence wanting in a certain determinacy, clarity, or fullness (for example, a feeling, in its purely immanent phase) is called adequate if it is "genuinely limited" (whatever *that* means) to the immanent.

Now, one might justifiably argue at this point that Husserl is unduly impressed with spatial perspective, and that, in consequence, he tends to overlook other important considerations in the evidential explication of objectivity. Spatial profiles should figure prominently but not exclusively, along with factors such as clarity, specificity, and levels of differentiation, in determining the possibility of evidential completeness. If we pursue this course of inquiry, not at all incompatible with Husserl's mature phenomenology, we can then discern the fundamental *logical* similarity which obtains for *both* immanent and transcendent objects: namely, that regardless of their profound *phenomenological* differences (differences articulated through the process of their genetic constitution), they are both, *as types of objectivity,* transcendent to and other than the objectivating consciousness itself. Both types fail to exhibit, for essential reasons (clarified within the framework of transcendental logic), an evidential completeness in one respect or another. Spatial configurations, profiles perhaps infinite in number, entail only one type of possible inadequacy *among many.* From the standpoint of knowledge, less than perfect clearness and less than total fullness in the intuitional presentation of an objectivity are just as much conditions of *imperfect* knowledge as is our acquaintance with some physical object through a limited set of its spatial profiles. These reflections will receive further support and amplification in later chapters. In particular, we will show that *essences,* though nonspatial (and, in this rather misleading sense, "immanent"), are *fundamentally transcendent,* to say the least, and *hence we cannot demonstrate that they must be adequately apprehended* in all respects *in spite of* the absence of any incompleteness due to spatial perspectives.

A second point of contention is Husserl's view that adequate evidence is at least to be won by means of the "Kantian Idea." Husserl's thinking runs as follows. The "real" thing is a unity of infinite perspectives; so much, our phenomenological understanding instructs us. It can be apprehended, for that reason, only through inadequate evidence. But there corresponds to the object thus experienced the *thought* of it as an experientially complete object, a full unity. We have an "Idea" of the object, which prescribes the *essential style* of our experience relative to it. This "Idea" is what Husserl regards as adequate. Similarly, the streaming, vital consciousness which is "my life," the "I," is a unified rushing of unlimited experiential contents and strata; we can therefore have only an inadequate knowledge of this life in its totality. But again, Husserl asserts that we do have an adequate "Idea" of this consciousness; we have an a priori "rule" or "law" (to translate what Husserl calls a "*Gesetz*") which predelineates the universal and purely formal unity and identity of this streaming consciousness through the "stylized" manifold experiences engaging it. The "adequate Idea" becomes, so to speak, a consolation prize for phenomenology, when the endeavor to rationalize fully the vital, flowing contents of consciousness and its formations has met with frustration.

Also, it might here seem reasonable to object that Husserl has made use of the concept of adequacy in an ambiguous way. For surely, one might say, the "Idea" is not adequate (and demonstrated to be so) according to exactly the same sense as that by which the transcendent object—or, for that matter, the whole of transcendental subjectivity—is held to be inadequate. In other words, it is not reasonable to suppose that the a priori rule for the complete object can be adequately given according to the same criteria which prove the object itself, in its concreteness, to be inadequate. The reasoning behind this objection could be, quite simply, that, since the "Kantian Idea" (an object of the understanding, and nothing more) is altogether different from the objectivity whose concrete unity it determines along essential lines, there must at least be a radically different paradigm for adequacy in each case.

But on the other hand, if one should steadfastly deny any such equivocation, then one might even begin to wonder whether it is so obvious, after all, that the "Idea" can be adequate in any (Husserlian) sense whatsoever. It is possible for me to know in general (let us say, in an essential way), exactly what it is for any object to be an object at all: that is, indeed, the very job supposedly accomplished by the phenomenological definition of objectivity as such. But it is not so clear that I can know exactly (with true adequacy) what it is for *this* particular to be just the very object it is, in all respects, now and throughout its career.[60] The former knowledge, where adequacy is to some extent plausible, belongs to transcendental logic (i.e., phenomenological inquiry into the logical structure and categories of the understanding in general); but the latter knowledge, where Husserl also affirms adequacy, involves phenomenology in transcendental description at a level much less universal and no longer formal: here, at least, our knowledge would seem forever doomed to incompleteness, just because such knowledge, though admittedly *about* the a priori and eidetic, will emerge only gradually and partially from continued reflection on our experience. Our eidetic knowledge, stemming from such reflection, will depend on the limitations, or contingency, which characterize our reflective grasp of this never-ending experience of the object's concrete contents.

Note, moreover, that we do not have to assume, for the purposes of our argument against adequacy (and consequently against apodicticity), that there *are* any such a priori "rules" ("essences"), nor, more particularly, what their exact nature and genetic constitution must be. Our whole argument can be formulated in a purely hypothetical way: If there are such a priori

60. We may consider this criticism to hold of the transcendental ego, as well, insofar as it is an object of reflective consciousness.

rules, what can we say about the possibility of an adequate and apodictic knowledge of them?

There is no reason to think that rules, whether a priori or otherwise, are necessarily articulated with optimum determinacy, clarity, and specificity such that no room is left for increasing differentiation and amplification. Rules, at best, can serve reflective consciousness as indicators, as guides to discernment and decision. Does the "possession" in knowledge of a certain rule ensure against error? Can a rule, having become the thematic concern of transcendental knowledge, truly recommend itself as at once fully determinate and yet without any unexamined, tacit presupposition? [61] In order to say that the a priori rule for the object x is adequately given, would one perhaps have to suppose the wholly gratuitous distinction between the (adequate) "form" of the rule and the (inadequate) working out of its "content," thereby preserving the adequacy of the rule (but merely in its form)? It would then be necessary to contend with the problem of differentiating, with respect to the rule (already, in a sense, a pure "form" or essence), its form and its content. A rule gains in power, in scope, in its resources as it gradually encompasses more and more experience within its assertion. But we cannot attribute this gain—which results from the functional application of the rule, prior to its thematization as a concern of phenomenological reflection—just to the "content," for it is nothing other than an increasing reflective *knowledge about* the rule (as a form). Let us express our objections as follows: first, the knowledge whose adequacy is here in question seems, if anything, to pertain to the content, rather than to the form; but, second, even if this were not the case, there does not seem to be any basis, nor in fact any procedure, for distinguishing, within an a priori rule of consciousness itself, its matter from its form. It is worth observing, now, that Husserl might

61. The author is indebted to J. Buchler for the kind of criticism he has developed here. See J. Buchler, *The Concept of Method* (New York: Columbia University Press, 1961). His investigations into the nature and function of rules, although conducted in a non-phenomenological context, are of sufficient generality to have some relevancy for phenomenological theory as well. Husserl might, for example, have profited from asking himself more conscientiously than he did: "What does it mean to say that in a certain discipline 'nothing remains hidden'?" It is revealing that Buchler directs this question at Descartes, by whom, as we know, Husserl was so inspired.

well have found this move of differentiation felicitous, at least prior to the time he started working on the *Logik*.[62] However, even if we should somehow be able to justify such a distinction on phenomenological grounds, the same problems could be shown to haunt our knowledge of the form alone; and an indeterminate regress would ensue. Why should the fact that the object of our knowledge is the pure form of an a priori rule entail the feasibility of adequate evidence? To formulate the question in this manner is to give expression to the more general and fundamental problem, namely: Is an adequate knowledge (satisfying the absolute norm of perfect and complete evidence) of any transcendent, thematic concern of consciousness, regardless of its purported a priori status, actually possible? The problems which attend the adequacy of the "Kantian Idea" of a "real" object (a "thing"), and which we have raised in a somewhat tentative manner, assume even greater force when a critical attitude is directed towards the "Idea" of the totality of a conscious life (what, in the *Meditations,* will be called the *eidos,* "transcendental ego"). Here, at least, one wants to say, the adequacy of the "Idea" is patently questionable.

Finally, it should be remarked, in keeping with the program of Husserl's radical phenomenology, that the a priori rule is itself a transcendent object of reflection, and must share the epistemic status of all other transcendents. It is true that it has no spatial dimensionality which could beckon us on to infinite exploration; it is true, furthermore, that it is a formation of consciousness engendered in the immanence (the vital activity) of consciousness itself. *But the immanence attributable to an a priori rule in its actual functioning cannot be transferred to the rule as an object of knowledge,* even when such knowledge is transcenden-

62. Cf. the first of the *Beilagen* (Appendixes) to *IPP*, p. 383, written in 1914. Husserl observes that every essence, like all objects generally, has a "form" and a "content." This is an instantiation of the more general matter/form schema so central to Husserl's early (and more "rationalistic") phenomenology. In later years, however, Husserl abandoned this schema, for example, in his analysis of perceptual acts. For a more detailed treatment of the matter/form schema in Husserl, see *FHCC*. Sokolowski carefully traces the sorry story of this rationalist schema, and shows how, time and again, it obstructed the maturation of Husserl's thinking in regard to genetic constitution. We may add that its grip on Husserl partially explains why the possibility of winning apodictic evidence seemed so persuasive to him.

tally purified and rigorously eidetic.[63] That this is the case should be recognized to follow from Husserl's own theory, once it is understood as emancipated from all rationalist presuppositions. The chapter on Husserl's *Cartesian Meditations* and, especially, the chapter on essential structures will pursue and develop the direction of critique adopted here, in this section.

[3] Apodicticity

It can be said with justice that, despite what amount to serious problems (relative to his later thinking), Husserl's *Ideas* marks considerable progress beyond the *Logische Untersuchungen,* with respect to the concept of apodictic insight. For, first of all, whereas he applied the concept in the earlier work in a naive way to mathematics, logic, and geometry, in the later work he explicitly calls for the execution of phenomenological reduction as a prerequisite to all investigations into these sciences. Geometry, for instance, may stand as a paradigm, for the beginning phenomenologist, of an eidetic and "necessary" science; but for the initiated phenomenologist, it must suffer bracketing, along with logic and mathematics.[64] Otherwise, its claims to universality (eidetic stature) and apodictic necessity are unacceptable. These exact sciences, too, must be clarified "on purely immanental lines," by reference back to the formative acts of consciousness. An indubitable, adequate insight into "what an axiom in mathematics states," for exam-

63. Thus Gerd Brand asserts that "I am always more and other than what I have or can have of myself as theme in apperceptive unity" (*WIZ*, p. 73). Similar views are advanced by Merleau-Ponty, *The Primacy of Perception,* ed. James Edie (Evanston, Ill.: Northwestern University Press, 1964), p. 64, and *PP*, pp. 219 and 345. On p. 345, he writes: "I know myself only in my ambiguity." A. de Waelhens observed: "Phenomenology denies, in fact, that consciousness can ever be purely present to and for itself. But in binding itself radically to the other, consciousness is obliged, in order to know itself, to substitute for its pure and definitive apperception, a laborious and complex coming to knowledge, wedding it thus to the countless metamorphoses which it derives from its correlativity to the countless modalities of this other, its constant companion . . ." ("Réflexions sur une problématique husserlienne de l'inconscient, Husserl et Hegel," in *Phänomenologica* (The Hague: Martinus Nijhoff, 1959), IV, 224. Also, cf. his "L'idée phénoménologique de l'intentionnalité," in *ibid.*, II, 119–20.

64. *Ideas* I, §§ 59–60, pp. 160–62 (pp. 140–43).

ple, is possible only by means of an analysis which uncovers the "immanent meaning" of the axiom.[65] Second, "insight," is explicitly determined in relation to the phenomenological concept of apodicticity, in such a manner that "insight" can no longer be employed to describe evidence for truths in the non-reduced sciences. Third, apodicticity is introduced as a kind of evidence appropriate only within the *eidetic,* as well as the phenomenological, reductions.[66] And fourth, apodicticity is presented somewhat more fully in its relation to adequate evidence, although this connection, from Husserl's own point of view, is not sufficiently clarified until *Erste Philosophie.*[67]

The first occurrence in the *Ideas* I of the concept of apodicticity is in the following context:

> Every eidetic division and individuation of an eidetically general fact is called, just *in so far* as it is this, an *essential necessity. Essential generality and essential necessity are thus correlates.* The use of the term "necessity" here vacillates somewhat so as to conform to the attached correlations: the corresponding judgments are also termed "necessary." But it is important to recognize these distinctions, and above all not to refer to essential generality (as is ordinarily done) as itself necessity. The consciousness-of-a-necessity, or more specifically, a consciousness of a judgment in which we become aware of a certain matter as the specification of an eidetic generality, is called *apodictic,* and the judgment itself, the proposition, an *apodictic* (also apodictically—"necessary") *consequent* of the general proposition to which it is related.[68]

The expressions "apodictic judgment" and "necessary judgment" are, we may infer, asserted to be equivalent. Here we should also note that Husserl has introduced "apodicticity" in terms of *propositions,* statements in *language.* Thus, it is clear that apodicticity belongs most definitely to the sphere of knowledge (i.e., positional and, in fact, *doxic* consciousness).[69]

65. *Ibid.,* § 25, p. 85 (pp. 53–54).

66. It seems, however, that Husserl does not regard *all* evidences reduced to the eidetic as entitled, for that reason, to claim apodicticity; see *Ideen* I, *Beilage* 27, p. 417.

67. And then, as we shall see, in the *Cartesian Meditations* Husserl proposes what he deems to be a major revision of the *Erste Philosophie* formulation.

68. *Ideas* I, § 6, p. 53 (pp. 19–20).

69. *Ideas* I, § 137, p. 354 (p. 337); see also §§ 103–5, 113–15, and 117.

Husserl then adds, somewhat cryptically:

> The propositions we have stated concerning the relations between generality, necessity, and apodicticity can also be conceived in a more general way, so as to hold good for any realm of discourse, and not only such as are purely eidetic. But with the eidetic limitation they obviously receive a distinctive and especially important meaning.[70]

He does not elaborate the more extensive purview of these concepts; nor does he give any illustrations. In any case, however, it may be surmised that apodicticity is at least associated with, though perhaps not logically bound to the fruits of eidetic research. In other passages, he binds together "necessity" (the "*absolut unentbehrlich,*" as he here expresses it) and "insight." [71]

Not until the end of the first volume of *Ideas*—that is, the crucial chapter entitled "The Phenomenology of Reason," which, as one should expect from the title, consummates the preceding phenomenological investigations with a sort of substantive methodological critique—does one find any ramified phenomenological analysis of apodictic evidence which can be considered to develop it significantly beyond the formulations in the *Logische Untersuchungen.*

Husserl notes that evidence (or "self-evidence," to render best his term, "*Evidenz*") is treated in customary discourse as equivalent to insight (*Einsicht*), and thereby it is equated at once with apodicticity. Two correlative errors, he maintains, reside in these equivalencies: On the one hand, there is the identification of *all* evidence with apodictic evidence, and in this way we demand too much of certain quite legitimate but non-apodictic modes of evidence; while on the other hand, there is the degradation of apodicticity, in as much as it is no longer treated as a very special, methodically limited and superior mode of evidence, but is rather conceived as characterizing evidence as such.[72]

Husserl is thus consistent in proposing, from this standpoint, a total reinterpretation, on completely phenomenological grounds, of this special cluster of concepts—evidence, insight, and apodicticity. To begin with, he holds, one must distinguish

70. *Ibid.*, § 6, p. 54 (p. 20).
71. *Ibid.*, § 149, p. 382 (p. 367), and § 42, p. 122 (p. 97).
72. It would seem that, in the *Logische Untersuchungen,* indeed, both these errors constituted real temptations for Husserl.

between (I) a mere ("blind") seeing and (II) the genuine experience of evidence (*Evidenz*), wherein what is given is self-evident, "bodily" present itself.

He illustrates (I) with the recollection of a landscape, once visually perceived, but presently quite lost to recapture; and (II) is illustrated with an act wherein the "truth" of the proposition '2 + 2 = 4,' for instance, is recognized and affirmed "with right." [73] Presumably, in this context, the fact that the two examples are drawn from such different domains is not relevant: the landscape could have been seen in the second manner (as in a very "vivid" and strongly corroborated memory), while the arithmetical proposition could equally have been articulated in the first manner (as in the case of a child just learning to count). The difference between (I) and (II) is measured in terms of the fullness of meaning-fulfillment, and in terms of the presence or absence of primordial evidence.

A fundamental reorientation in our understanding of evidence derives from his thesis that "rational consciousness in general designates a *summum genus* of thetic modalities, in which 'seeing,' used in its widest sense, as pertaining to primordial givenness, constitutes a well-defined class." [74] He suggests that the term "evidence" (*Evidenz*) should serve to designate just this *summum genus*. There will then ensue two hierarchic orders of subdivision, falling under heading (II) as described above: (A) *primordial evidence* (which means "every rational thesis characterized by a *motivated* relation in regard to the primordiality of what is given"),[75] or (B) *non-primordial evidence;* [76] and (1) *assertoric evidence*, designating that evidence which pertains exclusively to the individual (the particular) or (2) *apodictic* (non-assertoric) *evidence.*

The term "insight" ("*Einsicht*") will then be associated uniquely with apodictic evidence.[77] "Insight" is defined as "a

73. See *Ideas* I § 136, p. 350 (p. 334).
74. *Ibid.*, § 137, p. 354 (p. 337).
75. *Ibid.*
76. The landscape being seen exemplifies the former; the landscape being recollected exemplifies the latter.
77. *Ibid.* This represents a distinct evolutionary advance beyond the *Logische Untersuchungen*. For in that work, "insight" and "apodicticity" were, in general, *used* as equivalent, but not by any explicit convention. See vol. I, chap. 5, p. 91. Moreover, from the standpoint of the *Ideas*, "insight" was there employed in the "natural attitude" to describe the evidence for quite non-phenomenological items.

positional doxic, and also *adequate* data-giving consciousness which simply 'excludes otherness'; the thesis is motivated in a quite exceptional way through the adequacy of the given material, and is in the highest sense an act of 'reason.'" [78]

Next, just as there is pure and impure evidence in general, so there is further the differentiation of apodictic insight into its (a) pure and (b) impure modes. The former treats exclusively of essences and essential relations; whereas the second (a sort of "mixed" insight) is "the cognition of the *necessity* of an element of fact, in its eidetic subsumption, the being of which need not be self-evident." [79] Mode (b) could perhaps be illustrated by a judgment asserting some *application* of the pure eidetics of Euclidean geometry *to* a particular posited even on earth. It is not the event itself, but the *relation* (of subsumption or application) between essence and fact which is an impure variety of apodictic judgment.[80] Since apodictic insight, both pure and impure, is reserved for the special seeing of the eidetic, any seeing which is about neither the purely eidetic nor the relation between the eidetic and the particular, will of course be merely assertoric.

In summary, it would seem that Husserl introduces apodicticity in terms of insight, necessity, and, finally, essentialities. Apodictic insight is the "rational" functioning *par excellence* of consciousness; it is the functioning form in which alone consciousness has satisfied its self-imposed responsibility to possess absolute and indubitable evidence.

Furthermore, although he is never sufficiently explicit, the force of his argument may reasonably be assumed to imply *some* sort of direct correlation between adequate and apodictic evidences. For adequacy can relate to apodicticity through the *eidetic:* Husserl observes that the primordial givenness of the eidetic example (as in the arithmetical proposition) can be adequate, in contrast to the example of the landscape, which is inadequately evidenced, whether in visual (and primordial) perception or in recollection; [81] and elsewhere he has spoken of grasping and fixing in "adequate ideation the pure essences" which concern the phenomenologist.[82] Adequacy can also relate

78. *Ideas* I, § 137.
79. *Ibid.*
80. See *ibid.*, §§ 5–7, pp. 51–56 (pp. 17–22).
81. *Ibid.*, § 137, p. 353 (p. 337).
82. *Ibid.*, § 34, p. 104 (p. 74).

to apodicticity through the concept of *insight*, which, as we found, has been defined as "doxic" and "adequate." It could be regarded as implicit in his statements that apodicticity *entails* adequacy; whether the converse also obtains cannot really be inferred. Nowhere, unfortunately, does Husserl explicitly pronounce the existence, much less the exact nature, of a correlation between adequacy and apodictic insight.[83]

Still another region of apparent indeterminacy pertains to the precise coincidence of the eidetic with the apodictic. In section 6, the eidetic is held to be especially important for the attainment of apodicticity; yet apodicticity is not confined to essentialities. But in section 137, where Husserl constructs, in effect, a table of evidential differentiation, the apodictic mode of seeing is decisively and exhaustively distinguished from the assertoric mode because of its preoccupation with the eidetic.[84]

Finally, it should be observed that, in contrast to the treatment of apodictic evidence in the *Logische Untersuchungen*, and even more severely to his treatment in *Erste Philosophie* and the *Cartesian Meditations*, both works of a later date, the introduction of apodicticity in the *Ideas* does *not* firmly establish that Husserl meant to assert an incorrigible, absolutely final and irrevocable mode of evidence.

In fact, we cannot be clear at all what he wished to claim, then, for his apodictic evidences, in respect of their phenomenological compulsion. For Husserl seems to think that even empirical, assertoric evidences, from which they are radically distinct, may have a very compelling certainty or indubitability (thus, plainly more than a merely psychological order of feeling), when found to constitute a harmonious system of reciprocally supporting and self-rectifying experiences, and articulated in terms of conventionally acceptable "good reasons." Now, the lingering "dubitability" of these evidences, from the viewpoint of transcendental rationality, is motivated, Husserl maintains, by the

83. For this, we must await his formulations in *Erste Philosophie*.

84. But see *Ideen, Beilage* 27 (from 1914), p. 417, and especially *Beilage* 26 (also from 1914), p. 415. In the latter, commenting upon § 137 in the main body of *Ideas* I, Husserl himself notes a certain terminological deficiency, and hints at some inconsistency between §§ 6 and 137. He distinguishes three modes of seeing: (1) empirical (*erfahrende*); (2) eidetic (which may or may not be apodictic); and (3) insight into universal, unconditional necessities. Only (3) is clearly *both* apodictic and eidetic.

transcendent, adumbrational nature of the intentional objects thus presented. Consequently, when a *stronger* certainty is claimed for the apodictic mode, we might well infer, with some justification, that what differentiates the compulsion of the assertoric from that of the apodictic can only be that the latter, as eidetic and purely immanent (i.e., absolute and non-adumbrational), affirms not merely the absence of *present* doubt, summoning the testimony of a relevant past, but indeed the destruction of *all* (logically and eidetically) *possible* doubts, now and forever.

On the other hand, it is possible in fact to find remarks which suggest an approach to phenomenological inquiry which is prima facie quite incompatible with the concept of apodictic evidence.[85] These remarks do not explicitly refer to the norm of apodicticity; they would seem to bear closely on Husserl's discussion of the ideal of adequate evidence, but again, nothing decisive for our understanding of adequacy and apodicticity can be elicited from them. It must be conceded, ultimately, that we look in vain for a resolution to our interpretative dilemmas. These issues represent, in other words, some crucial problematic domains to which Husserl's subsequent works in part, at least, address themselves.

85. See *Ideas* I, § 65.

4 / *Erste Philosophie* (1923/24)

[1] The Domain Is Defined

The title to appendix 13 of *Erste Philosophie* sums up in a succinct way the most pervasive concern of that work: "To what extent can, in general, the demand of apodicticity for a knowledge of existents (*vom Seiendem*) be proposed?" [1] Husserl recognizes two principal kinds of knowledge: that of the existence (*Sein*) of objects, and that of their properties, whether essential or contingent (*Sosein*). He inquires:

> Must knowledge of existence (*Sein*) and knowledge of properties (*Sosein*) be apodictic in order for us justifiably to claim that they are such and such? Must all truly existent objects, all objects of possible science, be capable of being apodictically experienced, and thus knowable as such? And, moreover, adequate as well? [2]

He feels that, at the very least, through copious phenomenological research,

> I can thus make clear what a rational goal of knowledge would mean, directed toward an objectivity; what, in other words, rational justification for the positing of an object with an existent sense would mean, even though the goal of knowledge, the true, cannot be given apodictically and adequately in any form of knowledge.[3]

Erste Philosophie should be understood as a devoted search for the answers to these questions. It takes the form of an

1. II, 396–97.
2. *Ibid.*
3. *Ibid.*

investigation into the various primary categories of being, and, correlatively, into their corresponding modes of being-for-consciousness. The ultimate goal is thus to uncover and ground at once a *being* and a *mode of evidence* exhibiting the rational property of apodicticity.

[2] Further Definition of Adequacy and Apodicticity

Erste Philosophie exhibits a development beyond the *Ideas* in the sense that adequation and apodicticity are not only more fully introduced in their respective functions; they are also more clearly defined in their relation one to the other. Developing his thought beyond the *Ideas*, Husserl clearly wants to show that the two modes of evidence are truly correlative and function interdependently. Furthermore, adequacy is given greater examination as a philosophical norm. It is conjectured for the first time that its philosophical role may be that of a teleological ideal for evidence—an ideal none the less impossible of fulfillment, given the subjective and intentional nature of our access to evidence.

1. *Adequate Evidence*

Let us consider, first, Husserl's views about adequate evidence. He recognized, as we know, that there are many styles of justification besides adequation; but it is, he thinks, the final source and arbiter of epistemic justification. It entails an absolute fulfillment or completeness in the total meaning, inasmuch as all partial meanings, all implicated marginal meanings, are exhaustively fulfilled in a closed constitution.[4] Further,

> As long as something is co-intended which has not been presented (*was der Ausweisung ermangelt*), it remains open that the intended may not be. On the contrary side, full adequation excludes not being, and is a judgment executed through and through with insight (*einsichtig*) that bears the truth in itself in it, and indeed with apodictic *necessity:* it cannot be false. That is, moreover, a truth (in principle a universality), and itself an insight both adequate and apodictic.[5]

4. *Ibid.*, p. 334.
5. *Ibid.*

Elsewhere, the ideal objects of mathematics are suggested as exemplifying this perfection of adequate givenness.[6]

An evidence which has this ideal perfection, and which accordingly is adequate, can always be recognized (hence justified) as such "only in a second, necessarily reflective evidence, which itself must be adequate." Husserl then adds:

> That it can be adequately consummated, that such adequate reflections *in infinitum* are possible and, as it would seem, require justifications *in infinitum*, should not cause any concern, although we must still consider this problem at some appropriate time, as well as the problem which brings with it the possibility of adequate givenness. Perhaps it might then become manifest that such self-givenness is a mere 'idea,' just as, analogously, we call pure red an idea.[7]

Once again, we find Husserl postponing direct confrontation with the problem of a critique of evidence, pursued through all its radical implications and ramifications.

Here, nevertheless, we discover tempting intimations of the idea of a teleology of evidence—an idea that gains in centrality as Husserl's thinking matures. That the ideal of adequacy may involve an *infinite* series of evidences not only seems a *reasonable* view, but a *fruitful* one as well. In the context of a quest for apodicticity, therefore, this possibility urgently demands investigation. And more consideration than Husserl gives is also due the related conjecture he very briefly entertains that adequacy may be a mere *ideal*. He writes:

> Perhaps there lies in each and every evidence as self-giving, as consciousness, as the apprehension of the 'meant' itself, a certain *relativity*, of such a nature that, wheresoever we speak of an adequate evidence and are certain of it as such, only a similar but continuing and freely developing process of approximation to relative evidences in fact lies before us.[8]

Husserl may indeed be correct that these questions are not "proper for the beginning"; [9] in that case, it seems especially appropriate to question the wisdom of proceeding *as if* there were a firmly settled and authenticated conception of adequate and,

6. *Ibid.*, p. 496 n; also p. 35, where Husserl gives a simple proposition from the domain of arithmetic to illustrate his argument.
7. *Ibid.*, p. 33.
8. *Ibid.*, p. 34.
9. *Ibid.*

particularly, apodictic evidence. Husserl shows himself to be less modest in his pretensions and less austere in his methodological comportment than he would like to think. Postponement of critique, in itself, is *not at all* a reason for reproach. In the event of such postponement, and consequently, perhaps, an unavoidable incompleteness, what surely seems illicit, however, is Husserl's premature claims for a truly *apodictic* science.

2. *Apodictic Evidence*

Husserl gives us some important statements on apodicticity in *Erste Philosophie*. Consider the following:

> An apodictic knowledge simply excludes the possibility of the non-existence of what is known. It is of course always understandable that, where absolutely nothing regarding the properties (*Sosein*), the content of determinations of encounter (*Erfahrung*) can be adequately given, there remains no hope for an apodicticity of mere existence (*Dasein*).[10]

And further:

> An *apodictic knowledge* [is] completely capable of being repeated, in identical validity. What is once apodictically evident yields not only possible recollection of having had this evidence, but in fact the necessity of this status now and forever: finality.[11]

Undoubtedly, the most crucial utterance specifically regarding the relation of adequacy to apodicticity is the following:

> Something else, besides, is to be noted as characteristic of an adequate evidence: It comes to light in the investigation of the passage through negation or doubt. If I attempt to negate an adequate evidence or to posit it as dubitable, then there appears, again in adequate evidence, the impossibility of the not-being or of the dubitability of the evident, of that which previously came forth as grasped in absolute self-giving. We can refer to this peculiarity (*Eigenheit*) of adequate evidence as its apodicticity. Plainly, *every apodictic evidence is, conversely, adequate.* Thus we can use both expressions as equivalent and single out the one or the other,

10. *Ibid.*, p. 49.

11. *Ibid.*, p. 380. See also p. 496 n and pp. 365, 366, 368, and 398, which likewise can be construed as supporting the thesis that apodictic insight is *infallible,* and pertains to the *thetic and doxic* domain of consciousness.

> according to whether we wish to place special stress on adequacy or on apodicticity.[12]

Apodicticity is not simply *related* to adequacy; this passage unmistakeably affirms their *equivalence.* Yet, in view of the fact that the one is not thereafter *substituted* for the other, we would expect from Husserl some more extensive explanation as to what distinction he wishes to advocate. No further explanation in that portion of the text is forthcoming. What is the stress which is important enough to be marked by two different terms? In what respect can we not reduce the one to the other? He does, in fact, give us the rudiments of an answer: an apodictic insight (judgment) is the outcome of a special process of modalization performed upon an adequate evidence. It will become apparent, subsequently, that this special process is eidetic variation (ideation).

By way of explanation we conclude that adequacy and apodicticity are thought to go hand in hand, as different dimensions (intensities, stages) of evidential inquiry. Whereas a claim to adequacy tends to articulate the completeness, the intuitional perfection, fullness and primordial authority of an evidence, a claim to apodicticity tends rather to articulate the (doxic) conviction, *grounded on* this very same evidence, and itself an act of "seeing," that *any* assumption of the non-being or dubitability of that which is evidenced is excluded in absolute evidence. Only complete (adequate) evidence could demonstrably sustain the insight that it is final, indubitable, apodictic; and equally, only an indubitable (apodictic) evidence will be found ever to be adequate. Apodicticity is the result of a reflective operation (critique) performed upon an evidence *already compelling* in its adequacy. In that sense, it represents a stage of greater "dignity" than that at which we have simply an adequate evidence.[13] Moreover, it seems reasonable to construe Husserl's remarks as equating apodicticity with infallibility. What else could be meant by expressions like "absolute finality" or "the exclusion of every possible (conceivable) doubt"? [14] Husserl's repudiation of psy-

12. *Ibid.*, p. 35.

13. In later writings, Husserl makes it clear that the principle of apodictic knowledge is given its greatest determinacy, and thus is most clearly distinguished from adequacy, by virtue of its unique function in the process of ideation.

14. See, for example, the strong wording of the definition in *Erste Philosophie,* I, 324, and again in II, 365–66.

chologism makes it plain we are *not* to understand these locutions in any psychological or subjective sense, referring merely to our relative capacities to *imagine* the evidence other than it is. But what, then, is this other sense?

[3] The Inadequacy and Non-Apodicticity of Outer Experience

Husserl finds, first of all, that there is an unavoidable inadequacy and hence, dubitability in the perception of spatial objects (and realities, generally). Such objects can, indeed, be apprehended in their "bodily selfhood" (in "*leibhafter Selbstheit*"), as in the case of a present visual perception; but they cannot be apprehended fully and in their totality. One acquires a sense of the "*Gestalt*" of the spatial reality, along with a certain content of its thing-determinations. But there remains nevertheless a content of unfulfilled co-meanings and anticipatory intentions (*Mitmeinungen* and *Vormeinungen*) which will only find fulfillment in the advance of further perception.[15] "Realities" of the world cannot satisfy the ideal of adequate evidence; nor can we, certainly, expect an incorrigible, *apodictic* knowledge to be founded in sense perceptions.

Could one perhaps suppose that, although our encounter with particular things can prove deceptive, the world *in general* would fulfill the phenomenologist's demands for adequacy and apodicticity? Husserl replies:

> No, I have no special ground for doubting that the world may not be. But I ask myself whether it is, then, so fully certain . . . and if I reflect on, say, mathematical evidence, then I become aware that we must distinguish here empirical from apodictic indubitability.[16]

The world is not doubtful insofar as the essence of empirical doubt entails that "something speaks against it." The whole continuing flow of experience, in its preponderant harmony, *supports* the existence and certainty of the world. But Husserl's concern is *radically different:* for *apodictic* indubitability, he maintains, "entails something else, and much more; it entails: where I see, how I see, and firmly keeping to my insight, I cannot

15. *Ibid.*, II, 44.
16. *Ibid.*, p. 311.

even think of the possibility that the seen not be or be other than it is seen to be." [17]

As we have already observed in our examination of the *Ideas,* Husserl acknowledges that the contingency of this world "out there" is perfectly *compatible* with the weight of testimony in favor of the world. The contrast with mathematical evidence is introduced in order to reveal another dimension of analysis; it is not intended, for example, to express an idealist's or a theologian's "contempt" for the world. Nor can it be construed as a paradox due to some muddle-headed insensitivity to the beliefs enshrined in ordinary language. Husserl must be understood as defining a novel standpoint: that of *transcendental rationality.* Measured by such a norm, belief in the world cannot be apodictic, because it is possible for me (the transcendental phenomenologist)to *conceive* of this world, just as it is, "out there," as not being, or as being quite otherwise, while my own existence—the now-present, actual existence of a consciousness who doubts the world—to whom this world is conceived relative, will and must still be.

Is it not significant, though, that Husserl chooses to make mathematical evidence paradigmatic of apodicticity, in establishing this thesis? [18] In the much earlier *Logische Untersuchungen,* Husserl, without any apparent misgivings, describes the exact sciences in terms of apodicticity, even though he has not subjected them to phenomenological reduction. These domains of inquiry, though obviously greatly different from the phenomenological domain of "fluctuating experience," are thus still foremost in Husserl's mind, when he examines the titles of putative evidence from the standpoint of radical "transcendental rationality." Husserl has not shown the relevancy of such a paradigm to phenomenological evidence. We are consequently quite justified in objecting that, insofar as Husserl continues to conceive the norm of transcendental rationality (and, correspondingly, its supreme mode of evidence, apodicticity) in accordance with the paradigm of mathematics, just so far has the concept of apodicticity remained stable, and outside the mainstream of Husserl's phenomenological evolution.[19] Of course, it

17. *Ibid.*, p. 50; and see further pp. 126–27.

18. See *ibid.*, p. 496.

19. Husserl does not introduce or make any use at all of apodicticity in his very earliest major work, the *Philosophie der Arithmetik.* This fact is interesting, but perhaps not very significant, given the

may still be recognized that there are strong reasons, quite apart from those adduced from the mathematical paradigm, for maintaining the dubitability, or at least the inadequacy of outer experience.

[4] Transcendental Critique as the Disclosure of Transcendental Subjectivity

The thesis that the existence of the world is contingent and dubitable is the outcome of what Husserl calls an "apodictic critique" of outer perception, conducted in conformity to the new rationality. His investigations are so designated for two reasons: first, because the inquiry itself is structured by the quest for apodicticity (thus, belief in the existence of the world is interrogated as to its indubitability), and, second, because the thesis into which the inquiry eventuates is supposed to be itself an apodictic, necessary insight.[20] Husserl argues that, if one examines in pure subjectivity the very essence of outer experience, one can recognize apodictically its contingent (non-apodictic), presumptive structure.[21]

In other words, the procedure of apodictic critique is a way of reaching transcendental subjectivity. This way has, as primary guiding principle of absolute justification, the following rule: "What I simply cannot negate, cannot put in doubt, shall serve as valid. That was at once conceptualized in its most explicit and sharpest form as the principle of apodictic indubitability." [22] Accordingly, transcendental subjectivity, as the object of methodic self-reflection, is seen to remain "even though the world were not to be." [23]

Contrary to the static, nonhistorical analyses of truth in the *Logische Untersuchungen,* he subscribes in *Erste Philosophie* to a more dynamic and historical conception, at least in its relation to outer experience: "True being builds itself out of moments of

---

nature and concern of the studies. At that time, he had not yet discovered the importance of the "problem" of evidence. Evidence became for him a central and haunting subject only after he had confronted the accusation of psychologism, and its attendant questioning about the origin of truth.

20. *EP,* II, 48.
21. *Ibid.,* p. 400.
22. *Ibid.,* p. 125.
23. *Ibid.,* p. 126.

truth, each lying in infinity."[24] In a declaration which boldly breaks with the ghosts of Cartesianism and intimates the centrality of genetic constitution, Husserl affirms:

> Consciousness is not a *lumen naturale* which illuminates something rattling around (*ein Darinsteckendes*) in consciousness, but is rather a system of thoroughly involved, interconnected functions—functions of consciousness—such that the intentional object which is its achieved formation (*Leistungsgebilde*) results in the mode of the given itself, and results not simply as a consummated, final formation, but rather as a formation which points to an unending system of further motivated performances in consciousness. These are not contingencies, but essential necessities, for any region of being whatsoever.[25]

In a statement of the utmost significance, he consequently allows that, even though this pure subjectivity deserves special epistemological status, it cannot yet be called an authentically apodictic indubitability:

> The bracketing of the world on the ground that it is not apodictically given merely turned our attention to the universe of pure subjectivity which is given in a new kind of experience—transcendental vision. But the *critique* of its apodicticity *must* be carried out; this was, however, postponed by us. That was our first way, the Cartesian, to the transcendental ego and to its apodictic critique, which we have before us still to be carried out.[26]

Husserl himself introduces the notion of a "transcendental naivete" to describe "not only natural cognition not effected by the transcendental *epochē*, but also *every* cognition grounded in transcendental subjectivity, so long as this does not undergo an *apodictic critique*, and every sort of question regarding absolute justification in transcendental knowledge is omitted."[27] And he

24. *Ibid.*, p. 386. However, Husserl does not completely abandon the more static matter-form schema. For, as we shall see, he differentiates the transcendental ego into an adequate and apodictic eidetic *structure* and a flowing, living "content."

25. *Ibid.*, p. 247.

26. *Ibid.*, p. 126.

27. *Ibid.*, p. 171. See the following consequent criticisms of Husserl: Iso Kern "Die Drei Wege zur transzendental-phänomenologischen Reduktion in der Philosophie Edmund Husserls," *Tijdschrift voor Philosophie*, XXIV (1962), 303–49; *WIZ*, pp. 56 and 73; and J. Broekman *Phänomenologie und Egologie: Faktisches und Transzendentales Ego bei Edmund Husserl*, Phäenomenologica, vol. XII (The Hague: Martinus Nijhoff, 1963), pp. 1–3.

asserts the need to complete this critical grounding.[28] To what extent is Husserl himself culpable? For nowhere in *Erste Philosophie* can we find the radical apodictic critique he calls for. The postponement of this requisite task can only signify, for transcendental rationality, that the apodicticity reputed to have been won is still insufficiently justified.[29] We shall discover, in fact, that even in the later *Meditations*, Husserl postpones a critique; and we shall examine the consequences for Husserl's project of an apodictic phenomenology.[30]

[5] Immanence as the Sphere of Adequate and Apodictic Evidence

One of Husserl's primary methodological principles is that "A critique of transcendence requires, if it is to be radical, a prior critique of immanence." [31] Phenomenological method enables us to discover the sphere of "immanence" (i.e., the "transcendental") as that which "grounds final knowledge; what it apprehends as existent cannot be surrendered." [32] At last, Husserl thinks, we can win our prized apodicticity and adequacy; for "immanent presence" (*Präsenz*), which results from reduction to the genuinely and primordially perceived in its present immediacy and compulsion, is both adequate and apodictic.[33] The primordial "originality" of the immanent is, in general, "the source of all apodicticity." [34]

At first glance, it would seem that we have uncovered an apodictic and adequate foundation in the sheer immanence, plain and simple, of the transcendental ego. But Husserl justifiably admonishes against any over-simplified understanding of the "pure" subjectivity that has been won. This transcendental sub-

28. Husserl, *EP*, II, 169. Husserl distinguishes, in fact, three styles of reduction: the transcendental, the phenomenological, and, ultimately, the apodictic. See pt. II, chap. 3, pp. 69–81.

29. *Ibid.*, p. 33.

30. See our discussion of this postponement in chapter 5.

31. *EP*, II, 378.

32. *Ibid.*, p. 486. Egological experience "has in itself its absolute title, and not merely a presumptive one." "Immanent experience grounds final knowledge; what it apprehends as existent cannot be surrendered." But this does not hold for the immanent past: it is not absolutely given, even though it is still immanent, in another mode of awareness. Cf. further p. 470.

33. *Ibid.*, p. 465.

34. *Ibid.*, p. 469.

jectivity has manifold strata (*Schichten*) of relative mediacy and immediacy.[35] Indeed, even the "immediate" evidence in which I am now given to myself as transcendental ego has its strata. Only in the primordial experience of my *living, streaming present* (what Husserl also calls the "I am" or, equivalently, the "I know" and "I experience") can I have an immediate evidence which is an absolute, adequate, and "apodictic ground of experience, secured by an absolute knowledge of its existence in its structural form (*Strukturform*)." [36] Husserl considers the disclosure *in evidence* of the "I am" to be the final stage of radical reflection. And he thinks it *apodictic* because

> while I live thus in the immanent and actual present, and attend purely to it, I cannot conceive it as a possibility that there might be thereafter some perceptual occurrences which could somehow modify the title of this experience.[37]

But we should notice here, as we have earlier (in our discussion of the *Ideas*), that in Husserl's transcendental investigations of immanence there is a serious confusion of which he is completely oblivious, and which consists in the *saltu mortali* from (1) simply living the immediate present in awareness to (2) the reflective (and doxic) dimension of consciousness, where it is thought to be *inconceivable* that the evidence for my existence might ever be cancelled. Husserl shows himself, in other words, to have sustained a certain commitment to Cartesian rationalism, though it is now, to be sure, purged of its deductive method. For the foundation of knowledge which he affirms through the concept of apodicticity is, literally, the *thought* that I exist and cannot *conceive* of my non-existence, while I think; it is not the *act* of thinking, the *existence* of the thinker, lived in a certainty

35. This explains why he maintains that adequate and apodictic evidences are not yet acquired merely upon the execution of the transcendental reduction. On account of the discovery, made through such reduction, of a multiplicity of immanent strata, a critique of this transcendental immanence is asserted to be absolutely requisite for the final possession, no longer naive, of these evidences.

36. *EP*, II, 398. Cf. also pp. 169 and 467–69. This is Husserl's answer to the query with which he opens Appendix 13: "How far, in general, can the demand for apodicticity in regard to a knowledge of what exists be pushed?" Attention should be called to Husserl's employment of apodicticity in regard to an existence completely held *within* the sphere of *knowledge* (the thetic and the doxic)—and only in its *formal* aspect, at that.

37. *Ibid.*, p. 486. Cf. also p. 272.

(awareness) altogether prior to and independent of any thematizations or any process of doxic modalization at the articulate stage of knowledge. This confusion bears witness to some serious tensions and conflicts in Husserl's late phenomenology. On the one hand, he seems committed to the view that apodicticity pertains to the reflective and doxic domain (i.e., knowledge), and consequently, to the view that the apodictic *foundation* of knowledge is to be sought *in the evidences of reflection.* But, on the other hand, he inclines to believe that the task of a genuine apodictic *grounding* is only accomplished when the (nonthetic, prereflective) immanent and actual present, fundament of the total streaming life of the transcendental ego, has finally been recovered.[38]

Husserl thinks that a critique of the sphere of immanence, disclosed through the transcendental reductions, shows that the transcendental ego, not as eidetic structure, but as streaming, vital totality,

> while *apodictically knowable,* namely, as bringing experience into the form of an apodictic positing of existence, is *not adequately knowable.* And every special judgment of evidence I can announce through my pure subjectivity, insofar as it extends beyond the experience of the apodictic . . . is likewise no more capable of apodictic grounding.[39]

38. The distinction between evidences merely lived in awareness and evidences of reflection is a crucial one for the existential phenomenologies of, for example, Sartre and Merleau-Ponty. But it is also true that this distinction becomes increasingly sharp and important in Husserl's own mature works, from the *Ideas* on. We must be sure, therefore, not to misrepresent the nature of this distinction. *Every* experience, including those belonging to the reflective and doxic modalities of consciousness, is of course lived in awareness; and noetic acts, lived in awareness, are also positional (objectivating), and through them there are constituted diverse thetic qualities. On the other hand, *not* all experience, lived in awareness, will necessarily be (or become) reflective (or doxic). Thus, for example, I can experience ("live") a headache, even though I may not (yet) have brought it to full objectivation, constituted it as an objective, enduring state of my body, discussed it with others, reflected on it, and so forth. The headache, as simply lived in awareness, is "philosophically prior" to the headache as a fully objectivated, fully constituted concern for consciousness. It belongs, so to speak, to a *founding stratum* of consciousness. See Husserl's discussion of "thetic" and "doxic" in *Ideas* I, §§ 103–5, 113–15, and 117.

39. *EP,* II, pp. 396–97.

My transcendental ego, as a vital whole (including, therefore, my past and future, as well as the actual present, in a total unity), cannot be given with adequate and apodictic evidence. As for my past, it is certain in its immediate retentional givenness, for "the past 'appears' in the present" and, in principle, can always be reawakened in the retained present.[40] As for my future, Husserl supposes that it is, in its immanence, apodictically predelineated in respect of a certain "style" or "form"; but obviously, it cannot be given in anything like an adequate and truly apodictic evidence, inasmuch as the future is always "open" and indeterminate from the vantage point of our knowledge.[41] The transcendental ego is a whole constituted by a stretch of past moments which recede into obscurity or oblivion, and by a forward-streaming consciousness with its unfulfilled horizonal anticipations.

But Husserl also holds that this transcendental ego *may* be phenomenologically differentiated into a "form," or *eidetic structure*, on the one hand, and an inadequate, non-apodictic *flowing, vital content* on the other hand.[42] Such differentiation has, for Husserl, the advantage that it permits eidetic investigations which, by their very nature, *are* capable of adequate and apodictic evidence.[43] Moreover, when the vital streaming of the transcendental ego is reduced to the primordiality of its lived, actual *present*, here, too, Husserl believes an adequate and apodictic evidence is won.[44]

40. *Ibid.*, p. 469.

41. *Ibid.*, pp. 386 and 489–91.

42. Brand quotes Husserl as asserting: "When I begin self-explication, I find as first certainty: I am. This certainty, though, is still altogether indeterminate in its content; it pertains to me only in—but also despite—the unfamiliarity of myself. I am indeed certain that I am; but what I am and how I am—that I don't know in its particularity with real certainty. I have now, indeed, an apodictic certainty of my own being, but that does not mean I experience then and there everything which belongs to me . . . in my streaming self-experience, nor that I can't deceive myself in this regard" (Ms. B I 5 IX, p. 14, cited in *WIZ*, p. 59). Cf. also *CM*, p. 65.

43. *EP*, II, 470 ff. We shall subject this position to a critique in the final chapter, where we are specially concerned with the evidence through which eidetic structures are presented.

44. We shall propose a refutation of this thesis in the next section of the present chapter.

[6] A Critical Study of the Theory of Evidence Presented in *Erste Philosophie*

Let us now consider the four distinct domains in which Husserl thinks his phenomenological investigations have exhibited adequacy and apodicticity in their evidentially correlative modes of functioning.

1. First, we have seen Husserl contend that *the evidence through which the transcendent world and all the thing-realities in it are presented can be neither adequate nor apodictic.* And we have acknowledged strong reasons for the conclusions of Husserl's critique of outer experience. But Husserl further asserts that the intentional "Idea," the "form," so to speak, of the world, and similarly, the intentional "Idea" of all realities as such, can be both adequate and apodictic. He reasons that what, in these cases, we are really concerned with, *after* the reduction of these intentional objectivations to their corresponding transcendental noetic acts, is simply the a priori essential structure of transcendental subjectivity itself—our consciousness of the world and things, not the world and things "in themselves." Consequently, in order to find adequate and apodictic evidence, Husserl *must* retreat to the essential (eidetic) *structure* of the transcendental ego.

2. Second, therefore, we must recognize that Husserl thinks the transcendental ego, *in the fullness of its streaming vitality,* cannot be apprehended with adequate and apodictic evidence, while, by contrast, the "form" or *eidos* of this ego is adequate, and moreover apodictic. The question to be adjudicated, on phenomenological grounds, may be expressed thus: Can the transcendental ego be grasped through reflection in an adequate and apodictic evidence? [45] We suggest that this question calls for a phenomenological demonstration (a) that there are sufficient phenomenological grounds for Husserl's content/form schema in regard to the transcendental ego, and moreover (b) that there is an *absolute* and *static* connection between (what Husserl has

45. Iso Kern, for one, seems to be nearing the same issue when he questions whether we can have an apodictic knowledge of the *eidos* of transcendental subjectivity while we cannot have such knowledge of the "purified" (truly immanent) facticities of this same subjectivity. See "Die drei Wege zur transzendental-phänomenologischen Reduktion in der Philosophie Edmund Husserls," p. 321.

differentiated as) the content and the structural form of the transcendental ego, such that (c) this structural form, as independent of content and hence accessible in a purely *a priori* way, can be known with both adequacy and apodicticity. In the previous chapter, we presented some objections to Husserl's claim that the a priori "Kantian Idea" of the transcendental ego is adequate and apodictic. We argued that it is not enough to *distinguish* an eidetic structural form from a certain vital content, in the language of reflection. We are not anxious, of course, to refute the possibility of making *some* differentiation of that kind. It is only that, if there *were* to be an apodictic evidence here, the distinction would *have* to be absolutely fixed and maximally determinate, with a finality exclusive of all further (relevant) evidence; it would have to be possible, in a truly phenomenological sense, to isolate the two constituents in the most complete manner. There would have to be, in other words, *a total bifurcation.*[46] Is this actually the case? And is this even possible? Should we not rather understand the conditions for the possibility of this distinction as *relative to the effectuation, in various stages, of reflective phenomenological inquiry*? In recognizing such relativity, or fluidity in the differentiation of content and form, would we not really be doing greater justice to Husserl's analysis of the Cartesian method of "doubt" into a number of *distinct but interdependent steps* ("reductions")? [47] Would it not be best to acknowledge that, even in its *eidos*, the transcendental ego reveals itself to us only through evidences having a partial clarity, opaque and in some respects fugitive? What we are proposing is that eidetic structures, as objectivations of and for reflective consciousness, can also be subject, like transcendent "realities" generally, to a kind of evidential indeterminacy and inadequacy, although they have neither spatial dimensionality nor the inherent mutability and openness of the streaming

46. As mentioned earlier, Husserl did not seem distressed (at least as late as 1914) by the form-content bifurcation. See his *Beilage* I, p. 383 to *Ideas* I.

47. Consider Husserl's *Ideas,* chap. 4, § 33 and Q. Lauer, *La Phénoménologie de Husserl* (Paris: Presses Universitaires de France, 1955), pp. 340–41, on the plurality of reductions. The fifth leads to the transcendental ego, while the sixth discloses the reduction that Lauer describes as the living flow of consciousness. Along these lines, Merleau-Ponty observed that the great lesson of the phenomenological reductions is that they are never finished. See *PP,* preface, p. xiv.

transcendental "life" itself. Furthermore, we contend that the very differentiation of content and structural form is a *transcendent,* and therefore what Husserl should call a *dubitable, formation of reflective consciousness.*[48] In fine, we hold that phenomenological investigation of the *genesis* of our knowledge of form (our *eidetic* knowledge) reveals the inadequacy of such knowledge; moreover, it shows how our knowledge of *content* amplifies, enriches, and alters our knowledge of *form* in such a way that inadequacy of content will *entail* inadequacy of form.

Here we have confronted our more general problem, which concerns the adequacy and apodicticity of eidetic structures *as such* (and, above all, the universal, a priori structures of consciousness itself). And it is to the intricacies of this problem that we shall devote our special chapter on eidetic consciousness and its eidetic noemata.

3. Consider, now, *the apodictic and adequate evidential status which Husserl claims for the living, streaming present of consciousness.* In his more mature works, Husserl entertains the possibility of a stage of reduction *more* radical than that which recovers for the first time the immanent sphere of the transcendental ego.[49] This stage will bring to evidence the domain of "pure immanence," the primordial and founding *"Ur-Ego."* [50] Husserl gradually came to regard *this* domain, and not the transcendental ego, as the ultimate, primordial, truly radical *foundation* for our knowledge. And it would seem that he considered the evidence of this living, streaming now-present to be absolute, adequate, and, moreover, apodictic.[51] According to Husserl, the pure immanence of this momentary present is the "existence" which "grounds final knowledge," for what is therein apprehended as existent "cannot be surrendered." [52] It is, in fact, "the source of all apodicticity." [53] Husserl believed that it is this *"Ur-Ego"* for which Descartes must have been searching, since it alone truly exhibits the evidence of Reason that Descartes originally posited as the goal of his investigations.

48. In fact, in his very late papers, Husserl comes close to this more "radical" position. For example, in "Phänomenologie und Anthropologie," p. 3, he describes the transcendental ego as an *abstract* stratum of the concrete man.

49. *EP,* II, 175; cf. *Ideas* I, § 81, p. 216 (p. 198).

50. See *WIZ* concerning Husserl's late manuscripts.

51. *EP,* II, *Beilage* 3, pp. 338–41; also pp. 272, 465, 469, and 486.

52. *Ibid.,* p. 486.

53. *Ibid.,* p. 469.

We must note, on the other hand, that Husserl presumably thought the evidence of the streaming, momentary present to be an evidence *anterior* to all doubt and all certainty (in the sense of a *modalized, doxic* certainty). This evidence must be, therefore, a prereflective, non-objectivated, noncognitive evidence, "absolute" only in the sense that it is lived in awareness as what it is, plain and simple. Yet Husserl did not recognize the nature of this evidence as clearly and as explicitly as we might wish. He failed to see that, since the momentary, streaming present is not, originally, an objectivation, posited with a transcendent sense, *it cannot assume the kind of evidential status which is feasible, if at all, only for the eidetic structures of the transcendental ego.*

Following Husserl, we want to recognize that there is a sense according to which the streaming, momentary present should be considered evidentially adequate, absolute, and indubitable. However, in view of the meaning Husserl has given to "apodicticity," it is questionable whether *this* certainty, an evidence merely lived in awareness rather than objectivated and modalized through reflection, should be called "apodictic."

Now, we shall demonstrate first, that insofar as an evidence purports to be apodictic (according to Husserl's own procedures for determining the apodictic status of an evidence), it cannot be the truly radical *foundation* for knowledge which phenomenology, as Husserl conceives it, must disclose; and second, that if the streaming, momentary present, as lived in awareness, is to serve as the ultimate foundation, it cannot be described in terms of the concept "apodicticity."

A constant commitment to Husserl's own idea of a radical phenomenological science (at the heart of which, surely, reside the two intimately related principles of intentionality and objective transcendence) ultimately necessitates a *choice* between the goal of an apodictic evidence and the goal of an authentic evidential foundation. Although, to be sure, the ground for our argument is derived from Husserl's own very late writings,[54] it must be observed, nevertheless, that Husserl was not sufficiently

54. See Klaus Held, "Lebendige Gegenwart": Die Frage nach der Seinsweise des transzendentalen Ich bei Edmund Husserl (University of Cologne Inaugural-Dissertation, 1963), pp. 87–89. Held argues that the "now-present" cannot be apodictic in its endurance, for this involves its temporalization. And Husserl, he maintains, has clearly indicated that he sees temporality as destroying the possibility of an apodictic evidence. Note, in this regard, *EP*, II, 398–99.

aware of this dilemma, internal to his own phenomenological theory; for he never explicitly and decisively abandoned his idea of an *apodictic* foundation.[55]

The problem is that Husserl failed to recognize that the concept of "apodicticity," as it has been introduced and utilized in his investigations, is most definitely operative *only in regard to the objectivated, reflective, and doxic stage of evidence* (Let us call this PREMISE I). Indeed, apodicticity, if it be attainable at all, must belong to the *highest* and most articulate stage of knowledge. This does not, of course, preclude the possibility that it be, in some sense, a genuine mode of "seeing," a direct intuition or evidence. However, Husserl's employment of "apodicticity," as well as his (relatively few) remarks about it, unmistakably give it an eidetic, reflective, and, in fact, a doxic function. How, indeed, could it be otherwise? For if an apodictic evidence is an evidence in regard to which it is *inconceivable* that the intentional object thus evidenced could be essentially other than it is (or, for that matter, completely denied), then it must be the case that the ascription of "apodicticity" to this evidence could *only* emerge as phenomenologically justified through a very sophisticated process of reflection on this evidence. Apodicticity certainly would seem to be a doxic sense that can be authentically constituted, if at all, only through a complicated reflective process. Briefly, Husserl must acknowledge that, in his phenomenological researches, apodictic evidence is understood to be the outcome of a methodic, disciplined variation of envisaged compossibilities. The judgment that an evidence is apodictic logically *presupposes* an eidetic variation performed upon some originally *given* evidence, in order to establish the (founded) sense that it could not be otherwise. We see, now, that "apodicticity" could only designate an evidence constituted in a very special way through reflection; and it must be, in precisely *this* sense, not an immediate, simply lived evidence.[56] Clearly, an

55. Husserl could only have done so, it would seem, had he been as clear as some subsequent commentators have been (notably, Paul Ricoeur and Roman Ingarden) about the presence, in his late thinking, of two essentially divergent *tendencies:* one, fundamentally rationalistic, developed in his earlier work and was never fully repudiated in his later work; and the other, more distinctively phenomenological, emerged only in his later work and centers around the teleology of evidence and the method of genetic constitution.

56. *CM,* §§ 5 and 6.

apodictic *knowledge,* in the fullest sense, is what Husserl really wants. So the "apodictic foundation" he wishes to recover through phenomenological method commits him to an investigation conducted exclusively *within* the domain of knowledge itself. But this means that what his labors will yield is an *already constituted evidence of transcendence.*

Furthermore, Husserl's program for a fully rational science is not satisfied with an apodictic knowledge, in the usual sense of "knowledge." It seeks to win an apodicticity of *existence* (*Dasein*). In effect, Husserlian science aspires to an apodictic evidence which will represent the perfect *coincidence* of *knowledge* (construed as an intentional, doxic grasp of the eidetic) and *existence* (that dimension of consciousness out of which knowledge must emerge and to which, as it were, knowledge can merely *point*). And precisely here we discover the serious problem that undermines this "rationalistic" tendency in Husserl's thinking. For this aspiration irrevocably conceals *primordial consciousness* (simply living the immediate present in awareness) behind *a reflecting consciousness,* through whose activity of evidential presentation (i.e., constitution) it is found inconceivable that the evidence for some existence might be cancelled (denied).

The difficulties we have detected in the concept of "apodicticity"—its apparent ambiguities—correspond in a perfectly logical way to the presence of two distinct, but never clearly acknowledged tendencies in Husserlian phenomenology. On the one hand, we can discern what might be called an intuitionistic and rationalistic orientation, especially pronounced in Husserl's early steps into phenomenological research. Here, the announced goal of phenomenology is an absolute, rational *foundation* for knowledge, conceived in the manner of an indubitable "seeing," an indubitable, apodictic eidetic knowledge: a final and decisive possession of reflective consciousness, *somewhat* akin to a (Cartesian-style) deductive evidence that is simply *seen* as what it (necessarily) is. Within such a framework, of course, it is not at all surprising that mathematical knowledge, for example, should be considered apodictic. On the other hand, we can also find, as a later dominant tendency, an idealistic and, I think, truly transcendental-phenomenological orientation, according to which evidence is construed as *"Leistung,"* and the goal of an absolute foundation is not an eidetic knowledge, but the recovery of an anterior (philosophically prior) dimension of consciousness, namely immediate, sensuous existence, simply as lived in awareness. Evidence is understood, here, within the genetic, constitutive process of evidential presentation and clarification, conducted in respect of the unlimited horizons of evidential systems and interlocking styles of evidence. And from this point of view, we must recognize that *evidences which posit objectivities are necessarily meant as transcendent* in relation to their constitutive subjectivities (PREMISE II).[57] And we must recognize, moreover, that *these evidences,* falling within the unlimited horizons of evidence, *cannot be demonstrated to be either adequate or apodictic* (PREMISE III).[58]

Once we have acknowledged the truth of these premises, we are in a position to see that, in order to establish an authentic foundation for knowledge, we must recover that dimension of conscious existence which is absolute and "indubitable" by virtue of its phenomenological *primordiality,* and not by virtue of its *rational primacy* in the structure of knowledge itself. Deep into his transcendental-phenomenological investigations, Husserl finally brought to light the primordial, streaming, lived present. Unfortunately, however, he was still held in the grip of his early tendency toward rationalism, so he failed to see that he could not claim for this absolute, founding ego the title of an *apodictic* evidence.

Let us consider why this must be the case. Eidetic structures, of course, are given through objectivated evidences that carry a transcendent sense. But nothing could contrast more acutely

57. We understand this premise to be nothing more than a formulation of Husserl's broad and fundamental sense of "transcendence." Although Husserl did acknowledge the truth of this premise in the *Logik,* he apparently ignored the profound insight it purports, even in his late writings. Thus, by giving it articulation here, we have but recovered it from the darkness into which Husserl had abandoned it. We have simply allowed it to guide us in our critique of his quest for apodicticity.

58. We shall defend this premise in chapters 5 and 6. There it will be shown that Husserl's broad and fundamental sense of "transcendence," which is a crucial part of his mature phenomenology, entails (1) that differentiation into what Husserl calls "transcendent objects" and "immanent objects," though phenomenologically possible and even important, is not of primary significance from the standpoint of a transcendental logic, and therefore, (2) that it is necessary, for the most fruitful *transcendental* investigations of evidence, to group *all* these objects *together* under the category of evidences whose adequacy and apodicticity cannot be demonstrated.

with the reflective and (usually) doxic evidences through which these structures are given than the evidence of the streaming present, simply lived in awareness. Either this present is a lived evidence, merely lived in its prereflective, non-modalized certainty, or it, too, is originally an objectivated evidence, a reflective moment of transcendent knowledge. Now, if we say that the streaming present is simply lived, then clearly, we cannot describe it as "apodictic"; for the ascription of "apodicticity" requires, as we have already noted (see PREMISE I), that it be an evidence of a reflective and doxic consciousness. On the other hand, even if we suppose that the streaming, momentary present, as such, *could* be an objectivated and doxic evidence, it would still be a mistake to consider it apodictic, since we can demonstrate no absolute certainty (that is to say, a certainty beyond all *conceivable* doubt) in the domain of objectivated and transcendent evidence, even when it is purely a question of *self*-knowledge (see PREMISES II and III). Knowledge, as such, is always a knowledge of *transcendence;* it always articulates strata of sense (modes of evidence) that depend upon and "stand opposite" the living consciousness which has posited them.

However, we would be wrong to suppose that Husserl actually intended to treat the streaming, lived present as if it were, originally, a transcendent evidence of reflection. We would be most uncharitable, as well as textually irresponsible, to foist upon him a thesis so extremely paradoxical and in such patent conflict with the rest of his phenomenology. As we have already pointed out, Husserl, like the existential phenomenologists who succeeded him, eventually followed another, more radical tendency in his phenomenological enterprise, and sought the foundation for knowledge in the prereflective, lived present.

Nevertheless, it must be said that to describe this lived present as an apodictic evidence is, at the very least, to introduce a serious equivocation. "Apodicticity" cannot but function ambiguously when Husserl uses it to characterize both the highest stage of eidetic knowledge (the reflective and doxic spheres of evidence) and also the momentary, lived present (as it is simply lived in awareness). So that, although he certainly did not intend to confuse consciousness as "existence" with consciousness as "essence," his contention that the lived present is an *apodictic* evidence amounts to the view that the knowing consciousness, which is simply lived in awareness, *coincides* with the objectivated consciousness (let us say, the transcendental ego), which is perfectly known.[59] The "existence" or "presence" which Husserl claims to be apodictic is therefore not so much existence as it is *reflection on* (knowledge of) existence.

Apparently Husserl was unable to recognize with sufficient clarity that no evidence of reflection, giving an object of knowledge, could possibly function as the *ground* of knowledge, even if, contrary to fact, we supposed this evidence to be apodictic. This is so because, according to the principle of intentionality and the method of genetic constitution, any such evidence will point back to something more ultimate, namely, to that which has done the objectivating and followed the rules of eidetic and doxic reflection, simultaneously living in these acts through which the evidence was constituted. If, in order to be apodictic, an evidence must be an objective and methodically generated position of consciousness, then such evidence itself obviously *requires* a foundation (a "founding evidence"), and points back to a grounding in the lived immanence of pure, primordial subjectivity.[60]

The point is, even if apodicticity *were* somehow possible in respect of certain modes of evidence, we should have to withhold it, nevertheless, from that lived present evidence which is to be the authentic foundation. So if we should feel such a strong commitment to apodicticity that we cannot relinquish it, then we must either (1) deny the principle of intentionality, with its inherent orientation toward the subjectivity to which all its objectivities are genetically related in respect of their sense, or (2)

59. The living present could be apodictic only if, among other things, Husserl were able to show that reflection is an instantaneous and perfect act of consciousness, and that there can be a complete identity of this lived "*Ur-Ego*" with the objective ego we explore through eidetic procedures. See *WIZ*, pp. 57 and 71. In *Phenomenologie und Egologie*, p. 203, Jan Broekman argues, like Merleau-Ponty in this regard, that phenomenology must acknowledge that it can be no more than a philosophy of incomplete reflection, however much this may thwart the aims of rationalism. Husserl unfortunately seems to want, however, *both* an apodictic foundation (since nothing less will meet his ideal of Reason) and *also* a grounding in the absolute evidence of the living present. These two aims are mutually exclusive. He must therefore renounce apodictic evidence in order to recover the authentic foundation for knowledge in a truly primordial, founding evidence.

60. See Klaus Held, "*Lebendige Gegenwart,*" for an important discussion of this entire problem, central to Husserl's late phenomenology.

surrender altogether the transcendental quest for an authentically primordial foundation.

Working out the fruitful but latent implications of Husserl's own mature thought, there emerge from our critique, therefore, two related, yet quite distinct arguments for the thesis that the primordial, lived present cannot be apodictic (in Husserl's sense). The first, which we formulated in *Premise I* above, is a *logical* point, since it describes the logic or grammar of the concept "apodicticity" as it was generally employed by Husserl. The second is a profoundly *phenomenological* point, namely, that the lived present is not (nor does Husserl himself take it to be) an evidence of transcendence and reflection. The simply lived "*Ur-Ego*" is, rather, altogether anterior to such evidence, and precisely for this reason it can be the absolute ground for knowledge to which the radical transcendental investigations of Husserlian phenomenology so nobly aspired.[61]

4. Finally, we reach the fourth domain of evidence explored in *Erste Philosophie: immanent experience through which there is given an "immanent object."* Husserl contends that this kind of experience must be adequate and apodictic. We are in a position to see, however, that the criticisms developed in subsection 3 above obtain, *mutatis mutandis,* for this fourth domain. Immanent experience, simply as lived in its prereflective functioning, is perhaps "certain" (but *only* in a sense which does not at all presuppose any reflective and doxic positionality); but it cannot be called "apodictic." And the immanent experience of so-called "immanent objects" is just as little qualified for apodicticity, since it clearly is the evidential giving of an object that bears a transcendent sense. To repeat a point made earlier, Husserl's temptation to describe immanent object-giving experiences as adequate and apodictic has its origin in his confusion of lived experience and objectivated experience. The sphere of immanence becomes, for him, a thickened stream of objects already constituted, already fully "present" to consciousness. He

61. See *PP*, pp. 382–83: "Hence it is not *because* I think I am that I am certain of my existence; on the contrary the certainty I enjoy concerning my thoughts stems from their genuine existence." Also, "it is not the 'I am' which is pre-eminently contained in the 'I think,' not my existence which is brought down to the consciousness I have of it, but conversely, the 'I think,' which is re-integrated into the transcending process of the 'I am,' and consciousness into existence."

ignores the *living* experience *for which* these objects are objects. The sphere of immanence becomes an objectivation, completely explicit and lucid; and the task of constitution, the task of exploring and grounding objective significations relative to the living acts that presented them, is simply forgotten.

5 / The *Formale und Transzendentale Logik* (1929)

WITHOUT ANY DOUBT, the *Logik* represents a momentous development and maturing in Husserl's thought. It is the first of his published works to set out in detail the theory of genetic constitution; and it offers us at last a truly teleological conception of evidence, in which the essential history of the life of consciousness and its striving for knowledge is clarified. At the source of such development lies, quite simply, Husserl's "discovery" that there is an ineluctible historicity to consciousness. Consequently, phenomenology must attend to the genesis, growth and teleology of consciousness, if it is to understand its subject-matter. What is of greatest importance for his theory of evidence, in particular, is the new emphasis, deriving from this historical sense, on evidential *process* and movement, rather than on finalities, *finished* evidences pure and simple. A consequence for the theory of eidetic reduction and insight is that greater dignity is bestowed upon the facticities at the base of eidetic operations.

Husserl has become even more uncharitable toward the psychological relativists, whose theories he sees condemned to end either in mysticism or skepticism, as he has grown more confident in the efficacy and fertility of his own theoretical equipment. But now he is just as vehement in his repudiation of rationalist absolutism. The presupposition of a "truth in itself" is, for him, naive and without ground. "In short," he urges, "one must cease being blinded by the ideal notions, regulative principles, and the methods of the 'exact' sciences, particularly in philosophy and logic, as if the in-itself of these latter were really an absolute norm for the being of the object as well as for truth." [1] These words, as Husserl himself must surely have appreciated, can to some extent be addressed even to his own thinking, which, in its incipient stages, quite openly declared and manifested its profound indebtedness to the exact eidetic sciences of logic, mathematics, and geometry.

Escaping the Scylla of absolutism and the Charybdis of relativism, Husserl proposes his radical theory of teleological and genetic constitution: there is a gradual and relative approximation to an absolute norm, located at infinity, and grounded at every stage in phenomenological evidence. He calls us to acknowledge "the infinite aspects of life and knowledge, the infinite aspects of relative being, and, taken uniquely in this relativity, of rational being, as well." [2] We must perceive "the relative truths of this rational being." [3] In consequence, he thinks, we gain "a living truth, drawn from the living spring of the absolute life and of self-consciousness turned toward this absolute life in its constant sense of self-responsibility." [4] What is significant, then, is that "one has thereby absolutized truth, but not illegitimately; one has rather absolutized its horizons—no longer neglected, no longer hidden, but rather systematically explicated." [5]

There are variations to evidence—degrees of perfection. Husserl discerned the existence of such variations as early as the *Logische Untersuchungen;* but only much later could he appreciate the full import of this observation. The *Logik* is the first attempt to focus on these differences in evidence and to draw out, in terms of genetic constitution, their real meaning, especially for his eidetic investigations. For he notes that these differentiations exhibit an underlying essential typicality, which it is the office of phenomenology, as eidetic research, to describe. Thereupon, phenomenology can discover the idea of perfect clarity, perfect evidence, something "which I 'can' approximate—this 'I can' having its own appropriate evidence." [6] And the "true" description of these essential types of evidence will be at the same time a phenomenological *grounding* of the various *essential regions* of *being* to which the evidences correspond.

1. *Logik,* p. 245. Note also p. 140.
2. *Ibid.,* p. 245.
3. *Ibid.*
4. *Ibid.,* p. 246.
5. *Ibid.*
6. *Ibid.,* p. 253.

In the *Ideas*, Husserl gave but passing recognition to the interdependence of modes of evidence and to their connectedness within a whole system of knowledge.[7] He still lacked some of the theoretical underpinning which would have enabled him to develop these ideas in a theoretically satisfactory manner. In the *Logik,* however, he maintains explicitly:

> As it is true that even in the simplest case of living internal experience, the essential form of the constituting flux of this experience implies that *evidences function together,* and in a continuous way bear upon one another and are variants of each other, the same is true generally for the vast sphere of the entire transcendental inner life. . . .[8]

He continues:

> But we should also show that evidence in all of its forms and at all of its stages is not only interwoven with other evidences, to form higher, founded performances of evidence, but also these operations of evidence are in general connected to non-evidences and thus in essence constantly form variants of evidence.[9]

These variants, he notes, are accessible to transcendental and eidetic investigation because they are "structural forms which belong a priori to the unity of a life." [10]

It would be completely in keeping with Husserl's direction of thought, as well as the temperament expressed in many of his statements in the *Logik,* were he to announce his abandonment of apodicticity. Evidences are interdependent; they refer backwards and forwards to other evidential decisions; they constitute a harmonious totality only in the infinite dimension toward which they continually advance. There is no place in such a conception for an infallible, absolute, final and unassailable mode of evidence.

Nevertheless, it must be conceded to Bachelard that Merleau-Ponty is not justified in claiming that Husserl meant to surrender apodicticity in the *Logik.*[11] What Husserl believed, in fact, is this: that experience alone reveals the possibility of illusory experience, and, in the correction or modification of previous judgments,

7. See *Ideas,* I, § 83, ¶¶ 4 and 7.
8. *Logik,* p. 254.
9. *Ibid.,* pp. 255–56.
10. *Ibid.,* p. 256.
11. See *SH,* p. 106; and *PP,* p. xvi n.

> the evidence of experience is thus always already presupposed. The conscious "destruction" of an illusion, in the original character of a "Now I *see* that it was an illusion!" is itself but a type of evidence. . . . Even an evidence giving itself as apodictic can be revealed to be an illusion, and therefore presupposes for that possibility an analogous evidence upon which it is broken.[12]

This is not in any way to be construed as a denial of apodicticity, as far as Husserl is concerned. The concept retains its central role in the phenomenology of evidence. For Husserl thinks that, while we must not *confine* verification to perfect, apodictic evidence, nevertheless it is the case that evidence is in its most "rational" form when it is apodictic. Imperfect experience is still experience, still a consciousness of having the "things themselves"; hence experience can "regulate itself by other experience and rectify itself on the ground of such experience." [13] Moreover, Husserl appreciates that perfection in evidence is not possessed in isolation from lesser forms of evidence; it has its background, its history, its relative dependency upon these other evidential titles. Thus, Husserl may be construed as simply observing that one apodicticity (but *only* an apodicticity) can cancel out another.

It is obvious that Husserl has changed his thinking in some crucial ways since the *Logische Untersuchungen*.[14] But, inasmuch as he is not prepared to yield on the norm of apodictic evidence, he is still plagued by some of the very *same* problems and obscurities which attend his conception of apodictic insight in the *Logische Untersuchungen*. One will recall that, in the absence of any procedure for adjudicating between two apodictic insights in conflict with each other, Husserl could really do no more than give the insight a hypothetical form of definition. Here we learn from Husserl that an apodictic insight can conflict with another such insight, and that, of the two, only one will be "true." We also learn that conflict is possible only between two insights each of which purports to have a legitimate claim to apodicticity. But Husserl is still unable to provide a *method* for adjudication. Consequently, it must be insisted that, with respect

12. *Logik*, p. 140.
13. *Ibid*., p. 144. Cf. also pp. 109–10.
14. Contrast the above cited remarks with, for example, Husserl's statements in the *Logische Untersuchungen*, I, 111 and II, 594. Cf. also G. Berger, "Thèmes principaux de la phénoménologie de Husserl," *Emm*, IL (1944), 22–43.

to any given putative apodictic insight, it cannot be *demonstrated* whether or not it has the epistemic status to which it pretends.

It would be considerably less objectionable, although still quite untenable for other reasons, if Husserl were to posit it merely as the ideal limit of evidences, a guiding norm for which there never could be any hope of actual fulfillment.[15] Even as norm, however, it would require phenomenological grounding, otherwise it could be no better than a presupposition, a motive which structures and defines inquiry without itself being examined. At the very least, apodicticity must be exhibited in its genetic development out of the lower "founding" types of evidence, if it is in fact the case that it is an attribute of the reflective and doxic posture of consciousness. To some extent, Husserl attempts precisely this, when he investigates apodicticity in the context of eidetic variation. Our examination of the eidetic process will disclose, however, that there is no warrant for claiming apodicticity even in the rigorously eidetic domain, and that, in fact, apodicticity is quite inimical to the process of eidetic formation.

It may be argued that, until the *Cartesian Meditations*, Husserl does not even *begin* the examination which will ground apodicticity. In this work, Husserl yields to the austerity of the Cartesian temper—at least initially. And at first he abstains from any real affirmation of apodicticity. The method will be, rather, to utilize it only as a structuring norm or guide, acceptable on phenomenological grounds only after it has been "discovered" (grounded) in some particular fruitful investigation. On this principle, then, all employment of the concept *prior* to such an endeavor should properly be considered inadmissible and speculative. It is commendable that, in the *Logik*, he does perceive the crying need for a critique of apodicticity.[16] But, this critique, effected in order to remove the last vestiges of naivete, is itself supposed to be apodictic. On what grounds is its apodic-

15. Iso Kern and A. de Waelhens agree, in this regard, that the apodicticity-styled foundation can at best be a goal, not a starting point. Cf. Kern, "Die drei Wege zur transzendental-phänomenologischen Reduktion in der Philosophie Edmund Husserls," *Tijdschrift voor Philosophie*, XXIV (1962), 303–49 and de Waelhens, "Science, phénoménologie, et ontologie," *Revue internationale de Philosophie*, VIII (1954), 254–65.

16. *Logik*, p. 255.

ticity to be shown? Would the apodictic critique itself demand a critique to disclose its apodicticity? How far-reaching is the naivete which Husserl expects to overcome? Could we not perhaps sustain the view, certainly compatible with some rather important aspects of his own thinking, that naivete (*in a quite harmless way*) is actually unavoidable, in the sense that, if inquiry is never at an end and extends into infinity, evidences (even insights) interweaving with evidences, what is naive is simply that which, at any given stage of signification, is open to further examination and development? In view of the hypothetical nature of apodictic insight (suggested in the passage cited above) and its openness to conflict and cancellation, this interpretation would indeed suggest itself as the reasonable one. Nevertheless, Husserl is plainly unwilling to adopt it.

What could have prompted Merleau-Ponty to believe that Husserl was deliberately abandoning apodicticity? Let us remember that we have seemed altogether justified, so far, in construing apodicticity to mean infallibility or absolute incorrigibility. All Husserl's pronouncements gave support to this interpretation, including those in the *Logische Untersuchungen*. For, in this work, although he speaks of conflicts in insight, he also maintains that only *one* of the two could *ever* have been a "*genuine*" apodictic insight. It was thus not a question of *two truly* apodictic insights coming into strife. The *apodictic* insight was, is, and always will be true and apodictic. But, how is one to know this? If a *genuine* apodicticity *can* be cancelled (as the *Logik* would seem to suggest), then it is not infallible, regardless of whether or not the cancellation be executed through another "apodicticity." And if apodicticity is *by definition* infallible, as we should suppose on the basis of his previous works, then the statement that even apodicticities can be revealed to be illusions would suggest, prima facie, that there are no (authentic) apodicticities whatsoever.[17]

Husserl's perplexing statement in the *Logik* accordingly

17. While Sartre is the first to institute, in *The Transcendence of the Ego,* the radicalization of Husserl's transcendental turn, he is inexplicably recalcitrant in perceiving that such radicality must demand a complete purge of the principle of apodicticity. Merleau-Ponty, perhaps on account of his deep interest in the problem of meaning, is more penetrating in this respect; but inasmuch as he (wrongly) believes Husserl to have abandoned apodicticity, he forbears engaging in any systematic critique.

leads us to the interpretation that Husserl does not (any longer) define apodicticity in terms of infallibility and impossibility of negation. Thereupon, we may argue (1) that he simply abandons apodicticity (in its one and only "true" sense of infallible judgment), or (2) that he is actually advocating a novel construction for that concept to replace the old and untenable one, or, finally, (3) that Husserl, being quite unable to abandon apodicticity outright, is not prepared to see that he is actually articulating a very different concept. Let us, for the sake of convenience, call the older meaning the "strong" sense, and the novel meaning a "weaker" sense. Then the burden of this study is to show that apodicticity *in the strong sense* is without phenomenological substantiation. A weaker sense does not seem to harbor similar problems.

In all fairness, it should be admitted that there is another possible interpretative position, not completely wanting in its persuasiveness, namely, that Husserl's concept *never* meant infallibility or absolute finality, and that, in consequence, there never was a strong sense of apodicticity. On this view, the remark in the *Logik* is not perplexing, and requires no *special* explanation.

Careful reading of the *Logische Untersuchungen, Ideas* I, *Erste Philosophie*, and even the very late *Cartesian Meditations* and the *Krisis* will not yield sufficient support for this position. We have given a fair sampling of Husserl's remarks on apodicticity and, too, of the contexts in which he employs the concept. Such a presentation can leave no doubt as to Husserl's meaning. Nevertheless, it is certainly extraordinary to think that Husserl should have introduced so fundamental and far-reaching a revision in such an "informal," incidental manner, without explanation, without elaboration. One would expect some statement on the motivation for such a change, and on its broader theoretical significance. Moreover, if there was in fact a radical revision, how do we account for the impression that the apodicticity which functions in the *Cartesian Meditations* and the *Krisis*, both first published after the *Logik*, is once again intended in its strong version? Reasoning thus, one might well be persuaded that the proper verdict to reach is that the strong version is just a fiction, not to be found in Husserl, and that a weaker version is in fact *preserved with consistency throughout* the corpus of his work.

In rebuttal, we can assemble the following plausible counter-arguments. First, although the *Meditations* were not published until 1931, the *original text* was completed in 1929, the very same year in which the *Logik,* just recently finished then, was published. And in fact, Husserl's preface to the English edition of the *Ideas* I, dated 1929, reveals that he regarded the *Meditations* as merely "an extended elaboration" of the four lectures which he gave in the spring semester of 1922, at the University of London. Consequently, the heart of the *Meditations* should be attributed to the formative years subsequent to the *Ideas,* but anterior even to *Erste Philosophie,* as well as the *Logik.*[18] Thus when it was a question of Husserl's presenting a coherent "Cartesian" treatise in 1929, even if we suppose his *complete* acceptance, without reservation, of the contents of those lectures delivered earlier in London, we have no basis for arguing that the doctrines contained in the *Meditations* come *after* those in the *Logik.*

The proximity of these two works, taken in conjunction with the fact that the historical roots of the *Meditations* return us to 1922, can in this way account for the fact that the revised conception does not figure in the *Meditations.* Husserl's well-known habits of research and writing—the profundity of his early commitment to apodicticity, belonging to his studies of mathematics and logic—and finally, the fact that the *Meditations* were expressly dedicated to Cartesian problems and were thus written under a certain "constraint" in focus and method as well as in spirit—these jointly comprise a solid explanation for the visible dominion of the strong version in the *Meditations.*

There is, besides, another consideration in defense of our interpretation, which bears on the *Meditations* and the *Krisis* together, and which is in a more fundamental way intrinsic to Husserl's phenomenology itself. Certain facts may seem to support the view that Husserl never committed himself to a doctrine of absolute incorrigibility. But much as one wishes to think that Husserl could never have been so wrong-headed or guilty of confusion and equivocation, scrupulous reading will not permit such charity. One simply has to confess that his conception, at this point, becomes confused, ambivalent, and in clear contradiction to other, more radical forces in his thinking.

18. See Husserl's Preface to *Ideas* I, p. 22. The French edition of the *Meditations* was available in 1931. The original German text, of which Cairns' work is a translation, was not published until 1950, in volume I of *Husserliana.*

It must be acknowledged, moreover, that the *Krisis*, written around 1936, and thus considerably later than both the *Logik* and the *Cartesian Meditations*, unmistakably presents the strong version of apodicticity, even though the historical and teleological dimensions of philosophical rationality (in spirit obviously hostile to apodicticity) are brought into special prominence. The only explanation is that Husserl's reflections on the apodictic principle are bound to his earlier, still rationalistic goals and commitments, and consequently he failed to perceive that the claim to apodicticity just cannot be tolerated by any norm of rationality which construes the philosophical "reconstruction" of knowledge as an infinite task, engaging us in a temporally determinate, genetic constitution of evidence.

And we submit, furthermore, that there is no justification for concluding that, in as much as our interpretation of the apodictic principle finds Husserl's position confused and conflicting, some weaker version must have been intended. For nowhere can one find apodicticity employed in a context exhibiting the determination of its temporality and setting forth the conditions necessary for its justification or annulment. Nor would it be reasonable to suppose textual support for the argument that Husserl sustains the apodictic principle as nothing more than a preliminary methodological norm, a merely provisional guide to infinite investigation. As a matter of fact, Husserl deems the ideal of apodictic evidence to be phenomenologically admissible if and only if it can actually be exhibited in some methodically constituted evidence. But further, he is plainly convinced that, in the sphere of pure transcendental consciousness, he has indeed disclosed such an evidence.

If the notion of philosophical maturation is not repugnant, but in fact both reasonable and desirable, then confusion, internal tension between contradictory viewpoints, and a certain amount of equivocation are to be expected and even welcomed, when one casts a comprehensive glance over the intellectual labors of three or four decades. Internal contradiction, in this case, is a symptom, even a cause of growth. Nor is it reasonable to suppose, in a thinker, utter lucidity or perspicacity in his understanding of the evolution, momentum and ultimate orientation of his research. Could a philosopher but have such understanding, his task would have ceased before it began.

Over many years, Husserl evolved a theory of evidence at the center of which is a genetic, dynamic, teleological process of constitution. Only gradually and painfully was he able to leave behind him a partially psychologistic, excessively rationalistic, and nonhistorical approach—an approach of the sort which is, perhaps, appropriate rather to a natural investigation of the exact eidetic sciences anterior to the phenomenological standpoint.[19] It is natural, although not philosophically forgivable, that the radical implications of his mature thoughts on constitution should have been overlooked, and that his commitment to apodicticity should have persisted, undiminished in strength.

19. It is not at all accidental, I think, that it was in the *Logik* that, for the first time, Husserl suggested a *weakened* concept of "apodicticity." Sokolowski certainly puts his finger on the most important reason. He notes: "The tension in *Ideas* I, between the higher and the lower levels of intentionality, is resolved in *Formal and Transcendental Logic,* where Husserl replaces the static structure of acts with a genetic process, and thus allows the process of inner time to reach into the higher levels of intentionality. In this work, objectivity is no longer explained by structural elements and their composition, but by a process in our conscious life that, beginning from the now instant, finally solidifies into the constitution of things and categorical objects. To explain objectivity, Husserl now traces the pre-objective, lived anticipations of it in our conscious life" (*FHCC,* p. 206). Still another reason, closely related to this, pertains to the fact that Husserl did not really become clear about the nature of transcendence (in its fundamental sense) until he had irrevocably entered the field of research carved out by the idea of a *transcendental logic.*

6 / The *Cartesian Meditations* (1929)

[1] Introduction

THE CONCEPT OF APODICTICITY acquired, with the *Cartesian Meditations*, its ultimate explicit refinement in Husserl's phenomenology. Husserl's subsequent works (for example, *Erfahrung und Urteil*) give us slight reasons to suppose any major conceptual reformulations. In fact, while his mature writings (say, from the *Ideas* on) exhibit a growing and eventually dominant tendency to consider many philosophical problems from the standpoint of their "historicity" and to provide analyses for them which are much less formal, structural, and therefore essentially "static," it would seem that, in a rather perplexing way, the concept of apodicticity was left almost untouched by these important systematic developments. However hidden, vague and abortive this tendency may have been, we cannot doubt that its inner logic is decidedly subversive to apodicticity. Constitutional analysis, a concrete, teleological and genetic process of clarification, governed by the principle of intentional transcendence and cognizant of its roots in the temporality of consciousness, plainly represents the operation of a transcendental rationality in which apodicticity cannot fruitfully and consistently figure.

In the *Cartesian Meditations*, Husserl explicitly advocates a fundamental revision in the apodictic principle defined and utilized in *Erste Philosophie*. On the one hand, this revision is both healthy and in order. Healthy, because it indicates Husserl's constant willingness to recognize and resolve outstanding theoretical problems; and in order, because it reveals the significance of Husserl's phenomenological recovery of primordial temporality, and implies an extension of Husserl's studies in genetic constitution. On the other hand, the revision is also rather unfortunate, for the attempt to resolve some of these theoretical problems is insufficiently comprehensive, and paradoxically, therefore, it serves only to conceal from Husserl the underlying weaknesses to which the apodictic principle is still exposed.

[2] Husserl's Confrontation with the Heritage of Rationalism

In both spirit and method, Husserl's *Meditations* are respectfully "Cartesian." This doubtless quite intentional approach can alone exonerate him somewhat of certain otherwise unaccountably rationalist utterances. Phenomenology, he believes, is a necessary moment in the development of responsible self-consciousness; for it heralds the emergence of the authentically "rational" norm of science, and sets about to actualize precisely this norm in a concrete manner as the foundation of knowledge.

The phenomenologist must search for "those cognitions which are first in themselves and can support the whole storied edifice of universal knowledge." [1] We must gain access to

> evidences that already bear the stamp of fitness for such a function, in that they are recognizable as preceding all other imaginable evidences. Moreover, in respect of this evidence of preceding, they must have a certain perfection, they must carry with them an absolute certainty.[2]

The centrality of apodicticity in the fulfillment of this rational goal cannot be overlooked: Husserl believes that in the apodictic principle we possess a complete and ultimate grounding on absolute "insights behind which one cannot go back any further." [3]

To Descartes, guardian of the indomitable will only a true rationalist could have, is attributed the methodic search for an apodicticity that would serve as ground for all knowledge. Husserl cannot offer enough praise for the Cartesian method, sublime in the "asceticism" of its mechanics and its aim, puissant in the richness of its accomplishments. But his commitment to a

1. *CM*, p. 14 (p. 54).
2. *Ibid.*
3. *Ibid.*, p. 2 (p. 44).

radical norm of science carried him far beyond Descartes, permitting him a lucid understanding of the insufficiencies in the Cartesian strategy of doubt and in its methodological presuppositions.

Husserl discerned the momentous subjective turn which Descartes originated. But he rightly adopted it only after introducing the transcendental dimension; and he departs from the Cartesian drama of doubt by repudiating the deductivism common to all traditional systems whose fundamental aspiration it was to articulate the pervasive "rationality" (specified in conformity to the model that the exact sciences of the day suggested) which governs the universe. Phenomenological *epochē* is very different from Descartes' doubt, and can thus open upon a dimension of "reality" heretofore concealed from us: transcendental subjectivity. Even more important, it is able thereby to effect or verify, in a visibly fecund way, a radically novel interpretation of the antique endeavor to find the rational source and meaning of our "reality." Husserl's transcendental turn at once creates and confirms a new conception of rationality—a new conception of what it is to describe, explain and clarify, in an altogether "rationally" compelling and satisfying way, the reality in which we dwell.

The mathematical sciences were long the idols and exemplars for traditional rationalism. One need only consider Spinoza's *Ethics*, Leibniz's *Monadology*, Hobbes' *Leviathan*, and Descartes' *Meditations*. Husserl, while sustaining respect for the rationalist vision and its underlying optimism, does not hesitate to accuse even Descartes of

> the prejudice that, under the name of the *ego cogito*, one is dealing with an apodictic "axiom," which, in conjunction with other axioms and, perhaps, inductively grounded hypotheses, is to serve as the foundation for a deductively "explanatory" world-science, a "nomological science," a science *ordine geometrico*.[4]

Phenomenology, he is convinced, must eschew the desire to deduce, from a "little tag-end of the world," the remainder of this world according to innate principles and formal logical arguments. A transcendental grounding of knowledge must, on the contrary, be wholly intuitive, descriptive, immediate. "And, indeed, instead of attempting to use *ego cogito* as an apodictically evident premise for arguments supposedly implying a transcendental subjectivity, we shall direct our attention to the fact that

4. *Ibid.*, p. 24 (p. 63).

phenomenological *epochē* lays open . . . an infinite realm of being of a new kind." [5]

The phenomenologist must relinquish the paradigm of an exact, deductive, formal science, without at the same time abandoning altogether the great ideal of science which is our inheritance from the past. It is necessary to conceive a different and, for the first time, legitimated norm of rationality. "All the rationality of the fact lies, after all, in the a priori." [6] Hardly the traditional innate knowledge, this is conceived as "the a priori of constitution." [7] It can be achieved only through the effectuation of a *genetic constitution* (clarification and grounding), in respect of the *transcendental eidetic* formations of consciousness.

The "highest imaginable form of rationality" imposes both an a priori–eidetic and a genetic method.[8] By means of such systematic clarification of objectivities in terms of their corresponding *essentially necessitated* intentional performances, "every sort of existent itself, real or ideal, becomes understandable as a 'product' of transcendental subjectivity, a product constituted in just that perfection." [9]

In spite of Husserl's modification of Cartesian method, and in spite of his determination to break with traditional rationalism, it must be said that there remains a decidedly strong rationalism which quite contradicts the radicality of the transcendental revolution. Nowhere is Husserl's fundamental commitment to the spirit of rationalism so apparent as in the *Cartesian Meditations*. What he has in mind, to supersede Cartesian rationalism, is, for all its intuitional immediacy and its concern with evident being, nevertheless still an order of *knowledge* bearing the dignity of *science:* "Now, however, we are envisaging a science that is, so to speak, absolutely subjective, whose thematic object exists, whether or not the world exists." [10]
The *Meditations* are aimed more at explicating a priori certain already-formed eidetic *structures* than at clarifying the *full genesis* of knowledge in regard to founding experiences lived in awareness. Husserl's new science will strive for absolute and apodictic cognitions; but for the first time, he thinks, this an-

5. *Ibid.*, p. 27 (p. 66).
6. *Ibid.*, p. 155 (p. 181).
7. *Ibid.*, p. 137 (p. 164). Cf. also p. 84 (p. 117).
8. *Ibid.*, p. 81 (p. 114).
9. *Ibid.*, p. 85 (p. 118).
10. *Ibid.*, p. 30 (p. 69).

cient philosophic ambition need not end in frustration. Indeed, the apodictic norm shapes his whole phenomenology. It is at once the most problematic, but also the least well-defended of his primary philosophical ideas.

In fine, Husserl's transcendental "revolution" is not sufficiently radical. Once the philosopher knows why he must repudiate all norms of rationality that demand an indubitable evidence, he has understood the reason for the "existential turn," and he can clarify and describe the worlds of intentional objectivation in their emergence from prethematic, non-objectivated, simply lived experience. From the standpoint of existential radicality, it follows, as we have seen, that intentional objects, as such, belong to the sphere of knowledge, and hence to the sphere of transcendence. "Opposite" transcendence, as its grounding and source, is consciousness simply lived in awareness and certain in its prereflective activity.

Now, if we can demonstrate the intrinsic untenability of apodicticity and, what is more, the extent to which it contradicts and subverts other, better confirmed and more fruitful elements in his phenomenology, we shall have made a considerable contribution to the overthrow of a very robust reign of rationalism in philosophical thinking. It should not require argument that such rationalism is wholly subversive to the peculiar spirit and method which define phenomenology as a new and radical philosophic movement.

[3] The Evidence for Objectivity

Husserl's historical sensibilities gave him to believe that perfect evidence and its correlate, "pure and genuine truth," are the common property of mankind, "lodged in the striving for knowledge, for fulfillment of one's meaning intention." [11] While truth and falsehood, confirmation and disconfirmation play an incessant part in our everyday life, in view of their "changing and relative purposes, relative truths and evidences suffice." [12] But science, so he imagines, looks for "truths that are valid, and remain so, once and for all and for everyone." [13]

11. *Ibid.*, p. 12 (p. 52).
12. *Ibid.*
13. *Ibid.*

Husserl recognizes, of course, the prima facie pragmatic and authoritative claims of our ordinary "certainties." He does not deny that, according to our everyday criteria, we know for certain that there is, let us say, an inkwell on my desk, and that we are, besides, entitled to this certainty. It is only when we abstract from the immediate concerns surrounding this judging situation and reflect, from the vantage point of an engaged consciousness, on the nature of evidence in general (i.e., on the essential structure of making and having evident), that we conceive for the first time the rational possibility that we may be wrong, that these evidences, not primary in themselves, can be deceptive.

Assuming the phenomenological attitude, Husserl interrogates our encounter with the world and the things in it. As before, he finds that our evidence can be neither primary, nor adequate and apodictic. External perception, though not apodictic, "is still an experiencing of something itself, the physical thing itself: 'it itself is there.' But, in being there itself, the physical thing has for the experience an open, infinite, indeterminately general horizon, comprising what is itself not strictly perceived."[14] At best, we can possess here a presumptive evidence. The world as phenomenon is an idea correlative to a perfect experiential evidence. Evidential adequation is impossible because of unfulfilled, expectant and accompanying meanings, all definitive of the thing's or world's objectivity and "reality." For the explicative phenomenological consciousness, however, there emerges the form, or system of actual and possible cognitions relevant to the objectivity in question. This provides an *idea* of total evidence which, were it attained, "would finally present the object itself in respect of all it is—an evidence in whose synthesis everything that is still unfulfilled expectant intention, in the particular evidences founding the synthesis, would attain adequate fulfillment."[15] This adequate idea of the object is an a priori necessity for the possibility of experiencing it at all, in the form of a coherent, objective system of synthesized experiences.

That "real" things are inadequately evidenced but nevertheless seem to be predelineated a priori as to their possible evidential fulfillments brings Husserl to reflect on the nature of objects *in general:*

14. *Ibid.*, p. 23 (p. 62).
15. *Ibid.*, p. 63 (p. 98). See also pp. 61–62 (pp. 96–98).

> Any "Objective" object, *any object whatsoever* (even an immanent one), points to a *structure, within the transcendental ego, that is governed by a rule.* As something the ego objectivates, something of which he is conscious in any manner, the object indicates forthwith a universal rule governing possible other consciousnesses of it as identical.[16]

Both the so-called "real" and the so-called "ideal" objects of our ontological universe are "products" of transcendental subjectivity. And every object, even an immanent one, is a temporal unity with an ideal temporal identity, and as such must transcend the objectivating performances of consciousness. We must eventually see that

> the object is, so to speak, a pole of *identity,* always meant expectantly as having a sense yet to be actualized; in every moment of consciousness it is an index, pointing to a noetic intentionality that pertains to it according to its sense.[17]

The object (whether "immanent" or "transcendent"), as pole of identity for the synthesis of intentional experiences, is always at best an "ideal immanence"—which is but another way of saying that it is transcendent (in the most fundamental sense of this word) to consciousness.[18]

These reflections point up the fact that a full understanding of objectivity calls for an antecedent elucidation of subjectivity, as the effective source of objective identity, unity and meaning. We shall soon follow Husserl into the sphere of the transcendental; but it is first of all to be observed that his investigations are really directed exclusively to the transcendental ego *in its fully objectivated dimension*—as an eidetic structure, in fact. He notes, for example, that the processes of consciousness, because of their flowing, amorphous, living nature, cannot be fixed in determinate concepts, but also that consciousness does exhibit an "essentially necessary conformity to type," which *can* be apprehended in strict concepts. It is thus to *structures* that Husserl devotes his attention.[19] Inasmuch as the transcendental ego *can* be objectivated, and, when constituted as *eidos,* is in fact thus, we grant that Husserl may properly subject it to structural analysis. What is lamentable is his reluctance fully to utilize the

16. *Ibid.*, p. 53 (p. 90).
17. *Ibid.*, p. 45 (p. 83).
18. *Ibid.*, p. 60 (p. 95).
19. See, for example, *ibid.*, p. 49 (p. 86).

results of his transcendental logic (in particular, his exploration of objectivity in general) in order to understand the evidential status of the transcendental dimension he has recovered. If it is truly a thematic *object* of consciousness, the transcendental ego will of necessity have those properties (among them, perhaps, an evidential inadequacy) which all other objects, as such, are said to have.

[4] Transcendental Subjectivity and Eidetic Structure

Expressing himself in a manner deliberately evocative of Descartes, Husserl guides his reflection from the world to the world as phenomenon, and from that to the *source* of this phenomenon in the intentionality of consciousness:

> But, no matter what the status of this phenomenon's claim to actuality, and no matter whether, at some future time, I decide critically that the world exists or that it is an illusion, still this phenomenon itself, *as mine,* is not nothing but is precisely what makes such critical decisions at all possible and accordingly makes possible whatever has for me sense and validity as "true" being. . . . And besides, if I abstained—as I was free to do and as I did—and still abstain from all believing involved in or founded on sensuous experiencing, so that the being of the experienced world remains unaccepted by me, still this abstaining is what it is; and it exists, together with the whole stream of my experiencing life.[20]

The inner logic of this methodic performance is indeed very radical, in that it is potentially disposed, as the wording of this remark reveals, to carry the process of clarification *behind* the objectivated dimension of consciousness right to its living, streaming present. We wish to contend that it is this present, the act of living it and livingly affirming it, which is the really indubitable foundation that Husserl sought. For the most part, however, Husserl obscures this radicality or else leaves it in the unpromising form of programmatic remarks.[21] Thus, when Husserl finally begins to elaborate the outcome of *epochē,* we find that he is concerned, instead, with experience *as structured,*

20. *Ibid.*, p. 19 (p. 59).
21. See, for example, *ibid.*, p. 20 (p. 60), where he speaks of acquiring the "living present" through the *epochē.*

manifesting the apodictic principles which delineate the pure *eidos*, "transcendental ego." [22] The intent of phenomenological science must be, he thinks, to articulate an "intuitive and apodictic consciousness of something universal," not conditioned by or even related to any facticity, hence altogether necessary. It will undertake an a priori and eidetic investigation of a pure possibility-consciousnesses, that is, pure eidetic possibility-variants of the transcendental egological structure. The ego under scrutiny is, therefore, the *essence* "ego," of which this or that *de facto* ego is but one of the compossibles.[23]

In a certain sense, however, Husserl's method does allow him to discern something outstanding about the evidence proper to the transcendental sphere. It is doubtful whether he could have understood his achievement nearly so well, had he not had at least some inkling of what it means (in the profound sense of a transcendental logic) to explicate the objectivated dimension. For, immediately following his explication of the open, indeterminate evidential horizons characteristic of "external perception," he admits:

> Something similar is true about the apodictic certainty characterizing transcendental experience of my transcendental I-am, with the indeterminate generality of the latter as having an open horizon. Accordingly the actual being of the intrinsically first field of knowledge is indeed assured absolutely, though not as yet what determines its being more particularly, and is still not itself given, but only presumed, during the living evidence of the I-am.[24]

In the complete portrait of transcendental subjectivity, there can be distinguished first the flowing *cogito* (the living now-present), then the ego as an empty pole of identity through time, the ego as substratum of habitualities (manifested formally for

22. *Ibid.*, p. 72 (p. 106).
23. *Ibid.*, p. 71 (p. 105).
24. *Ibid.*, p. 23 (p. 62). Even the life-stream is relativized and temporalized; but Husserl qualifies its transcendence with the term "immanent." The spatio-temporal world is a second, and nonimmanent transcendence. See Klaus Held, "Lebendige Gegenwart": Die Frage nach der Seinsweise des transzendentalen Ich bei Edmund Husserl (University of Cologne Inaugural Dissertation, 1963), pp. 106 f. He stops just short of recognizing the consequent impossibility of demonstrating an apodictic evidence for transcendental subjectivity, even with Husserlian manuscripts like C 1, p. 6, and C 10, p. 23, before him.

phenomenological inquiry as structural configurations of the ego), and finally, the ego taken in full concreteness.[25] The last two dimensions provide, as it were, the "flesh," the embodiment of the empty transcendental ego-pole. There are, Husserl maintains, not only poles in the *cogitata,* around which experiences that form objective meaning are synthesized and given endurance; there is also a second, and even more primordial polarization, or synthesis, whereby the various *cogitationes* are unified with the *sense* "belonging to the same identical ego." [26] One can, of course, attend to the ego as a mere pole of identity, and as ground for the diverse acts that correspond to the manifold *cogitata;* but one can also reflect on the ego-pole with all its abiding properties. For "by his own active generating, the ego constitutes himself as identical substrate of ego-properties." [27]

The transcendental domain perceived through the *epochē* is, in Husserl's own words, like "a Heraclitean flux." He thus concedes:

> The attempt to determine a process of consciousness as an identical object, on the basis of experience, in the same fashion as a natural Object—ultimately then with the ideal presumption of a possible explication into identical elements, which might be apprehended by means of fixed concepts—would indeed be folly. Processes of consciousness . . . have no ultimate elements and relationships, fit for subsumption under the idea of objects determinable by fixed concepts and thus such that, in their case, it would be rational to set ourselves the task of an approximate determination guided by fixed concepts.

But then he adds:

> In spite of that, however, the idea of an intentional analysis is legitimate, since, in the flux of intentional synthesis . . . an essentially necessary conformity to type prevails and can be apprehended in strict concepts.[28]

Husserl moves towards the flowing, lived now-present, which always escapes the congealing fixation of reflective analysis by retreating into a non-primordial past and bequeathing importance to the open novelty of a subsequent present. He insists that

25. *CM,* p. 67 (p. 102).
26. *Ibid.,* p. 66 (p. 100).
27. *Ibid.,* p. 67 (p. 101).
28. *Ibid.,* p. 49 (p. 86).

the immediate present can be perceived with an *apodictic certainty*. Still, as if with great relief, Husserl leaves the flux of consciousness, with its "infinite horizons of still undiscovered internal features," for the supposedly stable and eternal *structural* (eidetic) *properties* of this conscious life.[29]

The transcendental ego in its concreteness does indeed provide an unlimited field of experience; correlatively, the philosophizing ego is obliged to and can "explicate himself *ad infinitum* and systematically." [30] In this respect, Husserl says, the phenomenologist cannot hope for adequate evidence. Husserl sharply rebukes Descartes for his foolish attempt to win an adequate evidence for the transcendental ego in its total life:

> . . . though I am continually given to myself *originaliter* and can explicate progressively what is included in my own essence [that is to say, what is included in my full concreteness], this explication is carried out largely in acts of consciousness that are not perceptions of the own-essential moments it discovers.[31]

On the other hand, it would be a mistake, Husserl insists, to forsake the quest for apodiciticity:

> The ego, taken concretely, has a universe of what is peculiarly his own, which can be uncovered by an original explication of his apodictic "*ego sum*"—an explication that is itself apodictic or at least predelineative of an apodictic form.[32]

The most fundamental, most pervasive, and most universal feature of this apodictic structure which Husserl discovers is enunciated in the scheme: *ego-cogito-cogitatum*.[33]

It appears, then, that even after he has recognized the limits to adequacy in the transcendental sphere, Husserl continues to hope that it

> may be possible to show that the absolute evidence of the ego sum [that is, the egological form or essential structure] does, after all, necessarily extend into those manifolds of self-experience in which the ego's *transcendental life* and *habitual properties* are given, even if there are limits that define the range of those evidences. . . . More precisely stated: The bare identity of the "I

29. See *ibid.*, pp. 101–2 (p. 132).
30. *Ibid.*, p. 31 (p. 70).
31. *Ibid.*, p. 102 (pp. 132–33).
32. *Ibid.*, p. 104 (p. 135).
33. *Ibid.*, p. 50 (p. 87).

> am" is not the only thing given as indubitable in transcendental self-experience. Rather, there extends through all the particular data of actual and possible self-experience—even though they are not absolutely indubitable in respect of single details—a *universal apodictically experienceable structure* of the ego (for example, the immanent temporal form belonging to the stream of subjective processes).[34]

For Husserl, then, every explication of particular data manifesting the concrete life of the ego must be conducted within the framework of this a priori, eidetic, and apodictically evidenced egological structure. In this way, the flowing, concrete ego-life, originally elusive, is endowed with the sense of something firmly identifiable again and again; it is captured, so to speak, in its eidetic aspect, where an adequate and apodictic evidence can then be recovered. In summation, Husserl extends apodicticity and adequacy as far as he can into the living *content* of the ego, giving it full determination and indubitability *through the mediation of an egological structure.*

[5] The New Definition of Apodicticity in Relation to Adequacy

Husserl's conception of adequacy may appear to have undergone no significant modification since *Erste Philosophie.* In the *Meditations,* Husserl again introduces the ideal of perfect, adequate evidence, denies it to "outer perception" on account of its inherent transcendence, and differentiates lesser evidences that are one-sided and infected with "unfulfilled components." The ideal of adequate evidence is important, even though most evidences are intrinsically inadequate, because it serves as a guide to the improvement of these evidences. Husserl also believes, as before, that there is another, very different norm of perfect evidence, which has "a higher dignity" than adequacy. This perfection is apodicticity. It is an evidence "*absolutely indubitable* in a quite definite and peculiar sense, the absolute indubitability that the scientist demands of all 'principles.'"[35]

Any evidence, of course, is a grasping of something meant itself, meant as "the thing itself," and with a certainty of the

34. *Ibid.*, p. 28 (p. 67); also see p. 103 (p. 133).
35. *Ibid.*, p. 15 (pp. 55–56).

evidential moment that excludes any *present* doubt, then and there. This is the certitude which accompanies adequate evidence. "But it does not follow," Husserl argues, "that full certainty (of *this* sort) excludes the conceivability that what is evident could subsequently become doubtful, or the conceivability that being could prove to be an illusion."[36] For such certainty makes no pretension to comment upon, let alone guarantee, the *conceivable* (relevant) evidences which lie beyond the scope of the momentarily given. Hence, there is "an open possibility of becoming doubtful, or of non-being, *in spite of evidence* . . . [which] can always be recognized in advance by critical reflection on what the evidence in question does."[37] Immediately following this remark, the apodictic principle is introduced:

> An apodictic evidence, however, is not merely certainty of the affairs or affair-complexes (states-of-affairs) evident in it: rather it discloses itself, to a critical reflection, as having the signal peculiarity of being *at the same time the absolute unimaginableness* (inconceivability) of their *non-being*, and thus excluding in advance every doubt as objectless, empty. Furthermore, the evidence of that critical reflection likewise has the dignity of being apodictic, as does therefore the evidence of the unimaginableness of what is presented with apodictically evident certainty.[38]

Note, first, that Husserl suggests apodicticity is appropriated only through a special *reflective* (doxic) act performed upon evidences already somehow acquired.[39] Note, too, that since all evidence in its primordial state is said to exhibit certainty and to exclude *present* doubt (concretely motivated), the only property to distinguish apodictic certainty would seem to be that it is somehow the exclusion of *all possible* (conceivable) doubts, now and forever, *constituted* (justified) *purely on the ground of present experience*. Apodicticity must mean, therefore, an evidentially guaranteed *incorrigibility*. Finally, consider that Husserl's reference to *possible* (conceivable) evidence and doubt clearly implies that apodictic evidence is the outcome of eidetic variation. This fundamental aspect of apodicticity will therefore be treated to a separate critique in the next chapter.

36. *Ibid.*
37. *Ibid.*, p. 16 (p. 56).
38. *Ibid.*
39. Therefore, in respect of an apodictic judgment, these evidences are to be construed as "founding" evidences.

Thus far, our account of Husserl's introduction of apodicticity in the *Meditations* has not discerned any departure from the theory of evidence developed in earlier works. However, Husserl does in fact give us, in the *Meditations*, what seems (to him) a major revision of the *Erste Philosophie* formulation. He now thinks that adequate evidence and apodicticity need *not* go together. Apodiciticity "can occur even in evidences that are inadequate." [40]

What is the reason for Husserl's change of mind? And how profound a change is it? In the *Ideas*, as we saw, Husserl worked extensively with both the concept of adequacy and the concept of apodicticity, delineating through them the nature and boundaries of phenomenological investigation. But he made no attempt to define or clarify the logic of their relationship. *Erste Philosophie*, on the other hand, proposes to construe this relationship as an *equivalence*.[41] And the character of the equivalence, as well as the reasons for it, are set forth with clarity and precision. Unfortunately, however, the same cannot be said for Husserl's revised formulation in the *Cartesian Meditations*. He gives us not the slightest trace of an *argument* to support his new position. And since the earlier position seemed so reasonable, we certainly shall have to examine the prospects for such an argument. Furthermore, his presentation of the revision is exclusively destructive. He says little that can inform us *how* we are supposed to take the new relationship. So we are obliged to piece together a faithful interpretation by examining the way Husserl actually works with his concepts of evidence, and by observing the mechanisms and contexts that detail their intended meanings.

Obviously, therefore, we must be extremely careful in drawing any conclusions from remarks which communicate, in isolation, only a fragment or an aspect of Husserl's intentions. Otherwise, for example, we might hasten to welcome Husserl's "retreat" from adequacy as a bold move away from the vestiges of rationalism implicit in the largely structural and frustratingly formal analyses characteristic of his earlier studies. And we might suppose that, for Husserl, this retreat purports a decisive step towards a theory of evidence in which apodicticity is securely harnessed to *inadequate* evidence, and in which, consequently, apodiciticity in Husserl's *original* sense no longer could

40. *CM*, p. 15 (p. 56).
41. *EP*, II, 35.

function at all. But we must account for the curious fact that, even if we take him to abandon adequacy, the entrenchment of apodiciticity seems to be reinforced, not weakened.

To be sure, in the *Meditations* Husserl clearly entertains, as never before, the possibility that adequate evidence for the transcendental domain may be nothing but a dream, a normative (guiding) limit. But he insists (without argument) that, even if the transcendental evidences "should turn out to be inadequate, they still would have to possess at least a recognizable apodictic content, they still would have to give us some being that is firmly secured 'once for all,' or absolutely, by virtue of their apodicticity."[42] Is this remark just a formal demand, setting forth the desired goal for phenomenological inquiry, or is it the announcement of phenomenologically demonstrated results? Perhaps it betrays the confusion of self-deception: wishful thinking.

It is hard to avoid the suspicion that this is just another affirmation of the apodictic principle, and represents a deep-rooted "will," a vestige of the old Cartesian rationalism, to subdue the corruption of a temporally determined consciousness.

In *Erste Philosophie,* Husserl came to see that "no temporal being is knowable in apodicticity (*apodiktisch erkennbar*)."[43] The studies in this work are decidedly less structural, more surely genetic in their method; and they show a much greater attention than his earlier studies to the way in which temporality determines the modes and boundaries of phenomenological knowledge. Indeed, prior to the *Meditations,* as we know, Husserl decided to devote some important research purely to the problems of temporality and time-consciousness.[44] So it certainly can be supposed that in the *Meditations,* despite a strongly Cartesian orientation, Husserl has become sensitive to the profound significance of temporality.

Now, according to Husserl, adequate evidence must be defined by its moorings in temporality. Adequate evidence emerges

42. *CM,* p. 16 (p. 56).

43. *EP,* II, 398. If transcendental subjectivity is always encountered as a temporalized, objectivated being, except in the primordial, unthematized awareness of the vital present, how can it be *known* apodictically, even as *structure*? Isn't the desire to know this subjectivity in an apodictic manner very close, after all, to what is so objectionable in Descartes?

44. See VPZ. Also note the important remarks of R. Sokolowski, *FHCC,* pp. 189–90.

from the apprehension of an object in its temporal proximity; it is intentional completeness (fulfillment) and certitude of presence. Once the primordial moment of evidence has receded into the past, the object is obviously no longer held in this adequacy and indubitability.[45] But what if it should be possible to take this evidence *purely* in its moment of primordial presence and fully *see* that what it gives in a fulfilled intention, even though this will no longer be present, is such that no evidence in the future will ever be acknowledged as in conflict with it? And what if this aspect of the evidence is accorded a special (doxic) sense, and described as apodictic? Here, then, we would have a new stratum of meaning, a sense which could be said to be independent of the kind of intentional fulfillment required for adequacy, a sense in which the evidence could be indubitable, now and forever, and thus intrinsically trans-temporal, outside the flow of time altogether.

This is a tempting sequence of thought, and it may well have been the one which Husserl took. It suggests the following picture. At the same time that he recovered primordial temporality at the heart of transcendental subjectivity, and was compelled to see that he could no longer hope to obtain a demonstrably adequate evidence, he obviously grew much more confident of his insights into the *eidetic structure* of the transcendental ego. And it undoubtedly seemed to him that the *purely a priori elucidation* of this egological structure could be blessed with a certain freedom from temporal determination.[46] Now this freedom, as he saw it, is precisely the condition for the possibility of apodicticity.

Let us consider what Husserl himself relates:

> We remember in this connexion an earlier remark: that *adequacy and apodicticity* of evidence *need not go hand in hand.* Perhaps this remark was made precisely with the case of transcendental self-experience in mind. In such experience the ego is accessible to himself *originaliter.* But at any particular time this experience offers only a core that is experienced "with strict adequacy," namely the ego's living present (which the grammatical sense of the sentence "*Ego cogito*" expresses); while, beyond that, only an indeterminately general presumptive horizon extends, comprising what is strictly non-experienced but necessarily also-meant. To it

45. See Held, "*Lebendige Gegenwart,*" p. 86.
46. *CM,* pp. 102–3 (pp. 132–33).

> belongs not only the ego's past, most of which is completely obscure, but also his transcendental abilities and his habitual peculiarities at the time.[47]

Perhaps the most reasonable, and also most straightforward, explanation is that Husserl must have thought he would be able to preserve apodicticity if only he could somehow deny that the apodictic title of an evidence presupposes (requires) its demonstrable adequacy. In the next two sections, we shall explore (and question) the tenability of this move. Because, unless it is clear Husserl has shown (or at least, was in a position from which he *could* have shown) *either* (1) that the possibility of apodicticity does *not* at all entail the demonstration of adequacy, *or* (2) that the relevant transcendental evidences *are* indeed adequate, then he must do one of two things: *relinquish* apodicticity altogether, or else consider a *new* formulation *explicitly* built on the *non-demonstrability* of adequacy in regard to these evidences.

[6] First Criticism: Apodictic Evidence Must Also Be Adequate

It was suggested earlier that we can elicit from Husserl's works (at least) two distinct versions of the apodictic principle. According to the strong version (the one Husserl appears *most consistently* to have intended), apodictic knowledge is beyond all possible corrigibility, legitimated and guaranteed with the meaning, "valid now and forever, come what may." But according to some weaker version, it is construed, rather, as an evidence of such lucidity and compulsion that, *while the evidence is immediately present,* one cannot conceive of a *concrete evidential motive* for doubt or abrogation. At the same time, however, one will recognize that, despite its compulsion, *it is relative to (and thus dependent upon) the subsequent evidential positions which it has implicated (intentionally adumbrated) as transcendent.* This means that, in the most profound sense, one *can* conceive (in fact, *has* conceived) the possibility that the object evidenced might not be or might be significantly different; although, to be sure, this conceivability need not be *concretely*

47. *Ibid.*, pp. 22–23 (pp. 62–63).

motivated by any components of the immediately *present* evidence.[48] Under these circumstances, an apodictic evidence can, at best, provide the ground for a *provisional* judgment, firmly entrenched only so long as it can fruitfully systematize subsequent evidential positions. In this respect, an apodictic evidence cannot be at all different from other kinds of evidence. Nevertheless, it should be possible to differentiate stages of reflective and evidential inquiry, beginning with "simple" perceptions and eventuating in the (relatively) most articulate and methodically constituted forms of knowledge. And there is no reason why we cannot call those evidences consummated in eidetic variation and justified through genetic-transcendental critique—our most "rational" evidences, in sum—"apodictic." [49]

Now the reason we must inquire whether or not there can be, as Husserl supposes, an evidence which is apodictic but not demonstrably adequate, is this: the strong version of apodicticity plainly *requires* that there be a demonstrable evidential adequacy, whereas the weaker version we have sketched is formulated in explicit conformity to the *nondemonstrability* of adequate evidence (a consequence of objective transcendence). The weaker version, about which we have no serious misgivings, *adjusts* rational consciousness to the brute facticities of temporality, transcendence, and inadequate evidence.

Accordingly, the form of our argument, what we shall at-

48. It will be recalled that Husserl's argument for the non-apodicticity (the "transcendental dubitability") of our perceptions of material objects in the world is *not* that immediately present evidence *concretely motivates* a doubt (or makes such a doubt reasonable), but rather that the interdependency and flow (transcendence) of evidences make such doubt always (at least) *conceivable.* But why should the validity of this argument rest on the *kind of object* being evidenced? Husserl fails to explain or defend his position on this crucial point.

49. While it is not feasible to enter into any elaborate analysis, it does seem reasonable to suppose that this weaker version is actually quite strong enough to satisfy those philosophers anxious to preserve, e.g., the singular dignity of mathematics and logic. Because eidetic variation, though not giving us an apodictic evidence (in Husserl's strong sense), would still exhibit the evidential compulsion of these fields of knowledge in a special way. At the same time, this version also would seem to fit the position of those philosophers (e.g., W. V. Quine) who wish to dispense with the old bifurcations of judgments into "analytic" and "synthetic," "necessary" and "contingent."

tempt to show in this and the subsequent section, is as follows:

1. Husserl's strong sense of apodicticity presupposes (requires) the demonstration of adequate evidence (as Husserl originally thought in *Erste Philosophie*).
2. Husserl has neither demonstrated such adequacy, nor shown how it is possible for there to be (strong) apodicticity when the evidence is either demonstrably nonadequate or else not demonstrably adequate.[50]
3. Indeed, the *objective transcendence* of the items to which Husserl wants to ascribe apodicticity counts as weighty (though not, of course, apodictically conclusive) grounds for thinking adequacy is impossible, or at least not demonstrable.[51]
4. So either Husserl has to admit his case for (strong) apodicticity is thus far inconclusive, or he has to forego this sense altogether and embrace an explicitly weaker sense, a defeasible evidential claim defined in terms of inadequacy (or at least, the nondemonstrability, thus far, of adequate evidence.)

To see the reasonableness of our three premises, consider the transcendental ego. The transcendental ego recovered by Husserlian phenomenology is a temporally synthesized, "polarized," continually identifiable entity; it is, in short, an evidentially transcendent objectivation of and for a transcendentally reflecting consciousness. Our knowledge of this ego need not be dubitable in any empirical sense, as if there were concrete evidential motives for doubting its existence (or, for that matter, its being thus-and-so). But on the other hand, it cannot be claimed that such knowledge is demonstrably apodictic. Why so? Because Husserl has not demonstrated that this ego permits an adequate evidence. Let us recall that adequate evidence is an intuitional completeness and fullness corresponding perfectly to the noetic

50. Here, and also in 3, we want to avoid questions such as: "How can we determine (How have we determined) that an evidence is inadequate?" and "Is (our argument for) the inadequacy of object-giving evidences itself apprehended in an apodictic insight?"

51. If the *transcendent* character of an evidence entails its inadequacy (or the non-demonstrability of adequacy), then perhaps an adequate evidence is possible *only* in respect of evidences in which *no objects* are given. Such an evidence would be, for example, the evidence of the momentary, lived present. But, as we have seen, this evidence cannot be apodictic, even if it *is* adequate.

intentional sense. Adequacy for an intentional meaning occurs if and only if the meaning is exhaustively filled out by the evidence, so that there remain no partially unfulfilled components in the original meaning. Accordingly, inadequacy signifies that there is but an incomplete intuitional presentation of the object intended. Even if Husserl did not, we certainly *should,* count as modes of inadequate evidence indeterminacies of *various* kinds: vagueness, a certain want in clearness, differentiation, and fullness.

Now, the assertion of apodictic necessity, if it is not to be reduced to a mere (and unwarranted) psychological compulsion (e.g., the *de facto* limitations on our imaginative faculties), must postulate an evidenced state-of-affairs truly relevant to all (and any) evidential acceptances, not just at present, but forever: it is understood, after all, to be much more than the inconceivability of doubt motivated by *present* evidence and merely *presumed,* on this basis, to hold for subsequent conditions; it is an inconceivability of doubt *guaranteed by, and hence itself guaranteeing in advance* (*a priori*), subsequent evidence of a relevant nature.[52] It must *in fact* be the case that further evidence *will not* have any bearing on the present apodictic insight, in the sense that it could ever change, amplify, or cancel it. Otherwise, it must be conceded, in retrospect, that however compelling the insight happened to be, it could not have been truly apodictic.[53]

Husserl's authentically apodictic evidence would have to be, in fine, a perfectly adequate evidence; for only on the ground of evidence that has been demonstrated to be a complete fulfillment of intentional meaning could one be entitled to guarantee

52. We suppose inadequate knowledge to imply that, with respect to such knowledge, the future is truly open and indeterminate. "Relevant evidence" is here *defined* as any evidence capable of *either confirming or disconfirming* some possible given evidential judgment. If we look to Husserl for a clarification of the notion of relevance, we will be disappointed. This crucial problem is never sufficiently treated.

53. Of course, an evidence purporting to be apodictic will still be "relevant" to further evidence in the sense that its verification can be *repeated.* But this sense is not sufficiently strong for apodicticity as Husserl intends it. For verification (or, for that matter, the reiteration of a verification) is an empty, formal gesture, an unnecessary move, if it precludes, in advance, the possibility of disconfirmation.

the impossibility of negation or significant revision. As long as we have but inadequate evidence, or at least cannot *show* the adequacy of our evidence in *all* the requisite (relevant) ways, it cannot really be inconceivable that the evidence should be canceled or significantly revised; and we must, in consequence, abjure the apodictic principle.[54]

When unpacked thus, and clarified in its relation to the possibility of demonstrating adequacy, Husserl's principle reveals its intrinsic self-destruction. If, on the one hand, the apodictic evidence announced at some given time is held to be genuinely *relevant* to subsequent evidence (which we must assume if adequacy has not been demonstrated), then it must be possible, in principle, to conceive the apodicticity as negated. But if, on the other hand, it is argued that the putative apodicticity cannot be conceived as negated, then it must be the case that no phenomenologically significant connection of relevance and hence of implication (intentional adumbration) and interdependence, can obtain between the affirmed apodictic knowledge and the remaining corpus of one's evidence—past as well as future. Now if we should opt for the first horn of this dilemma, we must surrender the strong version of apodicticity; while, if we should choose the second, we are committed to a miraculous, quixotic, and indeed unintelligible notion of apodictic knowledge; and we shall have betrayed the fundamental insight of phenomenology that evidential consciousness is through and through intentional and transcendent. Husserl's broad and fundamental concept of transcendence surely holds true for *all* modes of evidence through which an *object* (*any kind of object whatsoever*) is intended. But objective transcendence would seem to entail (as Husserl saw lucidly enough in respect of *material* objects like candles and trees) *some* kind of inadequacy, or at least the nondemonstrability of adequacy. For the transcendence of an intentional object, its otherness in respect of the consciousness which

54. We must not suppose, on the other hand, that if inadequacy refutes apodicticity, the *demonstration* of a truly adequate evidence would automatically bring apodicticity with it. This is not the case; and Husserl shows due understanding in this matter. There could be, for example, a complete evidence, an actually fulfilled meaning *for the present*. But this fulfillment will not be apodictic, since the *present* fullness at once recedes into the "dubitability" of the retentional past.

intends it, is spelled out precisely (and concretely) in terms of *relevant* evidences which are *adumbrated (predelineated) but not yet present.* And although these relevant evidences could, in principle, be adumbrated with a presumptive certainty, it is hard to see how they could be absent and yet known apodictically.

It is clear enough that the second alternative would never have won Husserl's approbation. So it would seem that, in advocating the strong version, he simply failed to appreciate that it entails such an objectionable consequence, and that the alternative solution introduces a weaker version.

At the source of his recalcitrance we will find an insufficient working-out of the connection between apodicticity and adequacy. Curiously, the one and only finely examined aspect of this connection pertains to the domain of so-called "external (outer) perception." With both consistency and cogency, Husserl advances the view that such perception, precisely *because* it is transcendent and inadequate, cannot be an apodictic evidence for the objects in question. He is apparently shy to consider whether his reasoning on the subject of *outer* perception ought to be expanded to cover "inner" (immanent) perception as well. *A fortiori,* the grounds on which Husserl denies apodicticity to perception of material objects, namely (1) the entailment between apodicticity and adequate evidence, (2) the transcendent character of such perception, and (3) its consequent inadequacy, should obtain, *mutatis mutandis,* for the immanent perceptions through which the transcendental ego is brought to evidence.

The *Cartesian Meditations* betrays the fact that, in some ways, Husserl was facing in two directions. In the one direction, he saw the dark abyss of temporality; in the other, he fancied the dramatic flight of reason. With but one outstanding exception, his theory of rational evidence, Husserl's investigations of the major phenomenological problems move steadily, though with an often painful slowness, toward analyses which squarely confront temporality and come to terms with it. In fact, however, we have seen that, in the encounter with temporality, his theory of rational evidence, too, has been shaken, even to its foundations, since his retreat from adequacy is a potential subversion. But for some reason, Husserl remained quite blind to the urgency of a critique of rational evidence; thus, he was unable to remove its profound ambiguity.

[7] Second Criticism: Problems with Husserl's "Apodictic Critique"

At the earliest stage of his "meditations," Husserl sets forth the apodictic principle with a sober disclaimer: "As beginning philosophers, we do not as yet accept any normative ideal of science; and only so far as we produce one newly for ourselves can we ever have such an ideal." [55] On the other hand, he notes,

> this does not imply that we renounce the general aim of grounding science absolutely. That aim shall indeed continually motivate the course of our meditations . . . and gradually . . . it shall become determined concretely. Only we must be careful about how we make an absolute grounding of science our aim. At first we must not presuppose even its possibility.[56]

The norm of adequate, apodictic science is to serve as a tentative, precursory hypothesis, by which Husserl will be guided. He feels the obligation to discover an apodictic foundation *in advance of* any concrete accomplishments; but he is confident that his investigations will not be in vain. When discovered, this foundation functions to corroborate his initial normative hypothesis.

Husserl's attitude at the outset is not only provisional; it is questioning and relentlessly honest. His employment of the concept of adequate evidence in an ideal and normative capacity does not, for example, tempt him to refrain from posing "the question whether adequate evidence does not necessarily lie at infinity." [57] And once immersed in the exploration of the transcendental sphere disclosed through the reductions, Husserl confronts the need for an apodictic critique of the apodicticity he thinks has been won. Yet, as we have already seen in earlier writings, this critique is again postponed.[58] In view of the fact that the requisite critique is never effected, has not Husserl betrayed his own original methodological sobriety and asceticism? Has he not forgotten his vow to remain tentative and

55. *CM*, p. 86 (p. 49).
56. *Ibid.*
57. *Ibid.*, p. 14 (p. 56). We found that Husserl posed this very same question in *Erste Philosophie* without deciding it.
58. See *CM*, pp. 31 and 151–52 (pp. 70 and 177–78).

without ungrounded commitments? [59] According to Husserl's own adopted standards, he should abstain from announcing apodictic possessions until the requisite critique, itself apodictic, has been accomplished. Could it be, in fact, that the difficulties Husserl himself must have foreseen, to some extent, are actually of such magnitude as to preclude in principle the accomplishment of this critique? The point is, we must question whether apodicticity is possible even with a critique. Here, in fact, we may begin to appreciate that, regardless of what Husserl may think, the problem of apodicticity, and in particular the problem of an apodictic critique, necessarily *coincides* with the problem of adequate evidence. It is not surprising, therefore, that Husserl touches upon both these problems and sets them both aside.

In the preceding section, we argued against Husserl that we can sustain the claim to apodicticity *if and only if* we can demonstrate the adequacy of our evidence, and that, conversely, the failure to show adequate evidence is logically sufficient to entail the illegitimacy of a claim to apodicticity. In the present section, we shall appraise the decisive question whether an adequate evidence (conforming to Husserl's norm of phenomenological science) can in fact be attained without an infinite regress of evidential judgments. The urgent call for a *critique* of apodicticity would seem to imply that the legitimation of apodicticity is, after all, logically tied to a demonstration of adequacy. Therefore, if adequate evidence should lie at infinity—if, in other words, an infinite regress of evidence is possible—then the "apodictic" critique (which is itself, of course, simply a further but perfectly continuous stage of *evidence*, or descriptive explication) may well involve such a regress. Whatever we may discover to be the case, it is certainly plain that the transcendental sphere opened up for eidetic investigation in the later meditations is not *demonstrated* to meet those special requirements which the first meditation affirms to be essential, if it is to be the truly scientific foundation for knowledge.[60]

Let us examine Husserl's own utterances to substantiate our

59. In all fairness, we should note Husserl's confessed misgivings and self-criticism. Cairns mentions his marginal note to the original manuscript: "There seems to be lacking the apodicticity of the precedence belonging to transcendental subjectivity" (*Ibid.*, p. 21 [p. 61]).

60. See the "Bemerkungen von Prof. Dr. Roman Ingarden," in *Cartesianische Meditationen*, pp. 211–12.

argument. One of the first symptoms of distress occurs in his statement that it is possible to pronounce the *ego cogito* (the *sum cogitans*) in an apodictic judgment "only if my experiencing of my transcendental self is apodictic." For it is such experience which grounds all judgment. Descartes, he notes, sought a ground for the indubitability of just one *proposition,* or axiom: "I am." But the question is: What am I? Who is this "I" who can guarantee himself? For Husserl, this translates into the question: Does transcendental subjectivity at any given moment include its past as an inseparable part, accessible by memory? If the answer be affirmative, then we must show, he thinks, the apodicticity of memory. He believes that, even if memory were not apodictic, still the momentary "I am" (my existence, plain and simple), shorn of all past accretions, would remain as an unimpeachable core. He asks, then, how far the transcendental ego can be deceived about himself, and how far the absolutely indubitable evidences extend, in the face of possible deception (that is, *transcendental,* not empirical illusion). He admits, at last, that "in view of such questions, the problem of the range covered by our apodictic evidence becomes urgent." [61] There is, therefore, a certain presumptive character to the apodicticities disclosed through transcendental reduction, insofar as they have not received transcendental criticism (grounding) in respect of apodictic fulfillment and range—matters "which may," he thinks, "be apodictically determinable." [62] We are importuned: "When making certain of the transcendental ego, we are standing at an altogether dangerous point, even if at first we leave out of consideration the difficult question of apodicticity." [63]

Husserl distinguishes two stages of transcendental inquiry. The first is a "simple devotion" to the evidences inherent in the flow of transcendental experience and made accessible through the reductions. The second stage is none other than "a great task, *the task of a criticism of* transcendental self-experience." [64]

61. *CM*, p. 22 (p. 62). At the *close* of the *Meditations,* Husserl reiterates this problem, but has done nothing to resolve it. In a work so self-consciously propaedeutic to phenomenology, the claim to apodicticity becomes all the more unseemly.

62. *Ibid.*, p. 23 (p. 62).

63. *Ibid.*

64. *Ibid.*, p. 29 (p. 67).

When the great work of his meditations is coming to its conclusion, Husserl confesses:

> We have trusted transcendental experience because of its originarily lived-through evidence; and similarly we have trusted the evidence of predicative description and all the other modes of evidence belonging to transcendental science. Meanwhile we have lost sight of the demand, so seriously made at the beginning—namely that an *apodictic* knowledge, as the only "genuinely scientific" knowledge, be achieved; but we have by no means dropped it. Only we preferred to sketch in outline the tremendous wealth of problems belonging to the *first stage of phenomenology*—a stage which in its own manner is itself *still infected with a certain naivete* (*the naivete of apodicticity*), but contains the great and most characteristic accomplishment of phenomenology, as a refashioning of science on a higher level—instead of entering into the *further and ultimate problems of phenomenology:* those pertaining to its *self-criticism,* which aims at determining not only the *range* and *limits* but also the *modes of apodicticity.*[65]

We do not question the wisdom of postponing some phenomenological problems; nor do we wish to dismiss the prodigious insights accrued at the first stage precisely because of such concentrated and economic endeavor. We wish only to call into question the philosophic *justifiability* for Husserl's announcing the disclosure of the apodictic foundation *prior* to the critique which comes at the second stage.

As Husserl understands it, transcendental theory of knowledge leads back to a criticism of transcendental knowledge; and this critique requires, in turn, its own evidence. Husserl insists that "in this connexion, however, there exist no endless regresses that are infected with difficulties of any kind (to say nothing of absurdities), despite the evident possibility of reiterable transcendental reflections and criticisms." [66] This statement, made without elaboration or defense, cannot stand on its own. The fact remains that Husserl has not proved that there is no infinite regress of critique, nor even that, with just *one* stage of critique, an apodicticity no longer "naive" can be obtained. Indeed, since he admits "the evident possibility" of reiterable phenomenological analyses, Husserl is plainly not even in a position to contemplate the recovery of an apodictic evidence, naive or other-

65. *Ibid.*, p. 151 (pp. 177–78).
66. *Ibid.*, p. 152 (p. 178).

wise. We are obliged by the tentative spirit of beginning philosophers to consider his remark as scarcely more than an expression of defiant hope, born of the commitment of an indomitable will to surmount the impossible.[67]

Let us assume that Husserl is correct in maintaining that the (putative) apodicticity disclosed in the transcendental sphere is initially naive unless itself grounded in a higher apodictic critique. Now, in the first place, it is obvious that he does not effect the critique he has demanded. Therefore, the ultimate foundation for which he is searching—a grounding behind which one cannot inquire further—has not been won in the course of his meditations. That being the case, his assertion that there is no regress or, if there is one, it in no way calls apodicticity into question can be no more than an empty gesture. Its demonstration, of course, would bring him closer to the discovery of an apodicticity of unquestionable title.

Can Husserl remain satisfied with a "naive" apodicticity? Properly speaking, his own criteria do not justify him in declaring possession of an apodictic evidence. At most, what he has are tentative apodicticities. But a merely putative apodicticity does not comply with the strong version Husserl believes in. If a critique is indeed requisite, then Husserl cannot claim thus far to have found any apodictic principle. Indeed, we may go so far as to say that, in this respect, the concept of apodicticity has not evolved at all beyond the problems which we discerned in the *Logische Untersuchungen.*

On the assumption that, as Husserl notes, a critique is absolutely essential, would there develop an unlimited regress? In other words, can we find any phenomenological basis for affirming a terminus to the critique? If we cannot, then we are forever condemned to have putatively apodictic evidences which are increasingly, but never completely, purged of their naivete and presumptiveness. Such evidences would not, quite clearly, meet the standards demanded in the strong version. To what extent, therefore, would such a regress, even if it were limited to the first order, threaten the very possibility of apodictic evidence? Behind this question is the argument that, if even a "genuine" (though "naive") apodicticity requires a critique, by what evidential property are we to recognize that the apodicticity won

67. See F. Kutschera, "Über das Problem des Anfangs der Philosophie im Spätwerk Edmund Husserls" (University of Munich Inaugural-Dissertation, 1960), p. 70.

through the critique is not similarly naive? If we cannot hope for final assurance when we first confront an apodictic evidence, on what grounds can we hope for such assurance when we confront it again, mediated by the critique? The force of these questions is simply this: *The very necessity in the first place for a critique throws doubt on the finality and ultimacy of apodictic evidences, at whatever stage of reflection they may be claimed.*

Note that it will not do for Husserl to counter *these* objections with the argument that the regress terminates with the critique, and that once we "complete" this critique, we will have an evidence that is no longer naive but *fully* apodictic. For this would be to miss the point. If an evidence *initially* giving itself as apodictic requires apodictic criticism, then it cannot have been genuinely apodictic (in the strong sense) to begin with. So if we subscribe to the desirability of critique in general, we are brought to the conclusion that apodicticity cannot be obtained. The critique here intended simply amounts to the process of phenomenological-descriptive explication, a laborious and continual re-examination of the evidence. There is no room in this conception for an apodicticity, although the quest for foundational principles, rendered intuitively clear, will proceed as before.

From this point of view, the possibility of an infinite regress in evidential criticism is not, in itself, offensive; in fact, it simply testifies to the interdependency of evidences and explicitly acknowledges the incessant exploration and explication of consciousness (as a truly infinite field of study), to which the phenomenologist must surrender himself. The feasibility of an infinite regress of criticism (not, of course, an *apodictic* critique) should be regarded as altogether salutary. We will esteem it otherwise only if we be committed in advance to the norm of an incorrigible knowledge. Husserl is right in believing a regress poses no special problems and absurdities; but he is mistaken insofar as he feels inclined to deny any regress, or refuses to see how it does entail the impossibility of demonstrating an apodictic evidence.

There is no basis which we can discover for affirming a terminus to phenomenological critique. On the contrary, there are compelling reasons for believing that the regress of critique must, in principle, expand indefinitely. The transcendental ego is but an objectivated concern for Husserl's eidetic analysis. It is a transcendent structure in respect of which we cannot have demonstrably adequate evidence. We should realize, then, that a regressive series of intuitional appraisals, carried out within the transcendental reductions, and perhaps also within the eidetic, is wholly compatible with the most central and elementary concepts of Husserl's late philosophy. The reason Husserl was so disturbed by the problem of critique is that, in effect, any treatment of it which would be fully satisfactory, within the framework of his mature phenomenology, would really have to presuppose the abandonment of the apodictic principle. And this he was not prepared to see.

[8] Third Criticism: Apodicticity Is Incompatible with the Genetic, Teleological "Work-Concept" of Constitution

Paul Ricoeur's admirable study on the *Cartesian Meditations* serves well to introduce some outstanding problems in Husserl's theory of adequate and apodictic evidence, with respect to which it is possible to appraise the overall theoretical strains caused by the apodictic principle in the phenomenology of his late writings.

Ricoeur argues that the *Meditations* contains two contradictory tendencies: On the one hand, the "idealist" approach, which emphasizes *Leistung* (the incessant, infinite *process* whereby the structures of consciousness are evidentially constituted in their genesis and development); and on the other hand, the "intuitionist" approach, which focuses on *seeing* as the *terminus* and *justification* of knowledge. The latter approach, he argues, tends to undermine the important phenomenological developments of Husserl's maturity. It tends to ignore the sense in which the object is but an index for a process, never achieved, of phenomenological identification and explication; and it makes the object a plenitude of presence with a signification capable of full givenness. According to this schema, the *Ideas* is predominantly intuitionist, like the *Untersuchungen.* Husserl was interested at that time in discerning and categorizing the "irreducible" kinds of seeing. The *Meditations,* by contrast, shows greater concern for unpacking the presumptions implicit in seeing, and for setting out the actual and potential intentions whose interlocking styles and strata constitute the process of "making evident."

These two tendencies are delicately interwoven and poised in the *Meditations.* Constitution receives greater attention just because it is a relatively late development, and stood in need of elaboration. The act of seeing (the act *par excellence* of making evident) had already been submitted to prodigious examination and argument. What Ricoeur does not appreciate sufficiently is that these tendencies are contradictory and deleterious only in isolation and reciprocal exclusion; taken together, as they should be, they are complementary aspects of one and the same activity. For an evidential act of seeing is not a miraculous event; it is the *outcome of a process* of genetic constitution. The way must always be prepared for a true, phenomenologically grounded seeing. Conversely, evidence short of "seeing" does not amount to a genetic constitution, no matter how much mental labor has been expended. Moreover, at the highest stage of evidential clarification, the object of the act of seeing (in the full sense) is precisely the process itself wherein it becomes constituted as what it is. Intuition and constitution *together* comprise one unified situation in Husserl's novel conception of objectivity. "Objectivity" refers to the processes of consciousness out of which, or in correlation to which the object emerges, as well as to the ready-made, completed "end-product." This is because the *full* "possession" of an object includes, for Husserl, the component of its evidential clarification or grounding.

Nevertheless, Ricoeur's difficulty in understanding the function of seeing in Husserl's late work is genuine. It originates in the continuing importance of apodicticity. Perhaps, then, Gilbert Ryle's objection to traditional rationalism is relevant, after all, even to Husserlian phenomenology. Ryle wants, among other things, to refute the superstition that proper ratiocination ought best to be described by analogies to seeing, and that the model should be a "prompt, effortless and correct visual recognition of what is familiar, expected, and sunlit." [68] Ryle contends that philosophers too fond of the visual model rather ignore the *"work"* of perception and knowledge in favor of their finished, seemingly effortless *achievements.*

Is it not perhaps the case that Husserl's tenacious employment of apodicticity, despite a very advanced and radical theory of genetic constitution (emphasizing the "work" of objectivating consciousness), and despite the abandonment of a total ade-

68. Gilbert Ryle, *The Concept of Mind* (New York: Barnes and Noble, 1949), p. 303.

quacy, is the source of an excessive and illegitimate reification of evidence—a reification that vitiates the genetic, teleological view at which Husserl finally arrived? At its best, apodicticity still favors finality over process. It postulates a kind of evidence of such clairvoyance that there is absolute disregard for the infinite stretches of investigation. And it wrests a false freedom from the temporal facticity to which it, like all evidence or knowledge generally, must be bound. These criticisms have a two-fold significance. First, they derive from and extend our earlier arguments concerning the logical interdependence of adequate and apodictic modes of evidence, the regress of critique, and the actual attainment of genuine adequacy (according to the postulated Husserlian norm). And second, they obviously call into question the functional compatibility of the concept of apodicticity with the rest of (mature) Husserlian phenomenology.

[9] Fourth Criticism: The Claim to Apodicticity in the Predicative Sphere Is Not Justified

One further critical perspective deserves to be considered. It may be appreciated with what care apodicticity has been shown, in the preceding chapters, to belong to the domain of knowledge (i.e., to the objectivating, positional and doxic mode of consciousness). Consequently, we have yet to declare an important aspect of Husserl's employment of apodicticity which further reveals its jeopardy.

Since apodicticity belongs to the sphere of knowledge, and knowledge must be capable of codification and expression in language, we may conclude that it must be a kind of evidence available for expression in language (linguistic judgments).[69] But consider that language itself is a complicated structure, transcendent to consciousness, vague and ambiguous at times, and so forth; and that in consequence it creates its own peculiar problems with respect to its expressive (predicative) function-

69. Indeed, not only judgments purporting to be apodictic, but in general all results of phenomenological investigations must be expressed in language, if they are to belong to the philosophical community and are to receive acceptance as genuine, "scientifically accredited" contributions. It is certainly fair to have misgivings about the credentials of any insight claiming apodicticity which is not or cannot be given expression in language.

ing.[70] Thus, for Husserl to demonstrate the possibility of apodictic knowledge, it would seem necessary for him to show, through the actual accomplishment of phenomenological investigations, that it is possible to uncover and articulate *every* presupposition nourished by language, even after its peculiar adaptation to phenomenological method; and that, even if one supposes the discernment of all presuppositions, it is possible to examine and ground them as evidentially legitimated judgments, in such a way that *all transcendental* dubitability is overcome, and all normative perspectives are clarified through genetic criticism. Finally, Husserl must demonstrate that the process of criticism and clarification can attain finite consummation, beyond which there is no further relevant meditation. Apodicticity cannot be regarded as even remotely justified, without the resolution or dissolution of these problems. Husserl may not be completely oblivious to their existence, it is true; but in any case he does not extend his investigations to deliver us from them. Once again, it must be said that Husserl forgets the strictures proper to the phenomenologist's "beginner's discipline."

The *Meditations* offers us a distinction between antepredicative evidences (judgments) and predicative evidences (judgments). The latter are evidences which have received predicative expression in some relatively fixed language; they are "higher" formations of evidences, founded upon the anterior "silent" evidences. Thus, predicative judgments will exhibit their own evidence or non-evidence, their own good or bad way of fitting what is meant.[71]

These founded judgments immediately pose a problem: How is it possible for them to conform to the founding evidences? And what are the criteria involved? Language in general, but especially our common language, is notoriously ambiguous, vague and wanting in the stability and perfect determinacy so keenly desiderated for science. These qualities may even be virtues, from the everyday point of view; but from the phenomenological and the scientific, they cannot be tolerated. Husserl observes that there is entirely too much "complacency" about completeness and precision of expression, too much disregard

70. In the posthumous *Erfahrung und Urteil,* it is directly asserted that language is an outstanding exemplification of a "first" idealization and abstraction (see p. 58). Similar views also find their way into the *Krisis*.

71. *CM*, p. 11 (p. 45).

for its niceties, for the purposes of a rigorous phenomenological science. "We require," he holds, "even where we use its means of expression, a new legitimation of significations by orienting them according to accrued insights, and a fixing of words as expressing the significations thus legitimated. That too we account as part of our normative principle of evidence." [72]

Ordinary language, and even that "purified," codified portion of it which phenomenology has embraced for its special tasks, actually enshrines prejudices and presuppositions of all sorts (that is, implicit judgments without grounding or reflective examination). Husserl regards their elimination as of primary importance. "That signifies," he remarks, "restriction to the pure data of transcendental reflection, which therefore must be taken precisely as they are given in simple evidence, purely 'intuitively,' and always kept free from all interpretations that read into them more than is genuinely seen." [73]

Other problems also deserve consideration. Language, as a structure, and indeed as resembling an exquisite tapestry of interweaving significations, is inherently "abstract" or "ideal," relative to moments of actual evidential apprehension. It is not just that language is "open-textured," vague and imprecise; these traits can, after all, be ameliorated, though again, only through a gradual process of refinement, adjustment and amplification. Language is also forever motivating a transcendence of the given, of the momentarily and primordially perceived. This, let it be observed, is in no way altered by the effectuation of a transcendental reduction of language itself, so that it becomes simply a language-phenomenon. Its transcendence adheres to it even in its phenomenological bracketing; for that is the very nature and advantage of language, its singular excellence for depositing, creating and transmitting intentional meanings. How can one render faithful these conceptual expressions, where the meanings are prescribed purely by the object perceived? [74] Expression, Husserl says, requires a definite "*hic et nunc*" meaning, corresponding to the intuitive evidence. How can there be such an achievement, with the perfection requisite to establish the possibility of apodictic knowledge? (Note that we are not intimating that no progress here is feasible. We

72. *Ibid.*, p. 14 (p. 54).
73. *Ibid.*, p. 36 (p. 74).
74. See *Ideas* I, § 65, pp. 174–75 (pp. 152–53).

question only an absolute correspondence, of the sort that apodicticity would necessitate.)

When it is a question of apodicticity, we are not entitled to remain content with any mere program for a *progressive* terminological fixation, however characteristic this may be for the early stages of a new science.[75] In fact, Husserl quite confesses that even with the requisite precision and determinacy of language, the conditions of rigorous science are not fulfilled. The propositions settled upon still have to be arranged into an ordered system, that is, as knowledge properly so called. That means language must finally be correlated, he thinks, with eidetic structures: a job partially undertaken in his transcendental logic.[76] We do not propose that these tasks represent insurmountable difficulties for phenomenological science; but only with the folly of innocence can we choose to ignore their bearing on the affirmation of apodicticity. Husserl, on the other hand, is not reluctant to utilize his principle of apodicticity in its doxic, positional vocation in spite of the numerous problematic regions for study which he himself has discerned in language.

In his phenomenological analysis of language, Husserl does well to stress that "stratification" is just a metaphor, and that the stratum of expression is, in essence, at one with the expressed stratum. Expression, as he remarks, is not like "an overlaid varnish or garment"; it is rather "a mental formation," which accordingly exercises new intentional influences or functions, in a relatively autonomous way, upon the intentional substratum.[77] This being the case, one begins to perceive that the expression of evidence in propositional form is hardly a simple matter, allowing little space for deception and hesitation. In the niceties of phenomenological description, one would suppose, judgment must await a precarious, if privileged, fate. Such description, after all, must go according to standards much more demanding than those rough-and-ready forms at hand in the natural attitude.

It would seem reasonable at this point to question whether the sphere of unity which is the expressed-in-expression is subject to such a thoroughgoing constitutional analysis of its inten-

75. *Ibid.*, § 79, p. 210 (p. 191) and § 84, pp. 224–25 (pp. 206–7).
76. *Ibid.*, § 66.
77. *Ibid.*, § 33, also § 127.

tional genesis as to illumine, adequately and apodictically, the "density," so to speak, which characterizes this unity as it is given. A "mental formation" is both a temporalized objectivity and an historical entity. Can one then reconcile apodicticity with the process of genetic clarification? Only, it would seem, if apodicticity can adjust itself to a genetic, growing a priori, or necessity.

Husserl amplifies his discussion of expressional incompleteness with an illustration in which he entreats us to imagine the arrival of a carriage bringing some long-expected guests. Suppose next that one of the hosts should exclaim, as the carriage with its passengers draws close into sight, "The carriage! The guests!" [78] To be sure, Husserl regards the host's exclamation as a mode of incomplete expression; but he nevertheless does not feel that any consequential problems are created here, when the expressive stratum does not "cover" the lower expressed stratum.

Like many of Kant's renowned illustrations, this one is also most infelicitous, if not truly misleading. Visual perception, when adopted as an illustrative model, encourages oversimplification, for it is, of course, graced with an altogether singular excellence, as we all readily acknowledge. Moreover, the phenomenological and eidetic reductions create problems about expression completely absent when it is a simple matter of "fitting" everyday expression to everyday situations, according to customary criteria. Suppose, for example, that Husserl were confronted with the problem of expressing, in language, the phenomenological evidence attending some fine harmonic modulation in a musical system—say that of ancient Greece, or of the Orient—totally foreign to his acoustic sensibilities. Would he feel so secure in advancing the cause of apodicticity, even when the research had been confined to *eidetic* analysis?

We are not obliged to confront and resolve perplexities about the status of language (as it is utilized for phenomenological description) within the reductions. It suffices for our purposes that a certain obscurity should attend this issue, and that the only justifiable attitude is one of caution, patience, and care. In view of such problems with language, or in general, with the judgmental expression of phenomenological insights, apodictic knowledge becomes most doubtful.

Apodicticity is, in fact, no more compatible, in some re-

78. *Ibid.*, § 126, p. 324 (p. 310).

spects, with the *Ideas* than with the *Meditations*. In the earlier work, Husserl called for the method of "limiting and improving criticism," engaging one in a continuing critique of the relation between utilized concepts and what is given in evidence. He writes:

> Much of what we have described must certainly, *sub specie aeterni,* be described otherwise. But we should and must strive in each step we take to describe faithfully what we really see from our point of view and after the most earnest consideration. . . . [The phenomenologist] should be sure of bringing to expression what in relation to time and circumstance is the thing that *must* be said, and which, because it faithfully expresses what has been seen, preserves its value always—even when further research calls for new descriptions with manifold improvements.[79]

In an earlier section, attention was called to Husserl's recognition that the range and limits of evidence, especially of apodicticity, must eventually receive precise phenomenological formulation; but this critique of evidential scope was postponed and never effected. It would therefore prove impossible to advance very far in a critique of language, in respect of its adequacy to the evidence which it presumes to utter, *before* such an elementary stage of evidential critique and determination has been undertaken. Yet Husserl claims apodicticity even *prior* to the most basic level of critique, even prior, that is, to establishing the scope, limits and modes of apodicticity. And it is only upon this, of course, that we are able to assess the fidelity of the *founded, expressional evidences* (judgments), belonging to our system of knowledge, to the *founding, antepredicative forms* of evidence.

79. *Ibid.*, § 96, p. 259 (p. 241); see also § 65.

7 / Apodicticity in the Eidetic Mode of Consciousness

[1] Introduction

IN THE PRESENT CHAPTER we wish to demonstrate first that the fundamental Husserlian doctrine of the transcendence of intentional objectivities obliges us to acknowledge that a certain incompleteness may well attach to even the *best* eidetic evidence; and second, that the possibility of such incompleteness (a possibility Husserl has not refuted) calls for abandoning the principle of apodicticity (at least as applicable especially to the so-called "morphological" essences, and in its strong version, which we, for the reasons presented, have construed as logically entailing adequacy.) [1] Our demonstration stands unless it can be shown that inadequacy does not entail non-apodicticity, or unless the contention that adequate evidence is not feasible in the eidetic sphere can be refuted by a phenomenological analysis of the evidences involved.

When we have accomplished this aim, and have conjoined our refutation of apodicticity in the eidetic sphere of consciousness with our earlier argument against the apodicticity of the lived, streaming present, we shall have *exhausted* investigation into the domains over which Husserl thought apodicticity to reign.

In particular, we shall argue that Husserl's differentiation of transcendent and immanent essences, as well as his rather formalistic analysis of the essence into "higher" and "lower" regions

1. We are leaving aside, for the moment, the possibility that "exact" essences can, in *some* sense, be recognized as apodictic. But cf. below, § 6, pp. 164–71.

of eidetic description—moves whereby he thinks one can *preserve* an eidetic region for adequate and even apodictic evidence —are not phenomenologically sound. We shall also explore the methods of induction and ideation. Thus, without in any way concealing their important peculiarities, nor impugning the "rational" superiority of ideation, we may be able to establish the respects in which ideation is not just *continuous* with induction, but is, moreover, its methodic *supplement*. We shall conclude our inquiry with a direct examination of *the problem of apodictic critique*. One may, in truth, say that it is precisely *this* problem which is the constant object of each of our criticisms: Husserl's immanent-transcendent grouping of essences; his "internal" bifurcation of essences according to levels of universality and specificity; and the intimately related endeavor to construe ideation as radically distinct from induction.

It is necessary to observe that it is not our wish, nor, in fact, would it be coherent with the scope of this study, to call into question the view that there are any intentional objects answering to the phenomenological concept of essence. We shall conduct our investigations hypothetically, *as if* there were such entities. Our concern may be expressed with a question, thus: *If there are essences, can one have a knowledge of them which, within the framework of a basically Husserlian phenomenological theory, could ever justifiably claim apodicticity?*

[2] The General Phenomenological Significance of a Refutation of Apodicticity in the Eidetic Sphere

Eidetic consciousness is the outstanding, and perhaps exclusive dimension of transcendental consciousness in which Husserl thinks apodicticity possible. On this view, apodicticity will (at the very least) distinguish itself from adequacy chiefly in that it directs attention to a very special *operation* on the evidence, rather than to evidential completeness, or intentional filling out. It belongs to that stage of reflection at which consciousness, having executed the phenomenological and the eidetic reductions, is intentionally directed, through a non-sensuous kind of perception ("insight"), at essential structures and essential relations.

We have observed that, in the *Ideas*, Husserl differentiates assertoric from apodictic insight, according to whether the insight pertains to individuals or to essences. Yet many of his remarks do not explicitly and unequivocally *confine* apodicticity to the eidetic sphere.[2] Indeed, in the *Meditations* and *Erste Philosophie,* he inclines to hold that the "I am" (i.e., the living, flowing present) is also apodictic; but we saw that this certainly is not an *eidetic* evidence (although, to be sure, it is a component, or dimension, of the essential structure of consciousness). On the other hand, Husserl believes that if the eidetic sphere does not have exclusive prerogatives, it does at least have primary ones. Moreover, even where no mention is made of the method of eidetic variation, an evidence is designated "apodictic" if and only if there is a mode of consciousness such that the being evidenced cannot be conceived not to be, or to be (significantly) different. And the operation of trying to conceive nonbeing or being otherwise, in respect of some evidence, turns out, we discover, to define precisely the method of eidetic exploration. It would seem permissible, therefore, to connect the apodictic principle with an eidetically demonstrated necessary and a priori evidence. Consequently, our main burden in the present chapter must be to demonstrate that a priori intuition of essential structures has not been shown conclusively to be apodictic.[3]

[3] The Essence as an Object of Knowledge

For Husserl, phenomenology must become a *purely eidetic science*, confined to a descriptive, intuitional clarification

2. See *Beilage* 29, p. 419, to *Ideen.* In 1914, Husserl wrote: "One could say: even immanent being is given to knowledge only as an idea, since it requires a process of 'approximation.' Adequate givenness is just an idea, having the character of a frontier to which one can approximate, but gradually." In contrast: "Transcendent being, however, is transcendent in the sense that ideas in that domain can approximate but never reach adequacy." But "An *eidos*, though not every *eidos*, can be absolute and adequately given." And in *Beilage* 27, p. 417 (also from 1914), Husserl notes: "Apodictic seeing should not be used for every eidetic seeing." Not every essential judgment is apodictic. But does he think that every apodicticity is eidetic? Sections 6 and 137 of the *Ideas* would tend to give an affirmative reply.

3. It is interesting to note that, when Sartre was still deeply under the spell of Husserl's thought, as when he wrote, for example, *The Psychology of the Imagination,* and had not yet taken the distinctively radical existential turn, he assumed all objects of reflective, eidetic consciousness to be apodictically knowable and not capable of deceiving us.

of the transcendental sphere.[4] Its subject matter is, ultimately, essential being. Husserl wants to secure a *knowledge* of essences (*Wesenserkenntnisse*). In fact, essential knowledge assumes the rigorous function of a *paradigm;* all other styles of so-called knowledge are called upon to demonstrate their ground and their title in eidetic judgments or "principles."

Knowledge, in general, pertains to the thematic, objectivated, and usually doxic formations of consciousness. Consequently, one may *initially* describe essences simply as *objects* (or objectivities).[5] Of course, one must eventually discern all the important properties that further differentiate them from other kinds of object. Nevertheless, from such a simple point of departure, we can derive many properties of *generic* importance which define essences, quite in general, as objectivities for consciousness.

An object, as such, is a unity, an identical pole of meaning; it is always an object-for a consciousness which, in its sense-giving capacity, "is absolute and not dependent in its turn on a sense bestowed upon it from another source." [6] All objectivated formations of consciousness will therefore have a *relative* ("*dependent*") *being* over against the active, signifying consciousness. They will also establish a certain *transcendence,* when construed from the absolute point of the living conscious acts, in that they are meant as objective *identities* through time, as opposed to the *multiplicity* of acts which constitute them: they are always "there," accessible to recollection, further analysis or amplification, and reiterated identification and attention. Husserl chooses the term "ideality" ("non-reality") to designate this fact.[7]

But if all objectivities (including physical "things") are properly disclosed in their *ideality,* there is nevertheless a sense in which "reality" may serve to announce *every objectivated concern* of consciousness—numbers, headaches, the universal "red-

4. Phenomenology, he thinks, is "the theory of the essential nature of the transcendentally purified consciousness." See *Ideas* I, p. 161 (p. 142). The *epochē* discloses the immanent sphere of consciousness, which will then be subjected to an eidetic analysis, eventuating in descriptions that are "essentially transparent in their validity (*Wesensmässig einsichtig*)."

5. See *EP*, I, 129 and II, 309; *Ideas* I, pp. 83 (p. 51) and 192 (p. 172), where Husserl speaks, for example, of the "ideally self-same essence."

6. *Ideas,* pp. 152–153 (p. 134).

7. See the *Logik,* pp. 36, 119, and 139.

ness," as well as tables and chairs, persons and pomegranates—in short, whatever is understood to be an intentional objective concern of consciousness.

Ideality may also be expressed in terms directly marking the phenomenon of *transcendence:* "It is the general ideality of all intentional unities as opposed to the multiplicities which constitute them. . . . [Therein lies] the 'transcendence' of all species of objectivities, which stand opposite the consciousness of them." [8] On the basis of this broad and most fundamental conception of transcendence Husserl declares: "If we now separate immanent from transcendent objects, that can only signify, then, a separation *within* this larger concept of transcendence." [9]

If the noemata acquired through eidetic variation are objectivities, they will exhibit, as we have reasoned, a fundamental *transcendence* in relation to the conscious acts in which they are disclosed:

> As we have suspended individual realities in every sense, so now we seek to suspend all other varieties of 'transcendent.' This affects the series of 'general' objects, the essences. They too are in a certain way 'transcendent' to pure consciousness, and not really to be found in it.[10]

And quite in keeping with their transcendent nature, essences, though *ideal* (in the special sense of being *contrasted* with *spatio-temporal* "reals" like desks, dogs, and diamonds), declare themselves as enduring objective concerns through "horizons" of intentional meaning: "Here is the synthesis of fulfillment, leading back from the mere meaning to the intuitively given meant, in a synthesis of confirmation and preservation." [11] But, on account of these horizons and this synthetic process, "the meaning can encounter conflict, in its return to self-giving intuitions, which can, for example, reveal the nothingness of the intended regular triangle." [12]

It would be reasonable to conclude that, inasmuch as all

8. *Ibid.*, p. 148.
9. *Ibid.*
10. *Ideas,* p. 159 (p. 140). Cf. further pp. 164–65 (p. 145), where, in discussing psychological interpretations of essences, Husserl again affirms that they are not a "real part" (*"reelles Bestandstück"*) of the flow of consciousness. But this can mean just one thing: they are truly *transcendent* to this flowing consciousness.
11. *EP*, I, p. 130.
12. *Ibid.*

essences are objects of knowledge, and, indeed, are transcendents at a relatively *advanced* stage of objective formation (being founded on experience of individuals and recovered through eidetic method) they would remain, for Husserl, mere "presumptive" and incomplete acquisitions of rational consciousness. That this, however, is not, in fact, Husserl's altogether consistent position will become clear in the ensuing investigations. Seemingly overlooking the fundamental sense of transcendence we have noted, he divides essences into immanent and transcendent, and maintains the possibility of winning an absolute, adequate, and apodictic knowledge of the former kind.

[4] Further Determination of the Essence through the Process of Eidetic Variation

Every experience, every particular in the stream of consciousness, Husserl tells us, is accessible to objectivation through a special procedure of reflective (but still wholly intuitive) operations that he calls "ideation" or "eidetic variation." [13] In such a manner, he differentiates two modes of "being-for-consciousness": the being which is peculiar to particulars (individuals); and the being peculiar to essentialities. The former mode is contingent and factitious, whereas the latter is a priori and necessary.

A facticity (*Tatsächlichkeit*) could just as well have been posited with another spatio-temporal locus, with another shape, size, color, and so forth; there is nothing "intrinsic" to it that necessitates its being precisely *this* that it is, with just these properties and no others.[14] Since every facticity is also "essentially" just what it is (as just *this* particularity), it will always be possible to elicit the essentiality which corresponds to each respective facticity. Through eidetic determinations, one can eventually delimit and then analyze regions, or categories, of individuals. The essence will, first of all, disclose *what* a particular entity is, for every "what" can be grasped in the form of an "idea" (an *eidos*).[15]

The ideating act in which an essence is truly given is a *seeing* experience (*Erschauung*), a genuine intuition; it is a data-giving act, regardless of whether it is an adequate evidence:

13. *Ideas* I, p. 108 (p. 80).
14. *Ibid.*, p. 46 (p. 12).
15. *Ibid.*, p. 48 (p. 13).

> The essence (*eidos*) is an object of a new type. Just as the datum (*das Gegebene*) of individual empirical (*erfahrenden*) intuition is an individual object, so the datum of essential intuition (*Wesenerschauung*) is a pure essence.[16]

Thus, "essential insight is still intuition, just as the eidetic object is still an object." [17] Eidetic intuition resembles individual intuition in being, at its best, consciousness of an object which is "bodily" self-given in an intentional act and grasped directly as the very essence itself.[18] Furthermore, analogous to the case of a sensible seeing of facticities, its object can be presented (*vorgestellt*) in a *multiplicity* of *other* acts, "vaguely or distinctly thought, made the subject of true and false predications." [19]

But ideation obviously differs significantly from sensible seeing. For example, observes Husserl:

> One cannot see the universal, red, the way one sees an individual discrete red; but the extension of our terminology about seeing . . . is unavoidable. We can thus express the fact that what is common and universal to an arbitrary range of discretely envisioned particulars, regarded as essential instantiations, comes to us *directly* and *as it itself*, just like an individual particular through sensible perception, and in an altogether analogous fashion, though indeed only in that complicated vision of the actively comparing process of congruence.[20]

In spite of such fundamental differences between sensible and ideative intuition—differences which we shall presently bring to light in greater detail—these two activities of consciousness are not only analogous in the respects described, they are also complementary and interdependent. Essences tell us something important about their subordinate particularities; and conversely, examination of a range of facticities leads to the disclosure of their corresponding essentiality. However, under the sway of his apodictic vision, Husserl was also rather tempted to posit an unbridgeable chasm separating facticity from essence, in order to preserve the pure necessity (and thus the apodicticity) of the latter.

Here, then, it is of the utmost importance to note exactly

16. *Ibid.*, p. 49 (p. 14).
17. *Ibid.*
18. *Ibid.*, p. 49; cf. also *EU*, p. 421.
19. *Ideas*, p. 49 (p. 14).
20. *EU*, p. 421.

how an examination of facticities will (can) eventuate in the disclosure of an essence. For, the purportedly wide separation of the two kinds of intuition must rest completely on the explicit utilization of a very special *method* in conducting this examination.

To be precise, it is indeed the case, as Husserl expresses himself,

> that no essential intuition is possible without the free possibility of directing one's glance to an individual *counterpart* and of shaping an illustration; just as conversely, no individual intuition is possible without the free possibility of carrying out an act of ideation and therein directing one's glance upon the corresponding essence which exemplifies itself in something individually visible.[21]

And yet, Husserl often seems inclined to believe that ideation does not *in any way* presuppose the apprehension or recognition of the reality-status (existence-status) of those facticities invoked in the process of eidetic disclosure.[22] The latter must contain, he asserts, absolutely no reference to concrete existence (no *Daseinssetzung*).[23] Consequent upon this special kind of positional abstention, definitive of authentically eidetic judgments, is the condition that the essence may be exemplified intuitively *either* through the data of experience (including memory), *or*, just as satisfactorily, in freely fantasized (conceivable) states-of-affairs.

The process of ideation can be organized into three principal stages: (1) a running through of exemplary possibilities; (2) an intuition (seeing) of their congruence, or coincidence (*Deckung*); and (3) an active identifying of the congruent elements as constitutive of a unity, henceforth called the "essence." [24]

21. *Ideas*, p. 50 (p. 16).
22. For Husserl, this distinguishes at once a general natural law (e.g., "All bodies are heavy") from a genuine essential generality (e.g., "All material objects have spatial extension").
23. See *Ideas*, pp. 51 (p. 17) and 54 (p. 20).
24. See Alwin Diemer, *Edmund Husserl: Versuch einer systematischen Darstellung seiner Phänomenologie*, Monographien zur philosophische Forschung, vol. 15 (Meisenheim am Glan: Anton Hain, 1956); note especially p. 132. The recovery of eidetic evidences by the method of eidetic variation obviously involves the important work of *synthesis* (perhaps especially the so-called "associative sense-transfer synthesis"). The issue of synthesis is certainly extremely important, and it is therefore surprising and puzzling that Husserlian phenomenologists, as well as commentators on Husserl's work, have

The first stage finds consciousness taking some particular (which it presumes to be an instance of the essence that is sought),[25] and treating it as a mere possibility among others. Abstention from positing the particular with an existent sense allows consciousness to regard each chosen datum as pure exemplar, as just one arbitrarily selected possibility among many. For

---

ignored so outstanding a problem. Robert Sokolowski, for example, has devoted an entire book to the concept of constitution (*The Formation of Husserl's Concept of Constitution*), without helping us much to understand the work of synthesis in constitution. Eventually, this problem will have to be explored. On the other hand, we shall not attempt to deal with this problem here. There are two reasons for this decision. First, a satisfactory exposition and account of synthesis probably requires a more extensive, more detailed treatment than the scope of this study will permit. And second, there is an important sense in which we are not primarily concerned with the *process* through which eidetic objects are brought to evidence, *except* insofar as this should give us reason to think the *outcome* of the process cannot be apodictic. Our focus, ultimately, is on the possibility of describing these eidetic (object-giving) evidences, *once recovered,* in terms of apodicticity. It does not seem likely, as far as we can tell, that a deeper understanding of synthesis would significantly alter the conclusions to which our investigations have led us.

25. Some commentators have noted with great perturbation of mind that the possibility of initiating eidetic variation so as to arrive at the desired essence seems to *presuppose* a knowledge of the essence in question prior to the exploratory endeavor. The accusation of circularity is not justified. It betrays a fundamental misunderstanding of the point of and motivation for eidetic variation. It will be recalled that the way to transcendental subjectivity commences with perception of the real world, even though the reductions will ultimately bracket such perception. The transcendent world serves as a "clue" to the more profound investigations that lead us to pure subjectivity. In an analogous sort of procedure, Husserl rightly may presuppose a natural and ready-made understanding of essences. His point is that such understanding is critically naive, insofar as it does not (truly) *see* the phenomenological *grounding* of these essences in the constitutive performances of consciousness, and moreover, this understanding must remain confused, indeterminate, and without full clarity, unless the essence is clarified, both as to its genesis and as to its total content. Genetic constitution of essences through ideation provides the requisite scientifically rigorous understanding of such essences as consciousness has already at hand, but not yet accessible in their clarified, determinate, and genetically constituted and legitimated phenomenological perception, whereby consciousness recognizes its objective concerns as constituted in and through consciousness—there, only to be clarified and authenticated by profound *self*-examination (i.e., transcendental critique).

this reason, *any other* particular (within the essential limits of the eidetic region involved) could serve with equal reward as the starting point. Thereafter, consciousness proceeds to produce and run through a series of variations on the initial example, again treating each further variant as a purely arbitrary compossibility. Consciousness itself, therefore, is transformed into a pure possibility-consciousness, as it attends first to one, then another of the compossible variations, since to each *noematic* variant there corresponds a *noetic* variant.[26]

What makes the examples genuine *variants* is, of course, their difference, each from the others. For instance, when running through a series of color variations, one discovers a certain conflict among them. No two colors can at the same time exclusively occupy the same spatial extension. Consequently, the beginning of the second stage is consciousness of the respects in which the variations are interrelated through conflict (*Widerstreit*). As early as the *Logische Untersuchungen,* Husserl enunciated the fundamentals of eidetic variation (in terms, though, of genera and species), except that its functioning within the transcendental reductions and its preoccupation with the so-called "immanent" essences were yet to be spelled out. On conflict and coincidence, Husserl says:

> This relationship sets definite kinds of content into connection, within definite contexts of contents. Colors do not conflict with one another in general, but only in definite contexts, as when they are related to the same extension. A content of the species q is never simply incompatible with a content of the species p; the assertion of their incompatibility always refers to a content connection of a definite kind G (α, β, . . . , p), which contains p and is supposed also to contain q.[27]

Consciousness, as it were, darts across and through the conflict, to discern (and tie together) the resemblances which are, in fact, the very ground of their difference. To pursue the illustration from the *Logische Untersuchungen,* there is a unified intuitional consciousness of a generality, yielding "a unified possible species which unites p and q through conflict on the basis of G." [28] In other words, p and q conflict because they are sensuous characters of the same genus, and are at the same level of

26. See *CM*, pp. 70–72 (pp. 104–106).
27. *LU*, II, pt. II, Sixth Study, p. 108.
28. *Ibid.*, p. 109.

specificity. As consciousness runs through the series, living its freedom of play, it becomes increasingly aware of encountering a pervasive restraint. And, when it finally grasps the sense of the limits to its freely evolved conflicts, it has discerned an invariant coincidence as the *ground* of this necessity, this inner constraint. This constraint is nothing other than the a priori (self-generated) lawfulness of consciousness itself.

The third and final stage is that in which consciousness explicitly recognizes, in an intuitively clear and full ideation, the objectivated unity which underlies the coincidence; it has before it, at that moment, the essence (*eidos*) itself, as a self-same identical objectivity, positionally accorded the sense of enduring through time (though, as it may be, now with validity, now with invalidity).[29]

Consequent upon the method by which it is acquired, the essence exhibits "with an apodictic evidence a universe of the conceivable . . . such that any negation has precisely the same signification as the impossible." [30] The essence possesses a validity and endurance as such which is "unconditionally necessary." [31] Necessity is associated with the essence's "irreality": an eidetic object is nowhere in the stream of consciousness; for the ideating consciousness has deliberately attempted to free itself from the temporal flow, and hence from all temporal location, by surpassing the particularity, the facticity of its exemplifications. The essence is therefore called an "*Allzeitlichkeit.*" The synthesis of the manifold coincident and compossible variants is spontaneous, arbitrary, and outside facticity; in that sense, the *eidos* is outside temporal flow. Yet, on the other hand, it is plain that the conscious *acts* through which the objectivated essence is grasped as a unity *are* temporally determined. Moreover, each act of intuition giving the essence is both a presenting (*Gegenwärtigung*) and a temporalizing (*Zeitigung*); in that sense, then, the essence, too, is inevitably bound to the flow of consciousness—bound to the brute facticity of time and particularity.[32]

The way in which an essence is related to the temporal flow

29. See *Logik*, p. 219; and see also *EU*, pp. 412–14.
30. *Logik*, p. 220.
31. *Ibid.*
32. See Klaus Held, "Lebendige Gegenwart": Die Frage nach der Seinsweise des transzendentalen Ich bei Edmund Husserl (University of Cologne Inaugural-Dissertation, 1963), pp. 70–72.

is of great moment. We may say that, from the noematic point of view, an essence is a structure, an object of signification. But from the noetic point of view, it is an a priori law of necessity, prescribing "that without which an object of this sort cannot be thought." [33] The a priori law is contained in an executive and constitutive *capacity* of consciousness: "It is to these capacities that are related . . . the phenomenological a priori as a priori created out of the resources of corresponding essential intuitions." [34] The "I can" is "marginally" present as what functions correlative to any objective sense: for an objectivity is precisely what is always accessible to further intentional positing, modalization, analysis, and amplification.[35] Thus, the essence emerges from temporally determinate intentional moments to become, *as object*, and more specifically, as a (doxic) necessity, a trans-temporal entity. We therefore argue that its sense of objectivity endows it with a fundamental *transcendence*, relative to the temporalized and temporalizing acts of consciousness through which it *can* (always) be grasped; while (for Husserl) its putative apodictic necessity, its utter independence from all facticity as a result of the method of variation, is supposed to give it the property of being not merely (1) transcendent in regard to particular ideative acts, but also, indeed, (2) known as identically transcendent, with the *same* validity, in relation to *all possible* (conceivable) acts.

Husserl deemed the essence to be a necessity of conscious lawfulness, beyond change, prior to all change—"prescriptive" or "legislating" in respect of all noetic activity. Can he, though, provide a decisive justification for apodicticity, in view of this transcendence of the objects of eidetic knowledge? It is *this* transcendence (2), after all, which would be required for an apodictic knowledge of essences. We must inquire into the phenomenological source of legitimation for such an eidetic consciousness.

According to Husserl's late thought, there are, corresponding to the noematic and noetic perspectives, two correlative aspects of the a priori disclosed through ideation: on the one hand there is an *ontic* a priori, and on the other hand a *constitutive* a priori. Phenomenologically, they are inseparable, forming a concrete unity, just as, in a more general way, noema and noesis are an

33. *EU*, p. 411.
34. *FtL*, p. 218.
35. *Ibid.*, p. 139.

original, concrete unity. Accordingly, just as every noema serves as "clue" to its correlative noesis, so

> every a priori 'immediately' conceived refers us back to the a priori of its constitution; one must master the possibility of grasping in an a priori way the correlation between the object and its constituting consciousness.[36]

On this view, an essence, like all objects whatsoever, must be queried as to its genesis (*Sinnesgenesis*) in the performances of consciousness. Essences, that is to say, will yield a history; they are sedimentations of meaning. Therefore, *no complete and fully rational apprehension of the essence is to be considered possible without the articulation of its historicity.* "Thus, to a *static constitution* of objects related to a subjectivity already 'developed,' there corresponds the *genetic a priori constitution,* founded on this static constitution which must necessarily precede it." [37] The essence must ultimately be grasped, according to this view, in its truly "living" sense.[38]

[5] How Husserl's Theory of Ideation Avoids Both Psychologism and Platonism

Husserl's theory of essence, especially after the introduction of the method of genetic constitution, pretends that it can repudiate psychologism and subjectivism without at the same time falling into an arrogant Platonism. Let us consider first how he thinks it possible to sustain the view that essences are not mere psychological constructs. He observes that

> what is engendered in the spontaneous act of abstracting is not the *essence,* but consciousness of the essence, and the position here is as follows: that a primordial data-giving (*originär-geben-*

36. *Ibid.*, pp. 219–20.
37. *Ibid.*, p. 220.
38. See *ibid.*, pp. 25–26, 184, and 221. T. Seebohm maintains that facticities and essences are inextricably bound together: the essence has a genesis in temporally fixed acts, and relates to facticity through the historical life of consciousness itself. And, having historicized consciousness (especially, "reason") and essences, he goes on to historicize apodicticity, arguing (as he thinks) in line with Husserl's late philosophy, that it must be fitted into a teleology of reason. But Seebohm fails to see that in truth his suggestion signifies a radical reworking of Husserl's theory of evidence. See *Die Bedingungen der Möglichkeit der Transzendentalphilosophie* (Bonn: H. Bouvier, 1962), p. 143.

des) consciousness of an essence . . . is in itself and necessarily spontaneous, whereas to the empirical (*erfahrenden*) consciousness which gives us sensible objects spontaneity is not necessary. . . . Thus there are no motives discoverable except for those of mistaken identity, which could demand the identification of the consciousness of the essence with the essence itself, and therefore the reduction of the latter to psychological terms.[39]

To this argument it should be added that essences, though ideal in the strict sense that they are objectivated without any spatio-temporal meaning, are nevertheless transcendent, unified poles of meaning, which endure as identifiable *objects* through time. Consequently, to reduce the essence to conscious *acts* is to deny that the essence is a genuine intentional object. Only a narrow construction for the notion of an object, according to which it must have spatial as well as temporal existence (location) could offer a serious, if unfruitful, opposition to Husserl's critique of psychologism. In the fecundity and soundness of its investigations, phenomenology finds confirmation enough for the position that an objectivity is anything whatsoever which is transcendently correlative, and always available, to intentional acts of consciousness.[40]

He is similarly anxious to avoid a Platonic hypostatization of essences. He argues that, unless "object" is defined as "empirical object," and "reality" as just "empirical reality," and unless one ignores the prerequisite for a rational possession of the eidetic, namely, a priori genetic constitution, through which the essence is presented as an eventuality of conscious (intentional) performances, one cannot find cause to accuse phenomenology of a Platonic reification.[41]

39. *Ideas* I, p. 82 (p. 51). See also Paul Ricoeur's introductory notes to the French edition, *Idées directrices pour une phénoménologie*. Also see T. Adorno, *Zur Metakritik der Erkenntnistheorie: Studien über Husserl und die phänomenologischen Antinomien* (Stuttgart: W. Kohlhammer, 1956), pp. 130–31.

40. An object is defined as "anything whatsoever, e.g., a subject of a true (categorical, affirmative) statement" in one of Husserl's very uncharacteristic approaches to the matter. See *Ideas*, p. 80 (p. 48). It is incidentally interesting to observe the resemblance between this doxic, predicative-level definition and the corresponding one which John Locke proposes: An "idea" is "that term which, I think, serves best to stand for whatsoever is the *object* of the understanding when a man thinks" (*An Essay Concerning Human Understanding* [New York: Dover Publications, 1959], Introduction, § 8, p. 32).

41. See *Ideas*, p. 80 (p. 49).

We shall presently show reason for qualifying somewhat Husserl's view that eidetic variation (ideation) is *radically* distinct from and totally discontinuous with empirical variation (induction); but we do not wish to deny altogether the existence of a genuine *difference* between induction and ideation. What we shall argue is only that the difference is not total, and that they are continuous and complementary operations. Finally, it will be shown that apodicticity in fact destroys this kinship: induction does *not* differ from ideation in that apodicticity is refused to the one while dignifying the other.

Indeed, it will then become clear why the ascription of apodicticity to eidetic objectivations is precisely what would motivate one to think the choice must be between the two equally great evils, psychologism and Platonism. Apodicticity acts, in effect, to eliminate Husserl's otherwise persuasive and sound phenomenological alternative. For if one should seriously query the title of apodicticity, as we are doing, and find it wanting, he would be inclined to conclude that essences can have only subjective, psychological status. But if one should be reluctant to opt for psychologism, the most obvious alternative is some form of Platonism: apodicticity readily suits the view that essences are eternal, immutable, and completely independent realities.

The way to overcome *both* psychologism and Platonism is through Husserl's genetic constitutional analysis, which discloses the historicity of intentional objects and validates (grounds) them in terms of temporally specific intentional acts. But here, too, the dependency of essences on their elementary facticities becomes manifestly incompatible with the perfect freedom that an apodictic knowledge of essences would demand. As we have already found, it is for just such a way that apodicticity is especially subversive. It altogether precludes understanding essences through a disclosure of their "living" sense.

[6] Husserl's Differentiation of Exact and Morphological Essences

Pure geometry, pure logic, and pure mathematics are traditional paradigms for the ideal of an exact eidetic science. It might at first be supposed that, since phenomenology also is an eidetic science, it would establish its method and its principles after the model of these older sciences. However, phenomenology is fundamentally different from them; indeed, it must function as their transcendental (and immanent) ground. They are purely formal (structural) and exact eidetic sciences, while it is concrete, genetic and descriptive, as well as eidetic.

In Husserl's view, geometry, for example, does not depend on *single* intuitions. It is throughout a system of deductively coordinated general (eidetic) propositions. Briefly, there are certain primitive concepts and definitions; a finite set of basic axioms ("primitive laws of essential being"); and rules for deducing an unlimited number of theorems. The concepts with which the geometer operates, according to the classical picture, are exact, rigorously determined, fully explicit, and never of necessity associated with any particular intuitions. There is, as Husserl sees it, no formal openness to the geometric system or its definitions. Insofar as experience functions at all in geometry, it is not as ground, but only as efficient vehicle for thought; a merely conceived (imagined) instantiation often would serve with equal power and economy. Geometry is a traditional example of a *mathesis universalis*, exhibiting immediately "rational" (*einsichtig*) principles grounded in eidetic axioms, and containing further, mediately grounded contents, equally necessary in their eidetic modality.[42]

Whether or not Husserl's conception is fully consistent with our present understanding of geometry as a formal axiomatic system, one will surely grant that phenomenology, in spite of all it borrows, differs along essential lines from any one of the classical exact sciences. Husserl might never have founded phenomenology, had he not come to it by way of resolving certain perplexities about the nature and, especially, the foundations of logic and the mathematical sciences; but he is adamant in showing that phenomenology requires a novel and very different methodology. He remarks again and again that a radical philosopher should not have any a priori methodological commitments. Method and strategies of inquiry must be engendered by and corroborated through the subject matter intended for exploration. By now we should have, in fact, rather good reason to doubt Husserl's faithfulness to these principles of counsel and discipline.

The subject, for phenomenology, is consciousness and its

42. See *ibid.*, pp. 55 (p. 22), 186 (pp. 165–67), and 193 (p. 173).

intentional formations. Its only original commitment is to painstaking intuitive investigation, with the aim of adequate description. And, the nature of this peculiar science being what it is, such concrete description is also a genetic, legitimating clarification. Consciousness, Husserl observes, is not a mathematical manifold; nor can it be otherwise than incessantly in flux—and that in different dimensions. Hence, exactness and deductive procedure are absolutely precluded. Nor are the eidetic formations of consciousness capable of exhaustive definition, inasmuch as they are the essences of concrete experience (*Erlebniswesen*).[43]

Geometrical concepts are called "ideal" concepts; they give expression to purely formal constructions for which intuitive presentation need not, but may well be impossible.[44] The essences to which these concepts refer are termed "exact essences." Phenomenological concepts are always, by contrast, completely intuitive and descriptive, expressing the essential nature of things as drawn immediately from simple intuition. Husserl appropriately designates their corresponding essences by the term "morphological," thus calling attention to their origin in and their dependency upon the "configuration" of the intuited data, as it truly gives itself.

It is possible, and may prove illuminating, to differentiate these two kinds of essence in the following manner. In the case of the exact essences, their explicit *definition* functions as the *ground and exhaustive determinant* of their meaning (or, from an ontological viewpoint, their being). As for morphological essences, however, their *meaning* (and being) is the *ground* of their definition. They are given the sense of being somehow *more* than what is already explicated in the propositions which define them and the judgments which articulate them. Their definitions do not engender them by means of a priori deduction; nor are they created by explicit conventions or fiat, having all and only these properties (contents) specifically designated by the formal system in question; but they represent, rather, a gradual discernment and analysis of the essences involved, as

43. *Ibid.*, pp. 189 (p. 168) and 191 (p. 171).

44. Even where intuitive presentation is possible, for example, in the case of small numbers, the essences are "exact," and hence very different from the "morphological" essences. Their exactitude, as we shall suggest, is a function of their formative *genesis* through the intentional presentations of consciousness.

consciousness comes to comprehend its constitutive acts out of which these essences are seen to emerge.

Phenomenological definition, it is suggested, will then be a style of solicitation, a relentless devotion to the infinite task of exploring hospitable openings in the density of being and meaning. Once more, however, it is worthwhile to question whether apodicticity does not contrive to congeal and ossify these morphological essences—even, or perhaps especially the so-called immanent ones, such as the essence of perception, of the will, or of memory. One must not in haste identify the quixotic quest for apodicticity with the justified and properly rational endeavor to achieve greater precision, rigor, and determinancy in eidetic judgment, and greater clearness and fullness in the essential insight itself. It is *indeed* the case that the processes of consciousness cannot be fixed, as such, in their tenuity and caducity, in adequate and exact knowledge, codified for all eternity; whereas, happily, as Husserl observes, the passage of conscious performances allows of an essentially "necessary" conformity to type, which *can* be apprehended in a system of knowledge. But there is no warrant for believing (in the absence of a phenomenological demonstration to the contrary) that, with these morphological essences—thematized, transcendent structures of knowledge that they are—a perfectly adequate and, moreover, apodictic fixation *in language* can be anything more than a dreamer's dream.

Perhaps in a certain special and "degenerate" sense, therefore, *exact* essences, and more generally speaking, the subjects of eidetic propositions in the exact (formal) sciences, *are* capable of being constituted in an adequate and apodictic knowledge. For, if we concentrate on that aspect of apodicticity which defines it in terms of the inconceivability of the non-being or not-being-thus of the items evidenced, we can see at once that something of the sort *does* pertain to the exact essences and the eidetic propositions of the exact sciences, insofar as they *are* precisely what they are *defined* (and hence, known) as. Here it would seem there could indeed be no evidence of a contrary sort which would ever be *recognized* (freely posited by consciousness) *as relevant.* Fresh or different evidence will be admitted *only* through the adoption of a *new* definition, and a *different* evidence; and it must not be supposed that this procedure is totally arbitrary, a simple product of some isolated, whimsical decision.

But so far, we have totally ignored the transcendent character of these evidences and, in effect, their intrinsic relativity. From the standpoint of Husserlian transcendental method, with its radical norm of rationality, such properties should be sufficient to call into question their apodicticity (in the strong sense): exact essences and, more generally, the subjects of exact eidetic propositions are a species of meaning which, like other meanings, have been posited intentionally with a transcendent-to-consciousness sense; they transcend the flowing, momentary *cogito* and are, just as much as the meanings through which the "real" transcendent world is presented, altogether relative to a particular evidential moment in the life of consciousness. After all, Husserl has exhibited the systematic meaning of his ideal of reason by calling the evidence of the world into question, even though he acknowledges that no concrete evidence motivates a special doubt. This evidence is dubitable, he argues, only in the sense that the world for which it speaks is meant as transcending the momentary, lived *cogito*. But in what respect, or in what sense, then, do the exact essences *differ* from objects in the world, such that they are exempt from *this* method of doubt? Of course, there *are* many significant differences between our knowledge of the world and our mathematical knowledge. What we want from Husserl, therefore, is a phenomenologically grounded demonstration that these two kinds of knowledge truly differ, specifically *in respect of transcendental dubitabilty*, for it would certainly seem that, *at least from this standpoint*, they are *not* radically distinct.

We cannot deliver the apodictic, rationally necessary evidences Husserl most dearly wants, even when we have explored the exact and eidetic sciences; yet we can sustain without difficulty numerous legitimate principles of eidetic and a priori knowledge. It is feasible, after all, to describe the domain of knowledge uniquely engendered (constituted) through the eidetic method. Moreover, the outcome of methodically rigorous eidetic variation, though not able to present itself as a demonstrably apodictic knowledge in the strong sense, can indeed give us meanings of special compulsion and dignity, meanings at least *presumptively* true not for a mere collection of cases (as with probabilities), but for *all* eidetically possible (conceivable) cases.

In our rational reconstruction of knowledge, in our laborious task of mental stock-taking, we are able, apart from and after the grounding of knowledge in primordial, simply lived experience (awareness), to explore systematically the map of knowledge itself; gradually we are able to discern *within* knowledge, and as itself a fragment of this transcendent, and, in Husserl's special sense, thoroughly "dubitable" realm of meaning, what seem *provisionally* to be the necessary conditions for the unity and order of knowledge in general. Here we will naturally find the laws of logic, mathematical conceptions, and certain categories pervasive in human experience (e.g., identity, unity, and temporality).

Our knowledge of these putative necessary conditions, or uniformities, is both eidetic and a priori, the result of a special method at work on exclusively "immanent" materials, that is, the inner structure of knowledge itself; but the a priori necessities recovered in this manner cannot disguise their status of transcendent, forever corrigible meanings, constituted and justified as such relative to the whole system of knowledge.

Categorial analysis, conducted not as Aristotle or Kant conceived it but rather according to the canons of phenomenological method, will, in other words, deliver a "necessary," a priori knowledge (a "critique," or second-order knowledge), revealing those items which, after eidetic variation, recommend themselves as most pervasive, most fundamental, and most nuclear in the given structure of knowledge, but which, at the same time, have exhibited, through their genetic constitution, their one "existential" weakness. Knowledge designated "a priori" and "necessary" under the compulsion of rigorous phenomenological method will ultimately betray the fact that, even with its sublime pretensions, *it must be sustained in existence through the intentional activity of consciousness*. Such is the case, although it may well be that, as long as this knowledge is in fact sustained, things could not (seem to) be otherwise, and are thus, in this very *special* ("weak") sense, adequate and apodictic.

Husserl is correct in maintaining that the results of categorial analysis are not intrinsically doomed to offer us only a psychological compulsion, or mere feelings of brute necessity. Nor is it the case that we are here concerned with some purely formal compulsion, grounded on arbitrary conventions. Reason has its way. Husserl's method inaugurates a new mode of evidential compulsion. At once logical (based on the synthesis of all eidetically compossible cases) and phenomenological (based on the articulation of pure evidence), it gives expression to the insight—valid enough if not affirmed as an apodictic judgment—that "this is the way things are," given the nature of a human consciousness who dwells in the world.

However, it is equally true to say Husserl failed to understand that, whatever the compulsion of an evidence, we certainly *can* conceive the philosophical possibility of its annulment. It is not that we need have in mind any concrete or specific doubts, for these are, in general, quite absent; but rather that, once given the radical vision of the transcendental reductions, we can conceive the philosophically significant eidetic possibility of a different meaning for the transcendent world, just as we can conceive the possibility of a consciousness which, as structured eidetically in critical knowledge, may be very different from the familiar.[45] This vision was dramatically, if misleadingly, enunciated by Husserl himself, when he observed in the *Ideas*, for example, that the world could conceivably not be, while consciousness would remain as it is.

Once, however, we have followed Sartre in repudiating a transcendental ego which mutely remains in god-like detachment from the mundane, then we are in a position to discover an incarnate consciousness, painstakingly exploring what it can know about itself, aware all the while of its facticity and transcendence, its ineluctable "thisness" (and correspondingly, the eidetic possibility of its being quite other), and aware, too, of its exquisitely paradoxical freedom.

Mathematics and logic, and in general, knowledge of the "necessary conditions" for knowledge, are far from being dubitable in any sense which implies that there exist *reasons* for doubting, or *images* of a world in which these matters would not obtain. Nevertheless, for radical phenomenology, they are ultimately to be understood as orders of transcendent meaning-formation, as principles which consciousness freely, *but also with sufficient reason,* determines to sustain in existence, in accordance with the larger designs and value of the entire network of such orders. And though the reasons be compelling and the evidence both rich and disciplined, once given the rational demands proper to a system of knowledge, we cannot ignore the fact that it is to the decree of consciousness alone this system owes its existence and sustenance. It is in this sense that Husserl declared the *world* to be dubitable; and it is in exactly this sense,

45. See Appendix, below.

now, that (in opposition to Husserl) we pronounce such knowledge to be not demonstrably apodictic, notwithstanding its a priori, eidetic character. The living, momentary present, by virtue of its transitory appearance, is able to enjoy, on the contrary, a quite perfect self-sufficiency; and yet it, too, is not apodictic, but for reasons of a different kind.

It is, in summation, within the dialectic of freedom and facticity that consciousness, as reason, will discern simultaneously the resources and the limits of its efficacy: for freedom, constituting the reign of decision and justification, serves to fortify the ideal of reason; while facticity imposes the interrogations which, holding reason forever in thrall, conspire to mock its image of omnipotence and incorrigibility. In a sense, phenomenological investigation of the necessary and the a priori, in the domain of logic and mathematics, can bring about insights of greater clarity than is feasible through the corresponding investigation of morphological structures of meaning, more vulnerable, it would seem, in their evidential authority. Yet it would be a mistake to think that this special clarity and adequacy of evidence purports a genuinely demonstrated (or demonstrable) apodictic knowledge, any more than does the evidence which accrues through categorial and morphological analysis, conducted according to the most radical sense of transcendental phenomenology.

In keeping with this radical sense, which makes the momentary *cogito,* merely lived in awareness, the "starting point" of philosophy, and thus the condition for a science of reason, we have acknowledged an a priori bound to facticity, an eidetic reduction which should never claim adequacy (though the "closure" of its evidence can be warranted), and a necessity through and through hypothetical. But at the same time, we have guaranteed the demands of reason for a special, methodologically warranted evidence. Phenomenology could ask for nothing more.

[7] Immanent and Transcendent Essences

Husserl introduces the distinction between immanent and transcendent morphological essences in the *Ideas.* Phenomenology is concerned, he maintains, solely with "pure descriptive theory of the essential nature of the immanent formations of consciousness, of the events under which the limitations of the phenomenological suspension can be grasped within the stream of experiences." [46] Everything which is transcendently individual, and also all the so-called transcendent essences, must be excluded from the field of study, except insofar as they have suffered reduction to the transcendental sphere.

What exactly is he differentiating? Immanent essences, he writes, are "essences of the formations of consciousness itself"; while transcendent essences pertain to "individual events which transcend consciousness, essences therefore of that which *only 'declares'* itself *through* formations of consciousness and 'constitutes' itself, for example, through sensory appearances." [47] Examples of the latter are the essences of "thing," "spatial shape," "movement," "color of a thing," "man," "human feeling," "soul," "quality of character," and "person." [48] The essences in geometry, kinematics, and what he terms the "pure physics of matter" must be bracketed because they pertain to transcendent "realities." [49]

Husserl contends that transcendent essences can indeed be given primordially, as the very essences themselves, but never with adequacy. With respect to, let us say, the (transcendent) essence of "thing":

> We can bring the noema of thing-meaning to the point of adequate presentation (*Gegebenheit*), but the various thing-meanings, even when taken in their fullness, do not contain the regional essence "thing" as a primordially intuitable constituent immanent in them. . . . In other words, whether it is the essence of an individual thing that concerns us or the regional essence of thing in general, in no case does a single intuition of a thing or a finite closed continuum or collection of thing-intuitions suffice to obtain in *adequate* form the desired essence in the total fullness of its essential determinations. And still, an *inadequate* insight into the essence is always obtainable; it will always have this advantage over an empty apprehension of the essence, such as can be set up on the ground of an illustrative, but obscure presentation (*Vorstellung*), that at least it has given the essence primordially.[50]

46. *Ideas* I, p. 161 (p. 143).

47. *Ibid.*, p. 164 (p. 146). Husserl notes in a footnote that this distinction was made only with great difficulty and contains some inconsistency, as it is proposed in the earlier work of his, the *Logische Untersuchungen*. That this should be the case is natural, in that he really had not yet inaugurated the full phenomenological turn at that time.

48. The examples are Husserl's. See *Ideas*, p. 161.

49. *Ibid.*, p. 162 (p. 144).

50. *Ibid.*, p. 380 (p. 365).

Inadequacy will, thus, always accompany transcendent essences, and in fact, not only in respect of clearness and distinctness, but in respect of completeness (fullness): "It belongs to the type of development peculiar to certain categories of essential being that essences belonging to *them* can be given only 'one-sidedly,' while in succession more 'sides,' though never 'all sides,' can be given."[51] *In spite of the fact that transcendent essences have no spatial extension,* Husserl holds them to be evidenced only in partial, incomplete configurations. By contrast, he thinks, immanent essences are always accessible to an adequate, apodictic, and absolute eidetic apprehension.

We may fairly surmise that Husserl differentiates immanent and transcendent essences precisely in order to demarcate an eidetic domain wherein adequate and apodictic evidence can be disclosed. However, our previous consideration of the fundamental concept of intentional transcendence should suggest that this differentiation is marked by certain inherent confusions of great moment. Perhaps the most pervasive is the confusion of the essence with the lived experience for which it is the correlative eidetic articulation. Experience itself, *as lived,* is plainly immanent; but the *essence* of that experience is an object of knowledge, an enduring nexus for a certain modality of experiences, and hence is always transcendent, relative to the immanent, lived acts of consciousness which confer upon it its essential signification. To be sure, the essence is an objectivity posited without any spatial locus. But, in the most fundamental sense of transcendence, the factor of spatial dimensionality should have no bearing whatsoever. It should make absolutely no difference, therefore, whether an essence pertains to some spatio-temporal "reality" (a transcendent in the *narrower* sense, like scissors and motor cars) or to some immanent, merely temporalized experience (such as a pain, a desire, a sorrow, a perception, etc.). In *both* types of case, the essences are and must be intentionally transcendent. And such transcendence can mean nothing other than inadequacy and non-apodicticity for a philosopher who has adopted the Husserlian norm of transcendental rationality and has, in consequence, seen fit to deny the adequacy and apodicticity of transcendent objects with the sense of spatio-temporal existence.

To be sure, one can designate essences as either transcend-

51. *Ibid.,* p. 48 (p. 14).

ent or immanent, but purely as an *elliptical* way of indicating whether the facticities convened by and subordinate to their respective essences, are spatio-temporal in their existence sense, or merely temporally enduring and accessible. In so doing, one must carefully refrain from forgetting the *ellipsis* and affirming thereby the possibility of essences in themselves genuinely immanent. For if we choose to interpret the evidence for our eidetic discoveries according to the broad and most fundamental sense of transcendence, we are compelled to acknowledge no ground for differentiating them: they are one and all transcendent. But even if, on the other hand, we should choose rather to construe this evidence according to one of those quite secondary senses of immanence (i.e., nontranscendence), which merely denote either reduction to the transcendental sphere or absence of spatial dimensionality, we are likewise brought to acknowledge no grounds for differentiation, since we may presume *all* eidetic meanings to be phenomenologically reduced and *none* to be spatio-temporal.

Consequently, while there surely is reason to differentiate, in terms of immanence and transcendence, the origin and epistemic status of *that for which* the essence is the eidetic modality of expression, the essences *themselves,* when founded upon facticities that have indeed suffered reduction to the transcendental, are one and all put on the same plane—as fundamentally transcendent. That Husserl, in the *Ideas,* does not clearly perceive this, despite his enunciation in that work of the fundamental sense of transcendence, is shown by his description of the essences which pertain to transcendent, spatio-temporal realities. These, he thinks, are always given "one-sidedly," incapable of being grasped, therefore, with an adequate evidence. But this position makes sense only if one confounds the essence with its corresponding individual exemplifications and, as a result, attributes to the essence those properties, such as spatial perspective, which are truly relevant just to the exemplifications. The house I dwell in has spatial perspective determining the perception I can have of it. On the other hand, if we consider just the question of intentional transcendence, then the spatiality of some exemplifications and the nonspatiality of others can have no relevance whatsoever. The *essence* of this house is neither more transcendent than, say, the essence of this particular act of willing, nor less transcendent than the particular "real" house, insofar as they are all posited as objectivities with a transcendent-to-consciousness sense, regardless of how much this sense will and, indeed, must differ in other significant respects, for example, with regard to the factor of spatial dimension (the house), or the factor of simple temporal endurance and identity (the essence "house," the essence "willing," and some particular act of willing, as an intentional object for reflective consciousness).

The *Logik* and the *Cartesian Meditations,* works written after the *Ideas,* no longer show Husserl attempting to differentiate essences in this way. Still, Husserl's persistence in attributing apodicticity to eidetic consciousness, or rather, to its noematic correlate, eidetic judgments, inevitably tends to perpetuate problems all too prominent in the *Ideas.* For, in this work, it is apparent that Husserl really *does* want to disclose and authenticate, as a privileged region for eidetic investigation, essences which are truly immanent in consciousness, and not just immanent in the sense that they have suffered transcendental reduction or in the sense that they are nonspatial; and that he wants to sift them out from those other essences "infected" with transcendence, so that he may ultimately present us with some real and validated apodicticities. This he apparently hopes to accomplish by isolating truly immanent essences which, by virtue of their absolution from the flaw of transcendence to which other essences (and thing-realities in general) are condemned, will thus be accessible to an absolute, perfectly adequate, and apodictic consciousness (knowledge). Of especial importance here is the alleged apodicticity of the *eidos,* "transcendental ego." Husserl chooses to ignore altogether with what toil and casting about he finally arrived, in the *Meditations,* at his insights into the basic structure of consciousness; he forgets how tentative and wayward his first steps were, many years before; and he betrays his own sense of the experimental nature defining phenomenology and, in so doing, contributing to its peculiar excellence as philosophical inquiry.[52]

52. Consider, for example, that some psychologists (Piaget will be among them) have offered substantial evidence for the theory that, in the early stages of infancy, there is no objectivation whatsoever, but only a totally undifferentiated, lived experience. If this be so, then it is in fact quite simple to conceive of a consciousness (a transcendental ego) which differs from the Husserlian model of structure, according to which there is an *ego,* a *cogito* and a *cogitatum.* What weight, then, can be granted to Husserl's apodictic knowledge of the *eidos,* "transcendental ego"?

[8] The Inadequacy of All Levels of Eidetic Articulation

Husserl remarks in passing that in the *Logische Untersuchungen* he operated with an excessively narrow conception of ideation: it demanded adequate insight, in the strictest sense. But by the time he set down his thoughts in the *Ideas,* he had come around to accepting the non-primordiality and inadequacy of eidetic insights as truly legitimate variants.[53]

In this interval, he had discovered the internal complexities of evidence, graded differentiations which still deserve acceptance as evidential modalities, once they are placed in the context of constitutional analysis. Especially in respect of eidetic intuition, he no longer felt inclined to describe it as if it had to be a uniform, encompassing, perfect and undifferentiated illumination of the essence; in fact, he sagely will acknowledge that, although primordial and even, betimes, adequate insight is possible and actually attainable, often the evidence will be inadequate in one respect or another—wanting in distinctness and specificity, clearness, and absolute presentational fullness—and in some cases, this inadequacy is inherent in the ideative situation, e.g., with regard to so-called "transcendent" essences.[54] He is willing to speak of "conjectural essences" and essences represented in symbol and maybe even falsely posited. And he supposes that a return to the intuition of the essence in its true givenness can disclose such cases of falsity. In the *Ideas,* Husserl explains why he attributes inadequacy to the ideation of *transcendent* essences:

> But if that itself which is vaguely known, the unclear floating image, let us say, of memory or fancy, produces its own essence, that which it produces can only be something imperfect; that is, where the single intuitions that underlie our essential apprehension are of a lower plane of clearness, so also are our essential apprehensions themselves, and correlatively the object apprehended has an "unclear" meaning, its disorderly mixtures, its lack of proper distinctions both within and without.[55]

It is to be regretted that Husserl does not make it sufficiently clear why such imperfection and vagueness can haunt *only*

53. See *Ideas,* p. 49 (p. 15), n. 2.
54. "Philosophie als strenge Wissenschaft," *Logos, I* (1910–1911), pp. 289–341.
55. *Ideas,* p. 177 (pp. 155–56).

"transcendent" essences. Why, in other words, these conditions do not also affect "immanent" essences, and hence essences in general. It is easy enough to accept his contention that the indeterminacies, openness, and inadequacy of our perceptions of individual realities provide a foundation of such a nature as to preclude the possibility of an adequate essential intuition based upon it. But to differentiate essences capable of absolute and adequate knowledge from those incapable of such apprehension on the basis of his immanent-transcendent dichotomy is to presuppose that the so-called immanent essences are somehow immune to the causes of doubt, error, and revision which assault the so-called transcendent essences.

We are willing enough to agree that the eidetic adventurer has no cause to despair. For, as Husserl notes, to every imperfect givenness, every inadequate noema, there belongs a corresponding noetic *rule* prescribing the absolute perfection of evidence towards which one may strive. We learned earlier that Husserl affirmed the availability of an a priori rule (a "Kantian Idea"), with regard to which it is always possible to perfect one's evidential holdings for objectivities generally. He is therefore simply sustaining a consistent and sound view, by explicitly applying the rule to the perfection of essential intuition. Thus, he writes:

> For every essence, just as for the corresponding phase of its individual counterpart, there exists, so to speak, an absolute nearness, in which its givenness is in respect of this graded series absolute, i.e., pure self-givenness.[56]

Eventually, determination of the marginal intuitive evidences, and an unfolding of further exemplary presentations, will bring the essential insight into "the brightly lit circle of perfect presentation."[57] He supposes, however, with less than compelling argument, that in the case of outer perception, fulfillment according to the rule is in principle precluded, while it is not so precluded in the case of non-sensible (eidetic) intuition, at least for the immanent essences. Can this be more than an ideal or norm? Can essences actually be grasped in their utter completeness, and apodictically?

Amplification and modification, or even, in more serious cases (at least with respect to certain categories of essence), complete cancellation of eidetic intuition, are firmly asserted to

56. *Ibid.*
57. *Ibid.*, p. 181 (p. 160).

be possible, even in Husserl's earlier writings on the subject. He correctly insists, though, that all criticism and fresh insight is "internal," and does not invoke sources of evidence different in kind: "It is only by an eidetic intuition that the essence of eidetic intuition can be clarified and legitimated." [58]

Husserl recognizes, moreover, that eidetic "singularities," in the very lowest region of description, often resist absolutely clear determination. However, he thinks this problem is counteracted by determination at the *highest* regions of generality:

> These are susceptible of stable distinction, unbroken self-identity, and strict conceptual apprehension, likewise of being analyzed into component essences, and accordingly they may very properly be made subject to the conditions of a comprehensive scientific description.[59]

He maintains that a self-evident apprehension of the essence happily does not demand that the subsumed particulars in their concrete fullness should be fully clear; the higher, more universal grades permit of clarification and determination quite independently of the intuitive eidetic presentations belonging to the more specific grades.[60] He argues that

> it is quite sufficient when grasping essential differences of the most general kind, as those between color and sound, perception and will, that the exemplifying instances should show a lower grade of clearness. It is as though the most general character, the genus (color in general, sound in general), were fully given, but not as yet the difference.[61]

And then, as if motivated by a presentiment of our outrage, he hastens to add that that "is perhaps a shocking way of putting it, but I could not see how to avoid it. Let the reader illuminate the situation for himself in vivid intuition (*Intuition*)." [62]

The finest eidetic nuances may be beyond us, yet he still affirms the possibility of an absolute, adequate and apodictic knowledge, considering the essence involved *as a whole*. Again, it would seem appropriate to consider this differentiation of

58. *Logik*, p. 220.
59. *Ideas*, p. 192 (p. 172).
60. *Ibid.*
61. *Ibid.*, p. 181 (p. 160).
62. *Ibid.*

higher and lower regions of eidetic description to be motivated, like the distinction between immanent and transcendent essences, by his desire to secure an adequate and apodictic evidence for *some* eidetic region, however circumscribed. But we must again show Husserl to be in serious difficulty.

There seem to be good reasons for Husserl's contention that the higher regions of essential differentiation are more susceptible to clear and distinct presentation and determinate conceptual expression than the very lowest regions. And if this should be the case, even a *relative* independence of higher eidetic regions from lower ones would function in a salutary manner. Thus, Husserl gives us the most universal region of the essential structure of consciousness in his schema *ego-cogito-cogitatum*, and he does so even without, for example, a satisfactory clarification of the role of the will in this schema, or of how, in its intricacies, the undifferentiating perception of the infant funtions, in contrast to the "fully matured" perceptual consciousness for which Husserl has provided a most general eidetic analysis. So, too, he believes we may grasp with pleasing fullness and clarity the essence of color, but have great difficulty differentiating fuchsia from magenta; we may grasp the essence of sound, but have great trouble discriminating certain modulations in key.

However, the acceptance of these facts should in no way commit us to affirm an *independence* of the higher regions from the lower of such magnitude and of such a nature that we are entitled, with but a full evidence for the most *universal* strata of a *morphological* essence, to assert that we have an absolute, adequate, and apodictic knowledge of the essence *as such* (i.e., as a whole). If the essence is truly a *unity* of meaning, then *any* suspicion of inadequacy entails that this independence can be neither demonstrably total nor itself demonstrably free from every ambiguity: delineation of such independence will be a non–a priori *function of progress* in specific differentation within the essence. Under these conditions, eidetic articulation of the higher regions of an essence can at best console itself with a presumptive, fluctuating and relative autonomy, contingent upon subsequent evidential accomplishments, and clarified as to its title only according to the increasing fullness with which the essence is gradually determined. In fine, since the inadequacy of eidetic evidence would *preclude* an absolute bifurcation of the essence, the absolute independence of eidetic regions cannot be sustained *prior* to a *demonstration* that the eidetic evidence can indeed be adequate, in the *fullest* sense of this normative principle. But in that case, Husserl's appeal to such independence (hardly presented in a phenomenologically compelling manner) as a *basis* for claiming the adequacy and apodicticity of his eidetic description is, at the very least, *not justified.*

If we think of the relatively high regions as the "form" of the essence, and of the relatively low regions as its "content," we may concede to Husserl that the form can become the focus of knowledge (even) where the contents are difficult to determine or specify with ideal clearness and distinction. But our concession will not tolerate any *bifurcation* of the essence, as a unity of meaning, into a fixed and absolute form and a rigidly circumscribed and contained region of indeterminate content. In view of an avowed inadequacy characterizing (much) essential insight, the assertion of apodicticity is *equivalent* to constructing a *bifurcation* of the essence which denies the fluidity of the distinction between form and its content, and runs completely counter to Husserl's description of the nature of *morphological* essences. Is it not precisely this fluidity and relativity which, after all, define morphological essences, in contrast to the mathematical and exact essences? In brief, can we not see that the espousal of apodictic insight into essences tends to blur the distinction between those essences which Husserl himself had asserted to be the real concern of phenomenology and the *exact* essences proper to the classical *sciences, par excellence*? Husserl was quite right, then, in anticipating how we would find it "shocking" to learn that the most universal regions are independent to such an extent that apodictic insight can become our abiding possession.

Let us consider the essence most fundamental for Husserlian phenomenology, namely, the transcendental ego. As one would imagine, it is a complex, elusive structure (so much Husserl admits), at least if one essays to comprehend it in its concrete life, with its willing, fearing, loving, perceiving, recollecting, and its countless habitualities. Husserl, first to understand this (and hence, in part, his objection to Descartes' deductivism, set in motion by the *axiom* "I am"), nevertheless effects an eidetic analysis of the transcendental ego which, he believes, confirms the view enunciated earlier in the *Ideas,* that *some* eidetic descriptions of an apodictic nature can be achieved, quite independently of the ambiguities and indeterminacy which infect lower regions of eidetic differentiation.[63]

He thinks we can at least possess an apodictic knowledge of the *most universal* structure of this essence, even though primary specifications, e.g., the perception of things, and lower regions of eidetic relations, e.g., the essential difference between perceiving (feeling) a "real" pain and merely imagining a violent and vivid pain, while believing it to be "real," or the essential difference between perceiving and willing, should remain unclear, vague, and inadequate. How is it possible to be absolutely certain, with a knowledge beyond revision as well as doubt, that some as yet unknown feature of, say, acts of willing or perceptual acts would result *merely* in an amplification, a confirmatory filling out of the essential structure already discerned, and not instead suggest lines of modification, sometimes relatively insignificant, but also sometimes vast? [64] It would not seem possible to adjudicate *in advance,* in a wholly a priori and noncontingent manner, just when the modifications one could envisage would be of such importance that we should not wish to regard them as amplifying the old essence, but as cancelling or negating the old and installing a different, truly novel essence.[65] Husserl requires, here, some *non*psychological criteria. In particular, it would seem that he could not argue his case without first spelling out the criteria which would enable him to distinguish, a priori, between *essentially important* revisions and *essentially minor* (trivial, insignificant) revisions.

It is reasonable to object, at this point, that his theory is *tantamount* to a bifurcation of the essence itself into essential and nonessential components. For if apodicticity should be feasible even with very *inadequate* knowledge (as our knowledge of the transcendental ego, both as concrete life and as *eidos,* surely is), that must mean that the results of further and more profound eidetic constitution are somehow *non-essential* (and are *known* to be thus), insofar as they could not conceivably introduce evidence the recognition of which would rationally compel consciousness to nullify (or *significantly* alter) its apodictic judgment. But it should be noted, here, that Husserl makes no

63. See *CM,* pp. 49–50 (pp. 86–87).

64. At this point, we confront head-on the crucial problem of critique, to be examined in the final section of the present chapter.

65. See Appendix, below.

attempt to provide any criteria for *deciding* what constitutes "exactly the same essence," before and after its possible modifications. One would think, however, that claims to adequacy and apodicticity logically presupposed some such criteria. A bifurcation of this order is obviously catastrophic and indefensible; and in any case, Husserl makes no satisfactory defense. Were he to have appreciated exactly where his theory leads to, he would doubtless have wanted to refashion it.[66] The only egress from this philosophical prison is through the abandonment of apodicticity.

It may be, of course, that, in the case of the most universal strata of certain essences, an eidetic insight of such fullness and determinacy is possible that a completeness or indubitability, always defined in terms of the *temporal present* of evidence, will deserve affirmation. A weaker version of apodicticity would here find its right, perhaps. But completeness and indubitability, like evidential primordiality, have acquired their right precisely *because* of their very specific relativity. Contrary to what one might at first imagine, the absoluteness of any evidence resides inextricably in its relativity. Husserl's apodicticity, by negating this

66. It might be objected that our interpretation of Husserl's theory of essences is unfairly rationalistic. There can be little doubt that, in the *Logische Untersuchungen* and *Ideas,* Husserl's treatment of eidetic method and its outcome (the recovery of essences and essential relations) is formalistic and excessively structural. In *The Formation of Husserl's Concept of Constitution,* Sokolowski carefully documents Husserl's progression from purely formal and structural analysis to a full-fledged method of genetic constitution. (Consider, for example, pp. 48, 54–56, 60, 70–71, 95, 97–98, 102–5, 138, 149, 162–63, 177–80, 202, and 204.) Sokolowski shows how, and with what difficulties, Husserl tried to cope with the nature of sensations, meanings, and the temporal constitution of immanent objects within a matter/form framework, and how he eventually recognized the need to abandon this framework altogether. So it is true that, in many ways, Husserl moved away from his early rationalism, as he developed the machinery of transcendental method and worked on the genetic constitution of phenomenological evidences. Nevertheless, our design in this chapter is to accumulate evidence for the thesis that Husserl's insistence on apodicticity requires, and thus leads to, an extremely formalistic interpretation of eidetic objects. But we do not mean to suggest that Husserl himself advocated a formalistic bifurcation of essences (although he sometimes seems inclined to do so), or even that he would have been comfortable with this treatment. We are interested only in showing to what doctrines Husserl's apodictic claims unwittingly *commit* him.

relativity, must abjure its prerogative to claim the *only* phenomenologically *grounded* absoluteness, namely, that which attends the perfection and wholeness of the moment of evidence. And it falls prey to the arrogance of its pretension.

[9] The Eidetic and Inductive Modes of Consciousness

1. *Antepredicative Typicalities Predicatively Constituted as Essentialities*

In his very late writings, wherein Husserl arrives at a full appreciation of the distinction between antepredicative and predicative consciousness, one is able to trace the formation of essences—that is to say, the formation of an explicit eidetic modality of consciousness—from their predicative articulation "back" to their constitutive origins in antepredicative, prereflective, lived experience.

According to the theory advanced fully in *Erfahrung und Urteil* and in pregnant, but not mature, form in the *Meditations*, essences (in the guise of typicalities and experiential "habitualities") are already operative *in potentia*, so to speak, within antepredicative experience. Thus, for example, we always encounter an individual object, even if it be an absolute novelty for us, as a such-and-such.[67] There is operative in prereflective experience a kind of "intimacy," a prefigured familiarity with kinds (types) of object. Perhaps, indeed, without such prescriptive lawful habitualities, there could be no objective encounter whatsoever.[68]

However, consciousness is so far merely passive, and want-

67. But, on the other hand, if there were no individuals to be encountered, there would be no essences, either. Merleau-Ponty observes that the essence is the "formula of an attitude, a certain modality of my hold on the world, a structure, in short" (*PP*, pp. 388, also 386). But, with equal right, one could say that the motivation and ground for any given essential attitude would be absent, were this world pervasively recalcitrant to that structure, that particular way of relating to the world.

68. This is the basis for Ricoeur's claim that Husserl avoids Platonism by introducing essences into a dialectical relationship with facticities. See his introduction to Husserl's *Idées*, p. 19. He overlooks the fact that apodicticity revokes and nullifies whatever dialectics there are, which the method of genetic constitution, on the other hand, so strongly encourages.

ing in a rational understanding or grounding of its motivation to typify experiences, until, in an authentically eidetic modality at the predicative stage of reflection (critique), and, besides, in the fullness of titled insight, it has *genetically constituted* (i.e., clarified) these subjective habitualities as essential structures of consciousness.

In this way, we are guided from familiar, but phenomenologically ungrounded, *empirical typicalities* to the corresponding *ideal essentialities* which underlie them. Typicalities function as the *starting point* of eidetic exploration; but, with the consummation of inquiry, that alone which is able to fulfill the demands, enunciated by rational consciousness, for a genetic constitution in the pure immanence of an active subjectivity, can serve as "true" starting point. Accordingly, essentiality must be disclosed as the foundation, as the *principium.*

The accusation of circularity referred to earlier is here shown to be misguided and based on a serious misunderstanding of Husserl's general method of inquiry.[69] There is nothing amiss in beginning naive eidetic investigations with a particular, antecendently supposed to be an example of the essence in question, and yet to be disclosed in essential intuition. For what we possess at the outset is not truly an essence, but only an empirical and as yet transcendentally unclarified typicality, the merest intimation of the authentic essence that must be fully presented in intuition. An essence has for Husserl the very special sense of being that sort of objectivity which is constituted for the first time through eidetic variation. It is only in a (loose) manner of speaking that he allows we *begin* our eidetic exploration with an illustration, either real or imaginary, of the *essence* involved.[70]

69. See § 6, above.

70. Husserl does seem rather naive, however, in that he assumes there are no serious problems involved in knowing precisely what are to count as genuine illustrations, genuine possibility-variants, of the essence specifically sought after. While he carefully elaborates the method of eidetic *variation,* he gives us no criteria for determining how we can recognize the "raw materials" with which we have to work. How, after all, do we spot the variants (the different particulars) to which the method is supposed to apply? Do we not, in a sense, have to know *already what* these particular variants are *essentially,* before we can utilize them in the variation process? Otherwise, how can we set the "outer limits" of eidetic variation, on the basis of which we are supposed to come upon the universal essence "hidden"

2. *The Question of Continuity from Induction to Ideation*

It should be clear, now, just what Husserl's essence owes to facticity, and how it emerges from experience. We may express our concurrence with Merleau-Ponty's assertion that Husserl recognized the fundamental homogeneity of induction and ideation, and also, therefore, the experiential (especially perceptual) ground of ideation; except that we should want to qualify it by observing that such homogeneity, and the humble genealogy of essentialities, function effectively for Husserl only in the most general articulation of his theory. Merleau-Ponty is not justified in believing that Husserl really thought the essence to be contingent, or that he thought empirical variation and ideation to be homogeneous, plain and simple, as if the latter were nothing but an advanced, more rigorous stage of but one continuous, seamless procedure. However, it is not in the least necessary to deny the validity of a certain fundamental difference between induction and ideation in order to affirm their yet more fundamental continuity and reciprocity. And just here is where Husserl has gone astray. One may, then, concur that

> the insight into essences rests simply on the fact that in our experience we can distinguish *the fact that* we are living through something from *what it is* we are living through in this fact. . . . In so far as the essence is to be grasped through a lived experience, it is concrete knowledge. But insofar as I grasp something through this experience which is more than a contingent fact, an intelligible structure that imposes itself on me whenever I think of the intentional object in question, I gain another

---

in all the relevant particular variants? Moreover, Husserl fails sufficiently to take into account the possibility that there may not be anything at all *in common* among any two (or more) of the "possible" variants. (See L. Wittgenstein, *Philosophical Investigations*, remarks 62–72 and 91–104). To be sure, we may be able to think of possible particular variants in a rough and "intuitive" way. But there is surely no reason to suppose our intuitive choices are necessarily appropriate or incorrigible: all the more reason not to countenance Husserl's extravagant claims to apodicticity. Richard L. Cartwright soberly appraises some aspects of the essentialist enterprise, outside the framework of phenomenology, and spells out problems logically similar to the ones we have discovered in Husserl's theory. See "Some Remarks on Essentialism," *The Journal of Philosophy*, LXV, no. 20 (1968), pp. 615–26.

> kind of knowledge. I am then not enclosed in the particularity of my individual life, and I can attain an insight which holds for all men.[71]

The Husserlian *Wesensschau*, in Merleau-Ponty's view, is simply "an intellectual taking over, a making explicit and clarifying of something concretely experienced." [72] It is a spontaneous, reflective organization of meaning.

Thus far, Merleau-Ponty has not expressed anything about essences to which Husserl would wish to object. But, as the ramifications of their views unfold, vast divergence is apparent. How, more exactly, does Husserl construe the *difference* between empirical and eidetic variation? That their respective *aims*, within the plan of rationality, are fundamentally different is, to begin with, plain enough; but it may not be manifest at once that they do involve *methods* so radically distinct. And yet, even so, Husserl may be unwarranted in supposing the epistemic status of the two procedures to be totally dissimilar and unrelated.

To see that this is the case, let us consider a hypothetical situation, reduced to its simplest conceivable analytic form. Suppose we wish to establish by induction the essence of "chair." To that end, we invite others to collect and present to us a large number of what they call "chairs." In that way we can further suppose that we have no foreknowledge about chairs at all. We, for our part, trust that their sampling is random and unprejudiced in all respects that would possibly mislead us, in some obvious way, as to what properties are essential to a thing's being a chair. However, it turns out, in fact, that all the chairs they chose, wishing to play a joke on us innocents, are upholstered in rose and gold damask.

Now, in actuality, the criterion of sincere randomness invoked when inductive generalizations are customarily formulated implicitly will utilize a kind of knowledge not strictly derived from deliberative induction—a "preacquaintedness" with the essence involved and some beliefs (not yet phenomenologically grounded) about what properties are essential to a thing's being what it is (say, in this case, a chair) and what properties are not. Thus, most rigorous induction, from Husserl's standpoint, already engages us in an activity that transcends the

71. Maurice Merleau-Ponty, *The Primacy of Perception* (Evanston, Ill.: Northwestern University Press, 1964), p. 54.

72. *Ibid.*, p. 68.

immediate knowledge at our disposal, and appeals to a crude, rough-and-ready ideation. Limiting ourselves exclusively to grounds justified by the sampling set before us, we should conclude well, and with reason, that among the properties essential to a thing's being a chair is that it must have rose and gold damask upholstery.

The obvious shortcomings of our deliberately crude inductive situation are intended, first, to point out that scientifically sophisticated inductive method actually introduces considerations closely related to eidetic variation (and, indeed, the starting point for such rigorous phenomenological inquiry) in an implicit, but not truly circular way; and second, to delineate those very inadequacies in empirical variation, reduced to its lowest and simplest form, which motivated Husserl to construct a theory of *eidetic* variation.

Eidetic variation could never lead to an outcome such as that of our crude induction. Even if it began with the very same sampling, its conclusion would be different, and differently justified; for it would have excluded upholstery as *non*essential on the basis of trial variations—just the sort of thing that *creditable* empirical variation will do, but without explicit recognition of its naively eidetic guidance.[73] Utilizing, say, only the empirical examples at hand, eidetic variation would at once have disconnected existential meaning, thereby transforming the examples into mere possibilities. The transformation is simply the adoption of a novel attitude (a method of relating intentionally to these objects) on the part of consciousness.

But the method of compossible variation introduces a spontaneity, a freedom from facticity which, though never total, still for the first time allows consciousness to explore its eidetic holdings. The exploration made feasible by this new attitude is actually nothing other than a self-exploration, a coming to self-consciousness, whereby consciousness uncovers and explicates, through the presentations of constitution, its a priori laws of eidetic accomplishment. In other words, consciousness possesses the ability to uncover, and precisely in this accomplishment, to ground (justify) its own lawfulness (its eidetic and rational nature). The eidetic modality of consciousness is that modality in which it sees, with the lucidity of intuitional fullness, those a

73. Conceiving a chair without legs, a chair without arms, a chair without a back, a chair in leather, a chair in blue velvet, etc.

priori necessary laws (essences) which, while effectively governing its intentional (but prereflective, unthematized) involvement with the world, were nevertheless as yet only marginally grasped, with the opacity, vagueness and indeterminacies belonging to a mere (empirical) knowledge of more or less inductively grounded typifying-habitualities. Hence, this eidetic method provides for a greater experimental *control,* a greater *range* of investigation, and finer *discernment* and *differentiation,* and thus a considerably more "rational" confirmation, than does the "purely" inductive method.

Husserl is therefore justified in arguing the necessity for a differentiation of induction and ideation. But does it *follow* that he is entitled to assert their utter discontinuity, to deny their underlying homogeneity and complementarity? It is our belief that the difference, real though it be, does not entail any discontinuity of such a nature that its presence could make possible the achievement of apodictic evidence. However, it must be stated further that the argument against apodicticity does not have to rest on the demonstration of such homogeneity, nor on any demonstration about the evolution of essences out of facticities. Even if ideation were capable of utter isolation from inductive procedures, there are other very compelling arguments against the apodicticity of eidetic consciousness.

Let us consider, first, the argument that the two processes are, in a certain sense, continuous.

1. According to the *usual* construction of the inductive method, it would inhibit the possibility of apodictic eidetic judgments *because it is confined to articulating particulars* (the domain of facticity) in a certain special way, that is, merely by generalization and extrapolation; whereas ideation treats of conceived compossibles, altogether detached from their conceivable mooring in facts.

Now, the late Dr. Alfred Schutz has argued well that "type" and "*eidos,*" induction from concrete facticities of experience and ideation based on the congruence of mere compossible illustrative variants, cannot be so radically isolated one from the other.[74] It is held that perception of individual facticities occurs through the efficacious mediation of antepredicative, passively constituted types (or, from the vantage point of the noesis,

74. Schutz, "Type and *Eidos* in Husserl's Late Philosophy," *Philosophy and Phenomenological Research,* XX (1959–60), 147–65.

through habitualities). And conversely, eidetic consciousness has its origins in facticity and builds upon its given resources of typification. The pure essence of the phenomenological and eidetic reductions, although quite distinct from and in no sense reducible to the empirical type which is its counterpart, nevertheless bears some traces of its primordial association with the empirical. It is not only that the eidetic functioning of consciousness is born out of the demands inherent in its involvement with particulars, but that the stage of reflection at which consciousness has "rationally" authenticated its eidetic posture seemingly cannot be reached *de novo,* but must instead be elicited from an attentive examination of singular exemplary possibilities. In other words, our involvement with some chosen set of facticities is what gives shape as well as direction to eidetic consciousness. It is in this sense, then, that the two methods are both continuous and complementary. But, whereas Husserl could recognize little more than that a certain functional correlation exists between them, and that universals and particulars implicate one another in actual experiential contexts, Schutz is anxious to disclose the *genesis* of the eidetic in antethematic typifying experience. Ideation simply represents, for him, a more rigorous articulation of the inductive types already operative, in a prereflective capacity, in our encounter with (but also within) the world. If we should now carry his argument one step farther, we see that apodicticity is in jeopardy. For apodicticity seems to require a *complete separation* of facticity from essence.

2. According to a somewhat different, but equally acceptable conception of inductive method, it would inhibit the possibility of apodictic essentialities *because of its intrinsic incompleteness,* rather than because of its *genetic confinement* to facticity. This is, in fact, the notorious "weakness" of induction that is forever lamented in rationalist and positivist schools alike. But Husserl is confident that ideation differs from induction in this regard as well as in the first. The process of eidetic variation, as he construes it, proceeds by absolutely arbitrary exemplars, mere compossibles. Therefore, he thinks, the series of variations, which in principle could continue indefinitely, can be terminated at any point, provided only that there have been enough variants to engender a satisfactory eidetic congruence for consciousness. Consequently, Husserl thinks he can argue that ideation, when it reaches the stage of a compelling eidetic insight, is in the fullest sense perfect, complete, and therefore apodictic. However, if we

can show that a form of *incompleteness* similarly accompanies ideation, then we have demonstrated that in this second sense of induction as well, ideation and empirical variation are more intimately related than Husserl prefers to think, and that ideation cannot fulfill the demands of any norm of rationality, whether positivist or transcendental, which stands philosophy under the ideal of indubitability.

This, our second argument, based not on the express homogeneity of facticity and essence, but rather on the incompleteness (inadequacy) of eidetic variation, calls apodicticity into question whether or not the earlier argument that the essence emerges from the type can be altogether sustained. It therefore functions quite as an independent argument against apodicticity, even though the two arguments are closely related, inasmuch as inadequacy is a concomitant of all evidence pertaining to facticity. Its independence stems from the fact that Husserl's doctrine of apodicticity must be shown defensible with regard to the *fully achieved* eidetic insight, regardless of the character of the *genesis* of such insight (i.e., regardless of how the *eidos* evolves from the empirical type). The crucial question is thus: Whether or not the essence is absolutely detached from its originating individual exemplars, can a knowledge of the essence finally won be truly apodictic? This question returns us to the question of the possibility that an essence, which is a transcendent objectivation, can be adequately evidenced. And this, in turn, introduces the key problem for Husserlian phenomenology: the achievement of a satisfactory transcendental critique.

[10] The Incompleteness of Eidetic Critique

The essence, we have said, is an objectivated, transcendent "nexus" of identity, around which a limited series of compossible variants have been synthesized into a unity of meaning, enduring as continually accessible through temporally successive intentional acts. What is asserted in eidetic judgment, namely, the essence, is posited with a meaning which, precisely as meaning, reaches *beyond* present evidence in its structural relatedness (a relatedness of *relevancy*) to other evidences esteemed to contribute somewhat to the "objective" sense of the essence.

It is not that the essence is ideal because it is the outcome of phantasy, and opposed to the modality of the physical thing, which is real because it is the object of outer experience, and bears the sense of existing in space-time. Rather, it is ideal in a sense not unlike the sense in which a physical object is declared ideal: both are poles of identity, *transcendent* to their constitutive acts, and functioning to synthesize certain experiences into a meaningful unit.

Since, now, it is through constituting the essence as identically enduring nexus of variations that consciousness first relates itself to a *transcendent object,* we are entitled to pose the problem of the apodicticity of such transcendence in the form of a question about the *formation* of the essence as an objectivity, or, what amounts to the same thing, in the form of a *critique* of eidetic variation.

The effectuation of a critique is demanded first, for the reason that Husserl argues eidetic consciousness can (at least sometimes) legitimately pretend to apodicticity, and in general apodicticity requires an apodictic critique; and moreover, for the reason that he claims for the eidetic modality of consciousness an arbitrary terminus to its variations, beyond which it is (apodictically) seen that further variations could not possibly (i.e., conceivably) introduce any more evidence, *relevant* in the sense that it might spur "essential" revision or annulment of the insight. The question of transcendence becomes, specifically, a query (critique) concerning the permanent validity of the coincidence (*Deckung*) posited as an identical entity.

We articulate the call for a critique so soon as we formulate the query: Is Husserl justified on phenomenological grounds in holding that eidetic variation, in principle open to an infinite series of variations, can eventuate in an essential insight that one may dignify with the title of completeness (adequacy)? And, if there is a sense according to which such insight is complete, is this sense sufficient to impose apodicticity? [75]

75. Along the same line of thought, consider these seminal criticisms: Adorno, *Zur Metakritik der Erkenntnistheorie,* p. 130; Q. Lauer, *Phenomenology: Its Genesis and Prospect* (New York: Harper & Row, 1965), p. 59 ff, and *La Phénoménologie de Husserl* (Paris: Presses Universitaires de France, 1955), p. 429; and F. Kutschera, *Über das Problem des Anfangs der Philosophie im Spätwerk Edmund Husserls* (University of Munich Inaugural-Dissertation, 1960), pp. 78–79. They argue that, precisely because of insurmountable problems with this apodictic critique, the principle of apodicticity cannot sustain the burden of foundation which Husserlian phenomenology has given it.

In the midst of effecting compossible variations, argues Husserl, we see that the process can continue for infinity; but we also see that we may conclude our exploration at any point, inasmuch as the variants are purely arbitrary, and hence all of equivalent substitutional value. After a certain number of variations, executed in the free play of consciousness, an inner logic of constraint (or, necessity) appears operative. This constraint is identical with the disclosure of a certain coincidence among compossible variants.

Eventually, there is a sufficiently compelling *insight* into the coincidence, which *presents* what is essential to the essence desiderated, and *excludes* all that is nonessential. Beyond the point at which insight is achieved, Husserl maintains, further variation would be more or less redundant and irrelevant, except in those cases where the insight is indeed consummated but wants in maximum clearness, distinctness, and fullness. The insight may well not be truly adequate in that sense, but Husserl thinks it is a *complete* evidence, nonetheless, in the special sense of being apodictic, and excluding, therefore, the merest conceivable modification that would motivate its destruction or annulment.

What justifies us in affirming that subsequent variations, if produced, could not conceivably (possibly) introduce *significantly novel* information—information of such a nature and of such weight that we would be rationally compelled to revise or abrogate the evidential authority of its insight? On what grounds can we affirm with peremptory certitude that, come what may, further variations could only amplify a preordained and unimpeachable signification, fill it out with *more of the same* evidence, but in no way *essentially* change it in its "rock-bottom" meaning? If vagueness, ambiguity, want in clarity, fullness, and differentiation at all levels are not just metaphors, they amount to genuine types of incompleteness, quite as much as does the fact that, in the case of physical things, there are an unlimited number of spatial perspectives, only a relatively small series of which have actually been explored.

We have argued that, although there certainly are some major problems in Husserl's theory,[76] there is at least no problem of circularity, with regard to how consciousness is able to *begin*

76. See n. 70, p. 184, above.

variation antecedent to its possession of essential knowledge: possibility-variation begins with a vague "shadow" knowledge of the essence, a rough-and-ready empirical typicality, treated as mere possibility. However, circularity does infect the grounds on which apodicticity is affirmed. Here is where Husserl should have been disturbed.

Might not the variations suggest themselves according to very different sets of criteria, relative, that is, to differing conceptions of what is *important*, among properties *f*, *g*, *h*, . . . , *n* to a thing's being essentially what it is? Such differences may well be of no practical consequence; nor must they reveal themselves in the operative typicalities. The matter will be otherwise in regard to eidetic judgments purporting apodicticity. In order for consciousness to claim apodictic insight into an essence, it must have a knowledge, beyond all conceivable doubt, concerning just *which* variants are really possible variants of the essence; it must know, not in a presumptive and rudimentary manner such as befits the initial stages of eidetic exploration but with absolute certainty, that *all* and *only* those variants have been brought forth which would deposit another aspect *essential* to the wholeness of the essence; and finally, it must have an apodictic insight (itself the outcome of an apodictic critique) into the apodictic indubitability of its original insight. It must, that is, know with utter certainty and necessity, in no way psychological or otherwise relative and subjective, that no further variants imaginable could ever be produced such that any *essential* modification would be in order. For *essential* modification, after all, would be tantamount to *revoking* or *negating* the essentiality in question, and installing a new and different essence. But this operation would entail the destruction of the apodictic insight.

Such a knowledge would seem feasible only if there were a prior vision into the essence, with which one could, as it were, in a totally mysterious way, "compare" the original insight won through eidetic variation. Yet, this type of comparison could only mean a special avenue of access to essences, independent of and outside eidetic consciousness—altogether the most non-phenomenological of notions. Moreover, if it is the case that insight pretending to apodicticity compels the execution of an apodictic critique, we encounter once again the difficulties created by Husserl's postponement of this critique. Circularity thus accompanies the problems created by the need for a critique, once apodicticity has been affirmed.

Even in the putative purity and freedom proper to eidetic variation, there is no apodictic guarantee, in the form of a criterion (or a set of criteria), that the variations chosen in a presumably arbitrary fashion are not the invisible manifestation of some as yet unexamined focus of interest. That is to say, the essence recovered may in fact (for all we know) be the product of an unexamined perspective, determining in an as yet unjustified way the upshot of the series of variations. Worse still, it may even be the case that *all* phenomenological explication *must* occur within the determination of some perspective or other, so that the essence would inevitably be a product that has been predetermined, perspectivally circumambulated in this way—and, it may well be, only *partially* examined in the light of reflective critique. But of this we can never be absolutely sure. As a result, the essence could never offer itself as more than a *presumptive* unity of all and only those variants truly bearing the "essentials" of the essence in question.

Let us further clarify our argument with an example for comparison. Suppose that I assert the proposition "The inkwell on my desk is blue." It may be, as a purely logical matter, that I am hallucinating, or dreaming, or otherwise in abnormal perceptual circumstances. But, unless I have some *special* reasons (of what we may call the ordinary sort, proper to the "natural," "mundane," everyday attitude) for doubting what I perceive, I am justified—our criteria for justifiable perceptual claims being what they are—in asserting that proposition. The evaluation of the justification for that proposition is *relative* to my present, temporally determinate evidential state, and my claim tacitly acknowledges this fact. Of course, it *is implied* in my assertion, and in the recognition of my being justified, that with respect to subsequent evidential states, my belief will continue to be found justified. For, in general, my being (ever) *justified* in holding a certain belief implies that there is some reason for regarding this belief as true, that is, as constituting an advancing *series* of warranted judgments. However, both our common and our philosophical understanding of perception disclose the possibility of error, so that there may come a time when I will no longer be entitled to sustain my belief. But such a turn of events does *not* call upon me to deny that I ever *was* truly justified, that I ever *was* in a position to claim justified belief.[77] That is because *the (generally accepted) conditions for justification have a built-in temporal and evidential relativity.* If I am indeed justified by the evidence at the time I make the assertion, then I remain so justified, but only in respect of *that* particular circumstance. The only question is whether I am ever in fact so justified. And, with the exception of extreme skeptics, it will generally be admitted that, our ordinary (natural attitude) criteria being what they are, when I am in the privileged position of looking *directly* at the inkwell and I see its blue color (that is to say, it seems to be blue and I "take" it to be blue, etc.), nothing more could reasonably be demanded of me, provided I have no special grounds for doubting my favorable position.[78] The point is, we must recognize that, correlative to the built-in relativity of our justification conditions, there is also an *implicit,* built-in relativity in our *claims* to knowledge.

Much more could, of course, be said here about these matters. Suffice it to say, for our purposes, that if we now distinguish conditions for truth from conditions for justification, it is only to clarify how it is that I may be justified at present, but not justified (and wrong) subsequently, in respect of the "same" evidential judgment. And it should already be clear that this distinction does not purport to deny that truth *is relevant* to the fulfillment of the conditions for justification. We mean, rather, that, since I cannot transcend the finite, temporally determinate

77. See John Austin, "Other Minds," in *Logic and Language,* second series, ed. A. G. N. Flew (Oxford: Basil Blackwell, 1955), pp. 123–58. Austin argues that I can claim to know (be justified in believing) that something is the case, and nevertheless be mistaken. He intends to articulate both our ordinary meaning (usage) of "know" and the conditions for knowledge. The point is that the conditions for the justification of a perceptual judgment are not (and need not be) identical with the conditions for the truth of the judgment, as far as our natural, mundane norm of rationality is concerned. Also consider, in this regard, Roderick Firth, "The Anatomy of Certainty," pp. 3–27; and John Pollock, "Criteria and Our Knowledge of the Material World," pp. 28–60, both in *Philosophical Review,* LXXVI, no. 1 (1967).

78. It is worth remarking that we may construe Husserl's view of our mundane criteria for knowledge (in the natural attitude), and of how they function in ordinary life-contexts, as essentially in accord with Austin's descriptions, and, more generally, with analyses of Wittgensteinian persuasion.

conditions for my knowing, fulfillment of the conditions for truth, in a philosophic sense, is not possible. Nor is this fulfillment in any sense requisite, when we can do well enough with *justified* belief. Justification does not coincide with truth, but it always points to it, and is measured by it as by an ideal index.[79] Thus it is that our ordinary beliefs can be regarded as philosophically "respectable," once their implicit logic has been exhibited.

Let us now consider the Husserlian claim to an indubitable, incorrigible evidence, the negation or cancellation of which is affirmed to be inconceivable. Here it is to be noted that such a judgment is really double-barrelled; for what is *asserted* is not just that some object x is evidenced thus and so, but also that the evidence is of a certain very special kind, namely, thus-and-so now and forever, with absolute finality. Thus, to assert at time t the proposition that x is apodictically P (where 'P' refers to some evidential description of x) is to make a judgment which, though in fact *relative* to a certain temporally defined evidential state-of-affairs, advances a *claim* about 'P' that is not *confined* to this state-of-affairs. Consequently, it does not seem possible even to *justify* this judgment, much less to satisfy the conditions for *truth*. For the judgment to be both justified relative to the evidence at t *and* true (now and forever), the eventuality of subsequent cancellation must somehow be absolutely precluded (in a logical sense).

Now, it seems clear that the justification of an apodictic judgment is perforce tied down to the evidential state of the judgment itself, defined by the moment t, and that there does not come to mind any other defensible conception of justification. And moreover, to the extent that we can discern a distinctive conception of justification in Husserlian phenomenology, we will discover it to be conceived within the *transcendence*, or the endless *interdependent evidential* horizons, of objectivity—that is to say, essentially the conception which has been invoked here.

We may also recognize that, whatever else can be said of truth, it is plainly bound to what is the case for an infinite

79. Consequently, it is not correct to assert that these conditions for justification gain their authority by *isolating* temporally determinate evidential states, or by suppressing their interdependency. Evidential states, though temporally defined as to their range, are "saturated" with protentional and retentional meaning, and hence can be said to be rectified in terms of this index.

number of temporally determinate evidential states; and it would seem to entail the *justified* assertion of an infinite network of evidential judgments. But it is logically impossible that we could have established, relative to some given temporally determinate evidential state, what all subsequent evidential states would posit; yet, the conditions for the justification and truth of an apodictic judgment would demand precisely this, such that an intolerable regress of apodictic critique would be engendered, just to guarantee the *present* judgment. This regress is, it will be seen, radically different from the harmless "regress" entailed by the *justified* assertion of a judgment such as "This inkwell is blue," with the scope of its evidential *assertion* conforming to the temporally determinant evidential state of the judgment.

One may attempt to elude these criticisms by denying the *inclusion* of any temporal variables indicating nonpresent evidential states. But, in that case, it seems impossible to maintain apodicticity (the doxic affirmation that *x* cannot *be* other than as it is presently evidenced). On the other hand, with this inclusion, and with the impossibility of any of the infinite series of judgments being found unjustified or false, the *relevance* of an apodicticity to subsequent experience becomes extremely circumscribed, and indeed paradoxical. For even in the *minimum* sense, according to which the apodicticity is simply reiterated, it must occur *through an evidential presentation;* and this presentation is a distinct and other temporally determinant evidential state, a temporally differentiated intentional performance of an endlessly streaming (self-transcending) consciousness. It does not make sense to suppose this performance of reiteration to be both genuine (i.e., a truly evidential presentation) and logically incapable of more than one outcome, insofar as our knowledge is concerned. Relevance, in the context of our knowledge (which is transcendent and not demonstrably adequate, or evidentially "closed") must mean genuinely open possibilities of discovery and decision.

The transcendent-objective sense of the essence envisaged must at once be recognized as playing a determining role in this issue. Transcendence (which, it may be recalled, describes Husserl's "immanent" as well as "transcendent" essences) entails the illegitimacy of apodictic insight in two senses, finely related: first, in that the essence is irrevocably *other than* consciousness, *relative* to it, and therefore without that perfect, absolute indubitability peculiar to lived experience as lived in prereflective.

prethematic awareness (i.e., the living, streaming present); and second, in that the essence is endowed with objective sense precisely because it is *not* something truly immanent and absolutely *present,* but is rather eternally incomplete, yet forever at hand, trans-temporally identical, accessible to further discovery or even just reiterative positing, in one modality or another. What is transcendent, i.e., objective, remains thus only so long as it has a meaning relevant to subsequent experience. And, it must be observed, this meaning is preserved not just through the possibility of further confirmation in experience, but through the possibility of disconfirmation as well. Conversely, this subsequent experience must not be denied its perpetual relevance to the objectivity in its *present* evidence. Apodicticity, on the contrary, functions to revoke objective, transcendent sense by precluding relevancy. Transcendence means simply that the objectivity in question is not fully present, hence, not fully presented (i.e., in some way inadequate). And what is not fully present has the sense of being *other* than consciousness; from the standpoint of radical transcendental rationality, it therefore *could* not be, while yet the living act of apprehension is. Within this picture, apodicticity cannot find a place. For even eidetic consciousness is perforce obliged to acknowledge its involvement with transcendent objectivities, and consequently to acquiesce in the abandonment of apodicticity. And this problem adheres to the apodictic pretensions of eidetic consciousness quite *apart* from any question as to the genealogy of such consciousness.

The only avenue of redemption for a consciousness guilty of perspectives either too confining or insufficiently examined and grounded (or both) would seem to be its recourse to incessant, laborious meditation in evidence, summoning novelty and extending its illumination into the depths of experience. But, of course, it is precisely these resources which the apodicticity of essential intuition would attempt to nullify. It is thus not only that apodicticity makes a claim which transcends the evidence, but also that it checks the one way by which it could rectify error.

To bring together some of our results thus far, an examination of the eidetic modality of consciousness has decisively revealed the transcendent character of the outcome of the method of compossible variation; hence this consciousness should rightly be described as an evidentially presumptive self-consciousness of its regulative (lawful) functionality. The synthesis which yields an invariant "nexus" (the essence, in short) is, first of all, *relative* to a particular fund of knowledge.[80] Second, inasmuch as it calls for a critique that is never, in fact, fully consummated, it is only provisionally independent of the facticities arbitrarily chosen to serve as mere possibilities. Third, the fact that the formalization (foundation) of essential definitions is, as Merleau-Ponty expresses it, "always retrospective proves that it is never otherwise than *apparently* complete, and that formal thought feeds on intuitive thought." [81]

H. J. van Pos gives felicitous expression to the conclusion at which we have, after much arduous journeying, finally arrived, and from which we have been able to evaluate the role and title of Husserl's apodictic principle:

> It is true that the essential *can* repeal itself in the encounter with a single concrete case, as mathematics demonstrates. But this peculiarity is perhaps unique in mathematics and cannot be accomplished outside of this domain. In the other regions of knowledge, the essential is not acquired in that manner, but only through the elaboration of as many data as possible. The essential, therefore, does not stand out with the first experience, and, *a fortiori,* does not precede it; rather, it exhibits itself through (*à travers*) experiences. And if indeed it should be thus, induction and essential intuition are not mutually exclusive.[82]

Husserl's phenomenology shows a gradual but continuous development towards a dynamic, genetic, historical orientation. When eidetic insight is declared to be more than well-grounded surmise—to be, that is, a justified apodicticity—this development suffers from a regressive force. Eugen Fink, investigating the a priori (hence, the eidetic) modality of consciousness, writes:

> Experiential knowledge is, however, always already embedded in an antecedent "a priori" knowledge, in which the universal structure of manifold kinds of things and their objective character are grasped in a pre-acquaintedness (*je schon vorverstanden sind*). Is this a priori of the human spirit timeless, a perplexing "innate" possession; or do the modes of a priori knowledge also change?

80. See Eugen Fink, "Das Problem der Phänomenologie Edmund Husserls," *Revue internationale de Philosophie,* I (1939), 264.

81. *PP,* p. 385.

82. "Valeur et limites de la phénoménologie," in *Problèmes actuels de la phénoménologie,* ed. H. L. van Breda (Paris: Desclée de Brouwer, 1952), p. 46.

. . . Is there a history not only for empirical knowledge, but also for knowledge of essences? [83]

Neither in its presumptive character nor in its historicity, does eidetic consciousness suffer any humiliation, any rational disadvantage. Even without being apodictic, eidetic consciousness is still a mode of consciousness with a very special title and dignity. It represents that profound stage of reflective and critical consciousness at which it has not simply articulated its evidences in predicative (and doxic) judgment, but has also appropriated a priori these evidences through the most intense, the most distinctively "rational" methodic contrivance: the evidences have been grasped with an eidetic, lawfully-structured hold; they have been recovered, animated and rectified through eidetic variation; and finally, they have been so constituted that doubt relative to the present, temporally determinate evidential state-of-affairs would be unwarranted, even absurd. This is quite sufficient to distinguish transcendental eidetic evidence both from "mundane" (a posteriori) evidence and from all transcendental (i.e., phenomenologically reduced) evidence of particulars and to invest it with a superior title.

This rational posture of consciousness cannot plausibly aspire to apodicticity. Consciousness cannot *know* its own a priori laws (essence) except through their *transcendence* as objects for it; nor can it hope to possess apodicticity because of the a priori prescriptive, regulative function of these laws. A priori structures of legislation (i.e., essences) may perhaps adjudicate in an a priori manner the "form" of experience; yet consciousness must learn frustration, if it wants to arrogate for itself an absolute, apodictic knowledge. For the essence sought after is not any mere formal definition; it will be, rather, the essence within the context of its "living" confrontation with the world of consciousness at large. Quentin Lauer contends that, insofar as Husserl succeeds in winning apodicticity, he has an "empty," merely formal achievement.[84] Apodictic knowledge cannot penetrate the ambiguity and the opacity which characterize the juncture where consciousness, in its a priori legislative function, encounters "objective" experience. There remains an infinite field, genuinely indeterminate (or at least not *demonstrably*

83. "Welt und Geschichte," in *Phänomenologica,* II (1939), 146. Cf. also *Logik,* p. 184.

84. *Phenomenology: Its Genesis and Prospect,* p. 128.

adequate) for the operation of conscious structuring. Eidetic consciousness cannot *know* with absolute indubitability what possibilities of significant amplification and revision lie dormant in this region where structuration is still to be accomplished; it cannot guarantee, regardless of its present powers of eidetic conceivability, the real impossibility of genuine novelty springing from this region of encounter.

In the *Ideas*, Husserl states that the work of "making clear to oneself" has two dimensions: (1) rendering an item intuitable in the first place, and (2) then enhancing the clearness, determinacy, and fullness of what is already intuitable.[85] Has Husserl's theory of apodictic evidence then merged these two stages of clarification? To what extent does the doctrine of apodicticity conceal the *task* of constitutional clarification and grounding behind the luminous *accomplishment* of infallible, maximally rational insight? The reader is reminded, in this connection, of our earlier mention of Gilbert Ryle's criticism of rationalist theories of knowledge.

Gaston Berger, approaching the subject with a background very different from Ryle's, expounds a similar criticism. Eidetic intuition, he maintains, is requisite for the *discovery* of knowledge, but it cannot be adequate for *guaranteeing the validity* of its discoveries. "No more than Descartes has Husserl distinguished with sufficient care the function of discovery from the function of justification, from the experience of validity."[86] We

85. *Ideas* I, p. 179 (p. 159).

86. "Les Thèmes principaux de la phénoménologie de Husserl," in *Études de Metaphysique et de Morale*, IL (1944), 42. Eugen Fink observed: "In Husserl, the meaning of 'transcendental constitution' fluctuates between formation of sense and creation." See "L'analyse intentionelle et le problème de la pensée spéculative," in *Problèmes actuels de la phénoménologie*. We are reminded, here, of Paul Ricoeur's parallel distinction between Husserl's later *idealism* and his earlier *intuitionism*, discussed in "Étude sur les *Méditations Cartésiennes* de Husserl," *RpL*, LII (1954), 75–109. Of course, these labels designate *tendencies* which overlap and often merge together, rather than two altogether distinct stages in Husserl's development. Sokolowski also notes the operation of two phenomenological directions. He points out that Husserl's earlier analyses tend to be static, formal, and purely structural, whereas the later ones tend to be dynamic, concrete, and fundamentally genetic (and thus, also teleological). See, in this regard, his book, *The Formation of Husserl's Concept of Constitution*. We accept these interpretations, but prefer to describe the evolution of Husserl's phenomenology in the following way. The

would modify this remark somewhat, in its application to the eidetic procedure, to recognize that the genetic constitution of an essence, which results from eidetic variation, is *both* a discovery of that essence *and* a kind of justification of its epistemic status; but this discovery and this justification cannot be identified with apodictic grounding; and to that extent, Husserl has encouraged the same confusion of which Descartes is here accused.

---

earlier tendency is a species of Cartesian rationalism, excessively formal and "intellectualistic" in character, and oriented in favor of "finished" acts and their final products. The later tendency, by contrast, emphasizes the *formative process* of evidential constitution; it is more attentive to the concrete phenomenological description of evidence, and attempts to recover the *temporal ground* of such evidence, as well as its sedimentation of sense-strata. In the opening chapters of *The Phenomenology of Perception,* Merleau-Ponty focuses on the former tendency in Husserl, arguing that its persistence even in Husserl's later work gravely subverts even the most promising investigations. It is hoped that our study locates the doctrine of apodicticity firmly within the context of Husserl's rationalistic tendency, and documents the severe tension between apodicticity and the later direction of his transcendental phenomenology.

8 / Conclusion

[1]

IN VIEW OF THE TENSION, so prominent and formidable, between Husserl's apodicticity (as we have construed it) and the very best in his mature phenomenology as a whole, one may be tempted once again to doubt our interpretation of the apodictic principle. Perhaps it does not mean infallibility, absolute indubitability now and forever; perhaps it is meant in a much weaker sense.

Doubtless this temptation can win support. Not unlike most truly monumental accomplishments that span a life-time of meditation or action, Husserl's work, by virtue of its creative energy and its organic development, will exhibit a certain ambiguity, a certain inner dialectical tension. Growth is impossible without such contradiction.

But preponderant evidence sustains the contrary interpretation: the strong version prevails. If the *Logik*, the posthumously edited *Erfahrung und Urteil*, and many of his untitled manuscripts, all representative of Husserl's last phase of thinking, could be regarded as the sole guardians of Husserl's "real" meaning; if, that is, we could choose to ignore the *Cartesian Meditations* and the *Krisis*, also of late vintage, then we would in some measure deserve censure for giving Husserl's concept a wayward meaning. This we could not do.

First, the way Husserl in fact utilizes the concept, according to its diverse range of contexts, testifies decisively in favor of our interpretation. If Husserl did not himself construe it in the strong version, he would not have been so tempted to demand, in the manner he did, an "apodictic critique" of all sciences, an "apodictic foundation," an "apodictic and truly rigorous first philosophy," and so forth. These expressions, if they meant nothing more than presumptive knowledge, simply could not conceivably have evoked that devotion, that fervor, that singular "apodictic will" to meditate and to know, which obviously define Husserl's peculiar philosophical temperament.

Second, if apodicticity were meant in some weaker sense, Husserl would have had to acknowledge the fact that he had not succeeded in demonstrating the adequacy of even the most rigorously grounded, and thus most "rational" modes of evidence. For it is nowhere plain that Husserl considers a legitimate claim to apodicticity as *compatible* with the possibility of inadequacy. In the beginning, with the writings prior to and including *Erste Philosophie,* apodicticity seems to obtain only in conjunction with adequacy. The possibility of the one necessitates (depends upon) the possibility of the other. Later, when confronted with a prevailing inadequacy, he attempts to sever the union of these two styles of evidence: apodicticity is thought to be possible *in spite of* inadequacy. One might infer from this that Husserl has truly rejected the position he held in *Erste Philosophie,* now maintaining the full compatibility of apodicticity and inadequacy. Were this the case, he would most decisively be advocating a weaker version of apodicticity. But instead, as closer scrutiny reveals, the thesis in the *Meditations* simply *restricts* the domain over which the reciprocal correlation between adequacy and apodicticity is thought to obtain. Henceforth, the correlation will hold *only* for the *eidetics* of the immanent structures of transcendental subjectivity. And this is precisely the region of adequacy. Husserl ministers to the principle of apodicticity first by *denying* any correlation at the point when its affirmation would entail an abandonment of apodicticity (to correspond to the abandonment of adequacy), and then, without much ado, *reinstating* it once its scope has been sufficiently delimited. Such an apodicticity is clearly to be understood in the strong sense.

And lastly, if Husserl intended a weaker version, he would have had to delineate much more rigorously the difference between it and the notion of adequation. If adequacy is also restricted to the eidetic sphere of evidence, what would differentiate adequacy from some weaker version of apodicticity? Only a strong sense of apodicticity clarifies Husserl's distinction: apodicticity is the outcome of eidetic variation, whereas adequacy is always under the compulsion of facticity and temporal immediacy. We do not wish to suggest, however, that there could be no weaker version which *would* be perfectly *differentiated* relative to the principle of adequacy, and which nevertheless would be, at the same time, wholly *compatible* with inadequacy (or with the failure to *demonstrate* adequacy).

Quite to the contrary, in fact, we submit that some weaker version of apodicticity, by whatever further properties it may eventually be defined, could be found admissible and moreover useful, if introduced, first, *within* the framework of, and hence as logically inseparable from, an inadequacy avowed intrinsic to any phenomenological evidence for objectivities intended as transcendent to consciousness; and second, as consequently capable of proper, grounded affirmation *if and only if temporally determinate conditions for justification have been fully satisfied.*

Of course, the exact nature of these conditions must be brought to greater precision and clarity. But, as a point of departure, we should consider here Husserl's fundamental and, so to speak, "primitive" concept of "seeing," serving to designate an evidence giving itself, at some favored moment of investigation, with an especially compelling presence and clarity. And we could go far to avoid psychologism—indeed, farther perhaps than Husserl himself in this regard—if we construe the special compulsion or weight of this seeing in respect of: (1) its confinement to evidence subject to the diverse stages of phenomenological reduction; (2) its temporally defined, *provisional* inconceivability, grasped as the outcome of a carefully controlled *a priori* method of eidetic variation; (3) its "horizonal" anticipation of and sensitivity to the confirmatory or annulling authority of subsequent relevant evidence, or, more generally, its function within an endlessly ramified network of interdependent evidential sedimentations ("acquisitions"); and finally, (4) its grounding, through genetic constitution, in the primordial, "lower," founding evidence of the intentional performances of consciousness.

It will be recognized that these requirements, sketching a "weak" version of apodicticity, do indeed delineate a distinctive, but also phenomenologically authoritative and legitimate species of evidence. Although one should rightly entertain misgivings about designating such evidence "apodicticity," this version is, like Husserl's apodicticity, both a reflective ("critical," or a priori) evidence and, for that very reason, a superior evidence. We may observe, in this connection, that Husserl unfortunately overlooked the fact that the reason for its superiority is its reflective, methodically contrived genealogy and nature. For to *see x* (to present *x* in evidence) is one operation, and to affirm that this seeing (evidence) is apodictic must plainly be a second, "higher," and specially reflective (doxic) operation. But, as such, it must also belong to what Husserl calls the "dubitable" sphere of knowledge.

[2]

IT IS HOPED THAT OUR CRITIQUE represents a compelling refutation of the strong version of apodicticity. This concept has so many ramifications within Husserlian phenomenology that any such refutation brings with it extensive consequences of great moment for his theory as a whole. There should be, however deep our criticism, sufficient testimony to the profound respect for Husserl's accomplishment which has been the constant motivation and encouragement behind our critique. The intention is, primarily, to unfetter his phenomenology: we have seen how apodicticity acts as a source of constraint and difficulty.

Husserl's great error is not that he sought to discern and to articulate with adequacy the rational principles inherent in and, what is more, truly prescriptive to experience; rather, it stems from his view that such principles, once elicited, can bring inquiry to a "final" evidence. Of course, all inquiry exhibits stages, points of satisfaction and rest, moments of decision and resolution. But these consummatory stages prepare for their own transcendence.

It would have been much more consistent with the current and temperament of his philosophical reflection, had he construed apodicticity as an ideal limit, a mere norm, at once structuring and liberating phenomenological meditation: ordering thought according to a determinate measure of evidence, but not rigidly confining it or trying to capture it in an exquisite act of mental acrobatics. Had he, in fine, introduced and utilized it in terms of the *temporality* of consciousness, he would have been advocating a norm of evidence *consistent* with the historicity of consciousness and its teleological, genetic method of clarification and grounding.

Philosophy is, as Merleau-Ponty believes, a summons to "vigilance," a personal and immediate commitment in a task to be done, but always anew, always unfinished. Nobody understood the philosophical calling better than Husserl. Yet somehow, in spite of himself, there remain in his phenomenology certain inheritances from an archaic rationalism which he could not, or would not repudiate. Apodicticity is the most salient of these. Husserl is more Humean and Cartesian than he suspects.

The plangency of Husserl's quest for apodictic first principles, his intense effort to preclude error and deception, can eventuate in an exquisite "purification" of reason only at the extreme sacrifice of existential signification, or content. "Truth" is sought in neglect of our *access* to it and our consequent obligations to *justify* our pretensions. There seems to be some special "presence" to truth that defies intentional analysis and genetic constitution. To purge transcendental subjectivity of all facticity, to attempt a grounding of knowledge in reason, the source of necessity, is tantamount to reducing the *being* of consciousness to *knowledge*. Existence (awareness) is transmuted into its corresponding essence. And with the absolute identity of the knowing consciousness which *is*, and the objective consciousness which is *perfectly known*, the fundamental doctrines of intentionality and transcendence are denied. Phenomenology becomes, then, a merely formal and abstract pursuit; it has forfeited the excitement and creativity of facticity, wonder and adventure. It has shown a greater affinity for "end results," final answers, "*having*" the truth, than for query and love of truth.

Husserl's commitment to a norm of apodicticity rationally motivates his search for a method through which it would be feasible to retreat or abstract from, and perhaps even deny, in a sense, the contingency and brute facticity (including temporal determination) which consciousness is compelled to acknowledge. In this, his attempt is fundamentally confused and misguided. For what jeopardizes the apodictic principle is the inexorably transcendent and temporalized nature of objectivity. Consequently, his eidetic method for purging facticity and acquiring the absolutely a priori is a futile gesture. So that even if we were to assent to the ideal that would overcome all "irrationality"; even if we were to demonstrate our confidence in the efficacy of reason to alembicate whatever contingency the universe confronts us with into a well-ordered system of eidetic necessities; even if we were to feel no nostalgia for the vital spontaneity of the prereflective, simply lived (*erlebt*) *existence* of consciousness—even so, we should be obliged to withhold outright acceptance from Husserl's theory. Moreover, inasmuch as the requisite apodictic critique is never truly executed, we are justified in maintaining, and precisely on criteria completely *internal* to his system, that a surd of "irrationality" persists. Consciousness eludes its own efforts to transform itself into apodictic knowledge, to rarify it out of existence. Perhaps, then, a more pliant, more self-consciously historical, but nonetheless transcendental conception of rationality would be in order, embedding the evidences of reason in the existential situations of philosophical inquiry.

Appendix

In loosening the grip an argument may have on us, it is sometimes philosophically illuminating to imagine a counterexample which, while admittedly at the extreme of probability, nonetheless will be recognized as a genuine eidetic and logical possibility. Here we see how the sheer extremity of an example can instruct us about the more ordinary and familiar aspects of experience, exhibiting them in a provocative and novel light.

Let us consider, to begin with, Husserl's view (advanced in *Ideas* I, and apparently never abandoned in later works) that certain of the "higher" eidetic regions and distinctions are capable of adequate and apodictic apprehension. Husserl chooses the absolute eidetic distinction between color and sound to illustrate his contention; and it certainly seems, *prima facie,* that he has found a clinching illustration. Now, it will be readily admitted that color and sound represent for us two altogether different eidetic regions and, further, that the evidence for their differentiation is compelling, indeed quite conclusive, by all ordinary criteria. But the point under dispute is whether or not this eidetic differentiation can be given, regardless of its high degree of universality, in an adequate and apodictic evidence. What we want to show, then, is simply that it is quite feasible to conceive a situation (or, if you will, a "world") logically and eidetically possible, however improbable, which will be such that either we should no longer wish to affirm this (kind of) evidence for the difference, or we should at least find ourselves in a giant labyrinth of meanings and interdependent possible decisions, quite unsure as to where, if at all, we ought to make our conceptual demarcations and build our meaning structures. And precisely because phenomenology is rigorously *descriptive,* it would seem to be altogether helpless in rendering a decision (a phenomenological "insight"), in this regard, that could have the status of an *apodictic* ruling. Husserl, on the other hand, gives to phenomenological description a kind of decisive power which it really cannot have: not just *showing* that something is the case but *demonstrating* that it is *necessarily* the case, as if the necessity of an evidence were a special kind of *property* that one could simply "read off," provided only that he be sufficiently attentive and disciplined.

The example proposed here for consideration is one which, in fact, has already been chosen to contribute to the demise of the tenacious distinction between analytic and synthetic judgments.[1] It derives its initial import from the scientific discovery that an amplifier, constructed to accept light waves picked up by a photocell and sound waves picked up by a microphone, will register the difference between colors and sounds only in terms of wave-length differentiation. In such a system, however, it makes no sense to speak of any absolute eidetic distinction between colors and sounds.

Now, suppose a considerable number of persons, having normal perceptual abilities (that is, perfectly able to see colors and hear sounds as we do), suddenly go deaf, and thereafter find that all the objects they were accustomed to call "red" looked grey to them. And suppose, further, that scientists, examining these cases, learned that things look red (to all of us) partly because they emit an extremely high pitched sound of which we are not aware, given our normal range of sensibility.

Of what relevance is this story for phenomenology? To be sure, it has no bearing on the descriptive, phenomenological articulation of perceptual experience, as it is lived in simple awareness. The evidence for distinct eidetic regions (namely, color perception and sound perception) remains untouched. But what *could* change, by virtue of these circumstances, is our assessment of our conceptual structurations. As before, they are experientially sustained and fortified; only now, they also appear thoroughly contingent.

Our experiences, as lived in awareness, are what they are. Phenomenology, as both descriptive and constitutive, must attempt to do justice to these primordial, prereflective experiences. But Husserl, when he chooses to confer an apodictic title upon a certain evidence, is not concerned with description or constitution in this manner; rather, he is working within the rules of a special method, totally intended for application to thematized, objectivated experience—in short, knowledge. Apodicticity thus raises the following question: *Given* that our *experience* is such and such, can we *know* that it *must* be thus and not otherwise?

It might prove helpful to entertain some of Wittgenstein's remarks on this subject:

> I am not saying: if such-and-such facts of nature were different, people would have different concepts (in the sense of a hypothesis). But: if

1. See Gilbert Harman, "Quine on Meaning and Existence," *Review of Metaphysics*, XXI, no. 1 (1967), 124–51.

> anyone believes that certain concepts are absolutely the correct ones, and that having different ones would mean not realizing something that we realize—then let him imagine certain very general facts of nature to be different from what we are used to, and the formation of concepts different from the usual ones will become intelligible to him.
>
> . . . .
>
> Compare a concept with a style of painting. For is even our style of painting arbitrary? Can we choose one at pleasure? (The Egyptian, for instance.) [2]

Wittgenstein's remarks raise many interesting and difficult questions. Prominent among these is the problem of determining the boundaries of our concepts, or (in Husserlian vocabulary) the evidential limits of eidetic regions and eidetic objects, and the corresponding ranges of their relevant possible exemplifications (i.e., particular eidetic variants). Outstanding, too, is the problem of demarcating between questions of convention, questions of "fact," and questions of conceptual analysis.

Consider, for example, the phenomenological essences described by the words "anger," "fear," and "jealousy"—which Husserl presumably would call "immanent eidetic objects"—and the various eidetic judgments which phenomenologists might want to make about them. Does it seem plausible to think we can apprehend these essences in evidences bearing the doxic sense of apodicticity (or the sense of adequacy, for that matter)? To be sure, we all know what anger, fear and jealousy are. We have experienced these mental states ourselves, in all likelihood, and can recognize them in other persons. And it might be fairly easy for us, upon deliberation, to come up with some criteria (necessary conditions, perhaps) for identifying these states when they occur. What can we hope for, then, in the way of phenomenological descriptions of the essential nature of such states? Even if it should be feasible to articulate (show the phenomenological ground of) the *essences* of fear, anger, and jealousy, it does not seem at all reasonable or conclusive that our judgments about these essences could be expressed in the form of doxic assertions that claim apodicticity.[3]

Suppose a phenomenologist concludes his investigations into the

2. Ludwig Wittgenstein, *Philosophical Investigations,* Part II, §xii. Cf. further his *Remarks on the Foundations of Mathematics* (Oxford: Basil Blackwell; New York: Macmillan, 1956), I, 113 and 115.

3. In the French edition of *Psychology of Imagination,* published but three years before *Being and Nothingness,* Sartre himself explains that one prime advantage to eidetic analysis is its power to recover apodictic evidences. Later, as we know, Sartre lost interest in essentialism, but he never subjected Husserl's doctrine of essential intuition, with its goal of apodicticity, to a direct and decisive assault.

essence of jealousy with the eidetic insight that jealousy exhibits essentially the properties ⟨*P*,*Q*,*R*⟩.[4] Is it inconceivable that jealousy should fail to exhibit all and only these properties? What if education and other social conditions should happen to produce a community of persons some of whose behavior and mental states we would wish to describe as exhibiting essentially the properties ⟨*P*,*Q*,*S*⟩, or perhaps ⟨*P* and (either *Q* or *S* but not both)⟩? The mental state described as essentially ⟨*P*,*Q*,*S*⟩ might be sufficiently similar to the mental state of jealousy described as essentially ⟨*P*,*Q*,*R*⟩, especially if *R* and *S*, though indeed essential properties, are somehow less significant than the properties *P* and *Q*. So we might be able to provide for this eidetic modification without too much trouble. But it is altogether conceivable that the mental state essentially described by the properties ⟨*P* and (either *Q* or *S* but not both)⟩ would have to be treated as a borderline case: a mental state very much like jealousy but also significantly different. Now, so long as this interesting community is a clear minority, we may be able to preserve our original eidetic judgment. As this community grows, however, our eidetic judgment could become increasingly periled. And if it should happen that the community of persons exhibiting jealousy in the paradigmatic sense disappears altogether, then it is quite conceivable that the property-set ⟨*P* and (either *Q* or *S* but not both)⟩ would become, straightforwardly, the essential meaning of "jealousy." At this point, we might of course insist that jealousy remains essentially ⟨*P*,*Q*,*R*⟩, and argue, in consequence, that jealousy simply exists no longer. However, since we have hypothesized a gradual change in the nature of the community at large, it is surely more reasonable to think that the concept of jealousy would be retained (for it is the nature of our world to favor inertia and conceptual conservatism), and that we would simply recognize the essence of jealousy to be significantly different from what it once was thought to be.

This story, of course, in no way necessarily causes trouble for phenomenology insofar as it remains rigorously descriptive of experience: as human experience changes, so our phenomenological descriptions should change. On the other hand, the situation we have envisaged, a perfectly intelligible possibility, should certainly make us suspicious of any claims to an adequate and apodictic insight into the essence of jealousy. (Apodicticity, after all, is alleged to obtain if and only if it is inconceivable that the essence in question could possibly be different from what it is.) And if all that Husserl means when he calls an eidetic insight "apodictic" is that it is a presump-

4. Notice that we are deliberately overlooking all the problems we mentioned earlier, concerning the adequacy (power) of eidetic method, as Husserl developed it, for conducting us successfully to any genuine eidetic insights whatsoever.

tively true description [5] of our actual experience, as we know it, then we are justified in feeling bewildered by his contention that variation of possibilities can provide an insight the abrogation of which is strictly and absolutely inconceivable, now and forever.

Now let us turn to a somewhat different sort of case. Consider the eidetic judgment, "All spatial extensions are (perceived as) colored." Here we have what Husserl, in the *Logische Untersuchungen*, would have called two "contents": *spatial extension* and *being colored.* If we ponder their essential connection, we shall conclude that the former is "dependent upon" the latter, and we can, in this manner, arrive at the above eidetic law. Certainly, as things are, this law is a true phenomenological description of our visual perception. But can we hold it to be an *apodictic* insight if it is true for all and only those who possess the faculty of sight? Suppose some peculiar alteration in our body chemistry brings it about that the entire human population suddenly goes blind. Suppose further that this condition is perpetuated genetically for two thousand years, and that, towards the end of the first millenium, the population lost all recollection and virtually all documentation of the visual perception which once was taken for granted among their ancestors. What would happen if, one fine day, an archeologist among these sightless people should chance to discover a stone tablet on which was engraved the sentence, "All spatial extensions are (perceived as) colored"? Would he readily assent to the apodicticity of that judgment? Would *he* find it *inconceivable,* in terms of his own experience, that spatial extensions not be perceived as colored? It is just an *assumption,* albeit one we must unfortunately be prepared to make if we hope to find an argument for apodicticity, that the archeologist should consider it at all reasonable, and should be willing, to decide whether or not the judgment is apodictic.[6] The point is, it seems perfectly conceivable that there

5. It does not seem unfair or out of place, here, to point out important phenomenological issues in regard to which Husserl himself had complete changes of mind. (1) His repudiation in *Cartesian Meditations* of the *Erste Philosophie* formulation of the equivalence of adequacy and apodicticity; (2) The question whether or not there can be sensations which are non-intentional (see *FHCC*, p. 49); (3) The question whether or not there is such a thing as a "temporal sense-datum" (see *ibid.*, pp. 102–3); (4) The shift from the *Philosophie der Arithmetik* view that we must reflect on our mental acts in order to form a category to the view in the *Logische Untersuchungen* that there is no need for this reflective act, since categorical forms can be given immediately in the exercise of a distinctively categorical act (see *ibid.*, p. 23).

6. Perhaps the archeologist we have imagined would treat this eidetic judgment as not conclusively apodictic for the same reasons that Gilbert Harman, in the essay mentioned earlier in this Appendix ("Quine on Meaning and Existence"), can suppose a world in which people would not

should be a person whose consciousness is *an authentic eidetic variant* in respect of our own, for whom it would not be reasonable to decide the question of apodicticity one way or the other, and for whom, therefore, non-apodicticity would be indeed conceivable. So if this kind of reasoning be permissible, then the argument for apodicticity turns out, in some cases, to be quite inconclusive. And if it should *not* be permissible, then Husserl must either weaken the concept of apodicticity by abandoning a definition based on inconceivability (possibility and impossibility) or else concede that, in the absence of sufficient criteria for limiting the range of possibilities, inconceivability (and thus apodicticity) cannot be demonstrated.

However, if we are inclined to persist in calling this judgment apodictic, are we ready to argue that the archeologist would *have* to recognize its apodicticity, even though the judgment could in no way describe his own experience? If so, perhaps this is because we tend to think that he must at least *know what it means* for someone to have visual perception, and *know what it means* for something to be colored, and thus can appraise the truth (and apodicticity) of the judgment purely in the light of a conceptual analysis. But this seems to imply that the sense in which *he* would have to acknowledge apodicticity could only be a sense which is intimately related to the sense in which some philosophers have wanted to call certain judgments "analytic."

The notion of analyticity, of course, is a troublesome one. Yet, even if we choose to set aside the current objections to this notion,[7]

---

recognize the analyticity of sentences such as "Copper is copper" and "For all *P*: Not both P and not-*P*," namely: although we cannot conceive of these sentences being false (and cannot conceive of any counterexamples), we can conceive a community of persons for whom, in regard to the *first* example, there is no linguistic expression corresponding to our word "copper," or for whom there is no "is" of identity, and for whom, in regard to the *second* example, the sentence "For all *P*: Not both *P* and not-*P*" simply has been assigned no truth-value, or for whom there is no obvious logically equivalent principle. Here we might say, though, that *for us*, it is reasonable to believe these sentences are analytic, but that it is conceivable that, *for others*, it should not be reasonable to believe the sentences are analytic. If we make an analogous move in regard to apodicticity, we shall have to restrict severely the Husserlian formulation, which is expressed in terms of what is conceivable and inconceivable, now and forever. But once we hold to this restriction, we have a *weaker* version of apodicticity than Husserl wanted. And of course, without this restriction, we are left with an apodicticity in regard to which the most we can say is that it is inconclusive.

7. See, for example, W. V. Quine, "Two Dogmas of Empiricism," in *From a Logical Point of View* (Cambridge: Harvard University Press, 1953), and "Necessity and Truth," in *The Ways of Paradox* (New York: Random House, 1968).

we are obliged to confront some important difficulties. After all, Husserl presumably intended his doctrine of apodictic insight in a different, stronger, and less "degenerate" sense; in any case, moreover, it is clear enough that he did not explicitly affiliate apodictic evidence with the traditional notion of analyticity.

Perhaps we should ponder the eidetic law about spatial extension and color in the light of a slight variation of our initial counterexample. Shoemaker has forcefully sketched a situation which shows us just what it would be like to discover a person about whom we should be inclined to say that he "sees" objects in space with (from a point on) the back of his head.[8] Now, if it is conceivable that some person should exhibit extraordinary skill in noting, recognizing, locating, and avoiding objects in the world around him, even though his eyes are not turned towards them and he is in no way touching them with his body, then it also seems conceivable (at least, we can say fairly well what conditions would have to obtain for it to be possible) that, since some part of the person's body other than the eyes is serving the function of seeing, the perception (and extensional individuation) of spatially extended objects could take place without any color perception of these objects. Perhaps the person in question has a patch of skin on the back of his head which is unusually sensitive to sound waves and air currents, and which can function as the organ of a kind of perception exactly like seeing, except that, of course, the eyes are not involved and the person is unable to describe the objects he "sees" with regard to their colors.

To be sure, the decision to deny that this illustrates a case of seeing (at all) is always open to us. But if the person's behavior is exactly like our own, except that he apparently sees (makes sincere and generally true perceptual claims about material objects) only when a certain region of the back of his head is directed towards the objects under consideration, it is not at all obvious why we should have to decide in this way. And if we do deny that this could be a case of seeing, then it must be because the use of the eyes is taken as *essential* to seeing. But how can this be *shown*? How can the counterexample be refuted, unless we advance a trivial (analytically true) argument that hinges on the ordinary *meaning* of the word "see"? It will be helpful to note what Shoemaker argues in this regard:

> But if, over a period of time, the person made a large number of egocentric statements, and we noticed that of all or most of these statements it would be true to say "If this is a true perceptual statement, he sees from point A," we would probably be strongly inclined, though we would not be logically compelled, to say that he does see from point A. In saying this, I think, we would not so much be drawing a *conclusion*

8. Sydney Shoemaker, *Self-Knowledge and Self-Identity* (Ithaca, N. Y.: Cornell University Press, 1963), pp. 170–82.

> from the observed facts as making a *decision* in the light of them. The decision would be to alter our criteria for the truth of perceptual statements.[9]

The important point is that the resolution of the philosophical problem raised through this possibility-variant of the *eidos* "seeing" may really amount to a decision, the adoption of a policy, or an a priori regulative principle. So-called "necessary truths," evidences with the doxic sense of apodicticity, can sometimes be clearly shown to derive their authority from the particular facts of nature we have come to think important, and too, simultaneously, from the conceptual boundaries we have drawn in order to live with these facts in a certain manner.

In other words, even if we decide to exclude the above example as a genuine case of seeing, and constitute in this way an invulnerable necessary truth ("All spatial extensions are [perceived as] colored"), the eidetic law will not have the finality and absoluteness which the apodictic principle requires, because its invulnerability rests on a decision to esteem certain facts and certain conceptual demarcations as more important than other facts and other demarcations. Moreover, what we would preserve through this decision would be a necessary truth for *all and only* those persons who have sight (in the ordinary sense); but the eidetic law would not be demonstrably apodictic, since (as we already discovered in our analysis of the blind archeologist) it would always be *conceivable* that the person to whom we have denied sight might reasonably refrain, in consequence, from assenting to its apodicticity (unless, of course, he be willing to assent to a merely analytic truth). On the other hand, if we cannot show that this example is not a case of genuine seeing, then it seems we have a genuine counterexample for the eidetic law. But there is still a troubling question to resolve *before* we can make such a decision: What could ever decisively *show* that our counterexample is not at all a case of seeing? When a person makes sincere and generally true perceptual statements about objects at a distance from him only when a certain region on the back of his head is turned towards these objects, there surely are *some* grounds which make it reasonable (though not logically compelling) to say that he sees things with this patch of skin; surely, that is, there are *enough* similarities with ordinary seeing to make it *reasonable* to say this. However, there are also *some* grounds for repudiating this example as a case of seeing, for the talent of this person does not make use of the eyes, and one *might* reasonably hold that this is what is essential to seeing, and that all other similarities are insignificant and accidental. Thus it would seem that any attempt to adjudicate the relevancy

9. *Ibid.*, pp. 178–79.

of our counterexample must ultimately rest on other (prior) decisions that settle what conditions (criteria) are essential for seeing. But this means that the argument for the apodicticity of the eidetic law would have to *presuppose* an apodictic insight into the *eidos* "seeing." And so we are led into a vicious circle. The claim to apodicticity therefore appears either inconclusive or else reasonable only in a weaker and defeasible sense.

Furthermore, it does not seem at all inappropriate to invoke here some of the arguments Husserl uses in the *Ideas* against the apodicticity of material objects. From the standpoint of transcendental logic, even the necessary truths expressed in eidetic laws are intentional products of reflective consciousness, constituted as what they are and as bearing the doxic sense they have through certain acts of consciousness. As intentional meanings, these truths *transcend* the acts of consciousness through whose reflection they are recovered and explicated. In precisely this sense, then, they are dependent upon and relative to the living consciousness which sustains and justifies them. Considered from this standpoint, it really seems no more impossible that an eidetic law should fail to hold while the primordial living consciousness which constituted and sustained it continues to exist, than that the world as we know it, or indeed all order and structure in external perception, should cease to exist while consciousness itself persists. So if Husserl thinks the world should be described as dubitable (non-apodictic) on these grounds, it would seem that we could plausibly argue that eidetic laws are likewise dubitable (non-apodictic), even though it would still be feasible to make sense (that is to say, give them a constituted sense) of their necessity.

Bringing together, now, the results of our analysis thus far, we conclude that, according to the foregoing interpretation of "eidetic possibility," the argument for apodicticity is either (1) inconclusive or (2) a question of pure conceptual analysis. Perhaps, then, the interpretation with which we have been working is somehow inappropriate or based on some misunderstanding of the peculiarly *phenomenological* character of eidetic variation. It is true Husserl observes that

> at first, even eidetic observation will consider an ego as such with the restriction that a constituted world already exists for him. This, moreover, is a necessary development. . . . [Later, however,] the ego varies himself so freely that he does not keep even the ideal restrictive presupposition that a world having the ontological structure accepted by us as obvious is essentially constituted for him.[10]

And it is also true that Husserl repeatedly detaches the eidetic variation of possibilities from all questions of fact, all descriptions of

10. *CM*, p. 77 (p. 110).

the *de facto* ego. On the other hand, the freedom of eidetic variation has its limits. Husserl affirms his loyalty to the "principle of pure evidence," which holds that evidences must be "free from all interpretations that read into them more than is genuinely seen"; [11] furthermore, he contends that "reason refers to possibilities of verification; and verification refers ultimately to making evident and having as evident." [12] And in his discussion of eidetic variation with respect to the essence of "table," he allows only those possibilities which are *genuinely possible perceptions.*[13] Finally, we should heed this obviously important formulation about the nature of eidetic possibility: "The eidetic laws of compossibility . . . are laws of causality in a maximally broad sense—laws of an If and Then. Yet it is better to avoid here the expression causality, which is laden with prejudices (deriving from naturalism), and speak of *motivation* in the transcendental sphere." [14]

Unfortunately, these remarks remain decidedly programmatic and raise more queries than answers. What is it permissible to claim as "genuinely seen"? Are so-called *logical* possibilities available to us in this manner? What, if any, are the phenomenological limits to the conceivable ontological structures which a "world" may exhibit? [15] How far does the *verification* of possibilities "in evidence" extend? What restrictions, if any, on the range of possibilities does the concept of *motivation* impose? In the *Cartesian Meditations,* for example, Husserl frequently mentions (but does not resolve) the problem of determining the limits of evidence in general,[16] as well as the special problem of establishing the "range," "limits," and "modes" of apodicticity.[17] Husserl also introduces and discusses the concept of *possibility,* but likewise fails to clarify sufficiently the limits, and therefore the meaning, of phenomenological possibility.[18] Clearly, eidetic variation is to free us from the dominion of facticity. On the other hand, we are not supposed to ascend with this freedom to the vertiginous heights where we can contemplate "worlds" that are purely logical possibilities. *What is the midway point?* Husserl's

11. *Ibid.*, p. 36 (p. 74).
12. *Ibid.*, p. 57 (p. 92).
13. *Ibid.*, p. 70 (p. 104).
14. *Ibid.*, p. 75 (p. 109).
15. Consider Husserl's cryptic remarks in *Erste Philosophie,* II, p. 213, about ontology and "possible worlds." Ontology demands, it seems, an investigation of the "disjunctively necessary forms of possible worlds." Apodicticity certainly *presupposes* the *results* of such an investigation.
16. *CM,* pp. 13 (p. 54), 15 (p. 55), and 29 (pp. 67–68).
17. *Ibid.*, pp. 151–52 (pp. 177–78); also see pp. 22 (p. 62), 23 (p. 62), and 31 (p. 70).
18. See *Ibid.*, § 25, pp. 58–59 (p. 94); § 27, p. 60 (pp. 95–96); and § 41, pp. 84–85 (pp. 117–18).

guiding criterion of *phenomenological motivation* is presumably intended to help us conceive a consciousness which "really" *could* be my own, even though it is not (and may not ever have been) my own. But *how much like* my own must it be? And how do I know that it *could* "really" be (or have been) mine? If it is *not* (and has *never* been) my own, then to say that it *could* be mine (or *could* have been mine) would seem to be reasonable if and only if it is logically possible that it be mine (be a variation of my consciousness). But then we need to know much more than Husserl tells us about logical possibility within the framework of eidetic method. Otherwise, it is not sufficiently clear just how the criterion of phenomenological motivation is supposed to guide us in excluding all sorts of logically possible counterexamples to eidetic laws for which Husserl wants to claim an apodictic evidence.

Thus, it would seem quite in order to maintain (1) that if Husserl intended an interpretation of "eidetic possibility" which would *not* authorize the interpretation we have used above, nevertheless he has failed to preclude our interpretation, and consequently has failed to give us sufficient grounds for ignoring the results to which this interpretation has led us; and moreover (2) that Husserl has failed to give his methodological concepts sufficient precision to allow for a meaningful and plausible *decision* about the apodictic claim of a genuine insight. In sum, whether we work with our interpretation, or assume instead that there is some other interpretation which Husserl must have intended, the verdict is the same: the claim that a phenomenological eidetic insight is apodictic has not been conclusively substantiated.

There are, in fact, countless eidetic judgments, grounded in phenomenologically describable evidence, which seem to require the resolution of these problems *before* we can recognize, or even understand, their purported apodicticity. Take, for example, the following insights: (1) "Objectivities accorded the sense of spatio-temporal existence must be perceived through intentional adumbrations." (2) "Temporal extension (location) is essential to (is a necessary condition for) the constitution of immanent objects." (3) "A pain of which we are not aware cannot exist." (4) "Intentional objects are accessible through a multiplicity of possible intentional acts." To be sure, these are insights which faithfully describe and explicate our experience; and it may be that, in order to see their truth, as well as their phenomenological meaning, we must submit our experience to eidetic analysis. But the question is, what are we claiming when we ascribe to them an apodictic sense? In what way are they such that their denial is altogether inconceivable? And exactly how far away from our actual experience can the free variation of conceived possibilities go?

Consider this eidetic law: "If a person experiences a pain, then he necessarily experiences it as a pain in his own body." (We might take this to be an instance of a human body which is not experienced as "his own.") Is this law an apodictic insight? What would it be like for someone to experience a pain (and know that he has a pain), and *observe* that this pain is not in his own body? [19] To the extent that we are inclined to say that this does not "make sense," it would seem that the eidetic law in question is construed as an analytic truth, *although it would be none the less phenomenologically descriptive, and in need of genetic constitution*. But to ground this law through eidetic analysis and genetic constitution is *not* in itself sufficient to show that a consciousness for which this law would not hold is utterly inconceivable.

Is the consciousness of a schizophrenic a genuine (permissible) eidetic variant of my consciousness? If so, then consider this tale about a person who is branded by a red-hot iron. Let us suppose, to begin with, that in the past, he has experienced pain, and that he understands perfectly well what pain, and the circumstances of pain, are for other people. Then, let us suppose he sees the iron while it touches him, understands that it is very hot, involuntarily winces and shrieks, and knows that he winced and shrieked. Now, it seems altogether conceivable that his visual perception of the iron, coupled with his knowledge about the pain which others normally experience and his extraordinarily acute sensitivity both to (what we know, but he does not know, to be) *his own* outward behavior (the wince and the piercing, blood-curdling cry, etc.) and to the behavior of the witnesses to this deed (their exaggerated expressions of horror, fear, and sympathy, for example) could actually induce in him an experience with the sense of pain, even though his awareness of his own body were such that he could not attach to this pain the usual sense that it was a pain in his own body.[20] Even if we *hesitate* to say outright that he really experienced a pain which he did not experience as "his own" (i.e., in his own body), we surely cannot *flatly deny*, under the circumstances, that he experienced a pain which he did not experience as in his own body. And this is why the claim to apodicticity is so perplexing. Perhaps we should recognize that apodicticity is not the full-fledged claim to inconceivability that it seems to be, and that, in consequence, it amounts to some weaker sort of doxic claim about our evidential descriptions. But if we do not make

19. See Shoemaker, *Self-Knowledge and Self-Identity*, pp. 97–98. And, as Shoemaker points out, if I had a pain which I could locate in the table nearby, that would not show that the pain was not my own (or not in my own body), but only that the table was a part of my somatic experiential field. See *ibid.*, pp. 114–15.

20. See Jean-Paul Sartre, *Being and Nothingness* (New York: Philosophical Library, 1956), pp. 55–56.

this concession, then we must grant that apodicticity, in Husserl's strong sense, is inconclusive (not demonstrable).

To see that this is so, consider what else we might possibly say here. (1) We might insist that, inasmuch as he has admitted he was in pain and *did seem* to experience pain, he has to admit that he experienced the pain he felt as a pain in his own body, for such are the conventions of our language and its concepts. And if he will not admit this, we might resort to saying (despite *some* evidence to the contrary) that he does not really know what pain is, or we might try an appeal to some explanation which postulates a pathological condition (although to do this is really a *petitio principii* which gets us nowhere). Or, on the other hand, (2) we might concede that he did not experience the pain as in his own body, and then argue that he merely *inferred* that he experienced a pain, and so he really did not experience a pain at all.[21] Thus, his refusal to recognize the pain as in his own body becomes simply a refusal to make the requisite *inference*, demanded by our conventional expectations. All these maneuvers, however, simply amount to our unwillingness to recognize a consciousness of pain which is not also a consciousness of this pain as an event in his own body. In sum, if we allow this case to be a genuine eidetic variant, then the argument for apodicticity is fatally jeopardized; while if we do not want to tolerate this case as a genuine eidetic variant, then it cannot be argued decisively that apodicticity purports *absolute inconceivability*.

21. But is it absolutely decisive, absolutely clear, that he did "merely" *infer* that he was experiencing a pain? Could it not be that his experience of pain was truly induced by what he observed in the behavior of others and by what he knew about his own (outward forms of) behavior?

Bibliography

[1] Husserl's Works

Cartesianische Meditationen und Pariser Vorträge. Edited by S. Strasser. *Husserliana* I. The Hague: Martinus Nijhoff, 1959.

Erfahrung und Urteil. Edited by Ludwig Landgrebe. Hamburg: Claasen, 1954.

Erste Philosophie. Edited by Rudolf Boehm. 2 vols. *Husserliana* VII, VIII. The Hague: Martinus Nijhoff, 1956, 1959.

Formale und transzendentale Logik. Halle: Max Niemeyer, 1929.

"Die Frage nach dem Ursprung der Geometrie als intentional-historisches Problem." Edited by Eugen Fink. *Revue internationale de philosophie,* I (1938–39), 203–25. Reprinted in *Husserliana* VI, pp. 365–86.

Die Idee der Phänomenologie. Edited by Walter Biemel. *Husserliana* II. The Hague: Martinus Nijhoff, 1950.

Ideen zu einer reinen Phänomenologie und phänomenologische Philosophie. Edited by Walter Biemel (vol. I) and Marly Biemel (vols. II and III). 3 vols. *Husserliana* III, IV, V. The Hague: Martinus Nijhoff, 1950, 1952, 1952.

Die Krisis der europäischen Wissenschaften und die transzendentale Phänomenologie. Edited by Walter Biemel. *Husserliana* VI. The Hague: Martinus Nijhoff, 1954.

Logische Untersuchungen. 2 vols. *Vol. I: Prolegomena zur reinen Logik.* Second, revised edition. Halle: Max Niemeyer, 1913.
Vol. II: Untersuchungen zur Phänomenologie und Theorie der Erkenntnis. Second, revised edition, issued in two parts, with the following subtitles:
Vol. II, Part 1: Untersuchungen zur Phänomenologie und Theorie der Erkenntnis. Halle: Max Niemeyer, 1913.
Vol. II, Part 2: Elemente einer phänomenologischen Aufklärung der Erkenntnis. Halle: Max Niemeyer, 1921.

Phänomenologische Psychologie. Edited by Walter Biemel. *Husserliana* IX. The Hague: Martinus Nijhoff, 1962.

"Philosophie als strenge Wissenschaft." *Logos,* I (1910–11), 289–341.
Vorlesungen zur Phänomenologie des inneren Zeitbewusstseins. Edited by Martin Heidegger. Halle: Max Niemeyer, 1928.

[2] Translations of Husserl's Works

Cartesian Meditations. Translated by Dorion Cairns. The Hague: Martinus Nijhoff, 1960; New York: Humanities Press, 1964.
The Crisis of European Sciences and Transcendental Phenomenology. Translated by David Carr. Evanston, Ill.: Northwestern University Press, 1970.
The Idea of Phenomenology. Translated by William P. Alston and George Nakhnikian. The Hague: Martinus Nijhoff; New York: Humanities Press, 1964.
Ideas: General Introduction to Pure Phenomenology [*Ideen*]. Translated by W. R. Boyce Gibson. London: George Allen and Unwin; New York: Humanities Press, 1931.
Idées directrices pour une phénoménologie [*Ideen*]. Translated by Paul Ricoeur. Paris: Gallimard, 1950.
The Paris Lectures. New York: Humanities Press, 1964.
The Phenomenology of Internal Time-Consciousness. Translated by James S. Churchill. Bloomington, Ind.: Indiana University Press, 1964.
"Philosophy as Rigorous Science." In *Edmund Husserl: Phenomenology and the Crisis of Philosophy,* by Quentin Lauer, pp. 69–147. New York: Harper & Row, 1965.

[3] Other Works

Adorno, Theodor. *Zur Metakritik der Erkenntnistheorie: Studien über Husserl und die phänomenologischen Antinomien.* Stuttgart: W. Kohlhammer, 1956.
Asemissen, Hermann. "Strukturanalytische Probleme der Wahrnehmung in der Phänomenologie Husserls." *Kantstudien:* Ergänzungshefte, no. 73 (1957).
Austin, John. "Other Minds." *Proceedings of the Aristotelian Society,* suppl. 20 (1946).
———. *Sense and Sensibilia.* London: Oxford University Press, 1962.
Ayer, A. J. "Basic Propositions." In *Philosophical Essays,* New York: Macmillan, 1954.
———. *The Problem of Knowledge.* London: Macmillan; New York: St. Martin's Press, 1956.
Bachelard, Suzanne. *A Study of Husserl's Formal and Transcen-*

dental Logic. Translated by Lester E. Embree. Evanston, Ill.: Northwestern University Press, 1968.

Behn, S. "Über Phänomenologie und Abstraktion." *Philosophisches Jahrbuch der Görresgesellschaft* XXXVIII (1925), 303–11.

Berger, Gaston. "Les Thèmes principaux de la phénoménologie de Husserl." *Études de metaphysique et de morale* XXXXIX (1944), 22–43.

———. *Le cogito dans la philosophie de Husserl*. Paris: Aubier, 1941.

Biemel, Walter. "Die entscheidenden Phasen der Entfaltung von Husserls Philosophie," *Zeitschrift für philosophische Forschung* XIII (1959), 187–213.

Black, Max. "Certainty and Empirical Statements." *Mind* LX (1942), 361–67.

Boehm, Rudolf. "Les Ambiguïtés des concepts husserliens d'immanence et de transcendence." *Revue philosophique de la France et de l'étranger* CXXXXIX (1959), 481–526.

———. "Zum Begriff des Absoluten bei Husserl." *Zeitschrift für philosophische Forschung* XIII (1959), 214–42.

———. "Zijn en tijd in de filosofie van Husserl." *Tijdschrift voor Philosophie* XXI (1959), 243–76.

Brand, Gerd. *Welt, Ich und Zeit*. The Hague: Martinus Nijhoff, 1955.

Broekman, Jan. *Phänomenologie und Egologie: Faktisches und Transzendentales Ego bei Edmund Husserl*. *Phaenomenologica* XII. The Hague: Martinus Nijhoff, 1963.

Buchler, Justus. *The Concept of Method*. New York: Columbia University Press, 1961.

Cairns, Dorion. "An Approach to Phenomenology." In *Philosophical Essays in Memory of Edmund Husserl,* edited by Marvin Farber. Cambridge: Harvard University Press, 1940.

Cartwright, Richard L. "Some Remarks on Essentialism." *The Journal of Philosophy* LXV, no. 20 (October 24, 1968), 615–26.

Celms, Theodor. *Der Phänomenologische Idealismus Husserls*. Acta Universitatis Latviensis, vol. XIX. Riga: Walters and Rapa, 1928.

Descartes, René. *Meditations on First Philosophy*. The Philosophical Work of Descartes. Edited by E. S. Haldane and G. R. T. Ross. New York: Dover Publications, 1931.

De Waelhens, Alphonse. "Science, phénoménologie, ontologie." *Revue internationale de philosophie* VIII (1954), 254–65.

———. "L'Idée phénoménologique d'intentionnalité." In Phaenomenologica, II, 115–29. The Hague: Martinus Nijhoff, 1959.

———. "Réflexions sur une problématique husserlienne de l'inconscient: Husserl et Hegel." In *Phaenomenologica* IV, 221–37. The Hague: Martinus Nijhoff, 1959.

Dewey, John. *The Quest for Certainty*. New York: Minton, Balch, 1929.

———. *Experience and Nature*. New York: W. W. Norton, 1929.

Diemer, Alwin. *Edmund Husserl: Versuch einer systematischen Darstellung seiner Phänomenologie*. Monographien zur philosophische Forschung, vol. XV. Meisenheim am Glan: Anton Hain, 1956.

———. "Die Phänomenologie und die Idee der Philosophie als strenge Wissenschaft." *Zeitschrift für philosophische Forschung* XIII (1959), 243–62.

Dreyfus, H. L., and Todes, S. J. "The Three Worlds of Merleau-Ponty." *Philosophy and Phenomenological Research* XXII (1961–62), 559–65.

Eley, Lothar. "Zum Begriff des Transzendentalen." *Zeitschrift für philosophische Forschung*, XIII (1959), 351–57.

———. *Die Krise des Apriori in der transzendentalen Phänomenologie Edmund Husserls. Phaenomenologica* X. The Hague: Martinus Nijhoff, 1962.

Farber, Marvin, ed. *Philosophical Essays in Memory of Edmund Husserl*. Cambridge: Harvard University Press, 1940.

———. *Phenomenology as a Method and as a Philosophical Discipline*. University of Buffalo Studies, vol. VI, 1928.

———. *The Foundations of Phenomenology*. Cambridge: Harvard University Press, 1943.

Feigl, H., and Sellars, W., eds. *Readings in Philosophical Analysis*. New York: Appleton-Century-Crofts, 1949.

Fink, Eugen. "L'Analyse intentionnelle et le problème de la pensée spéculative." In *Problèmes actuels de la phénoménologie*, edited by H. L. van Breda, pp. 54–87. Paris: Desclée de Brouwer, 1952.

———. "Die phänomenologische Philosophie Edmund Husserls in der gegenwärtigen Kritik." *Kantstudien* XXXVIII (1933), 321–83.

———. "Das Problem der Phänomenologie Edmund Husserl." *Revue internationale de philosophie* I (1939), 226–70.

———. "Welt und Geschichte." In *Phaenomenologica* II, pp. 143–59. The Hague: Martinus Nijhoff, 1959.

———. "Operative Begriffe in Husserls Phänomenologie." *Zeitschrift für philosophische Forschung* XI (1957), 321–37.

Firth, Roderick. "The Anatomy of Certainty." *Philosophical Review* LXXVI, no. 1 (1967), 3–27.

Funke, G., "Transzendentale Phänomenologie als Erste Philosophie." *Studium Generale* XI (1958), 564–82 and 632–46.

Gurvitch, Georges. *Les Tendances actuelles de la phénoménologie*. Paris: J. Vrin, 1949.

Gurwitsch, Aron. "The Problem of Existence in Constitutive Phenomenology." *Journal of Philosophy* LVIII (1961), 625–32.

———. *Studies in Phenomenology and Psychology*. Evanston, Ill.: Northwestern University Press, 1966.

Harman, Gilbert. "Quine on Meaning and Existence." *Review of Metaphysics* XXI, no. 1 (1967), 124–51.

Held, Klaus. "Lebendige Gegenwart": Die Frage nach der Seinsweise des transzendentalen Ich bei Edmund Husserl, entwickelt am Leitfaden der Zeitproblematik. University of Cologne Inaugural-Dissertation, 1963.

Henle, Paul. "On the Certainty of Empirical Statements." *Journal of Philosophy* XXXXIV (1947), 625–32.

Hirst, R. J. *The Problems of Perception.* London: George Allen and Unwin; New York: Humanities Press, 1959.

Ingarden, Roman, "Über die Gefahr einer *Petitio Principii* in der Erkenntnistheorie." *Jahrbuch für Philosophie und phänomenologische Forschung* IV (1921), 545–68.

James, William. *Essays in Radical Empiricism* and *A Pluralistic Universe.* New York: Longmans, Green, 1958.

———. *Pragmatism and the Meaning of Truth.* New York: Meridian Books, 1958.

Kant, Immanuel. *The Critique of Pure Reason.* London: Macmillan; New York: St. Martin's Press, 1956.

Kern, Iso, "Die drei Wege zur transzendental-phänomenologischen Reduktion in der Philosophie Edmund Husserls." *Tijdschrift voor Philosophie* XXIV (1962), 303–49.

Kutschera, Franz. "Über das Problem des Anfangs der Philosophie im Spätwerk Edmund Husserls." University of Munich Inaugural-Dissertation, 1960.

Landgrebe, Ludwig. "Husserls Abschied vom Cartesianismus." *Philosophische Rundschau* IX (1962), 133–77.

Lauer, Quentin. *La Phénoménologie de Husserl.* Paris: Presses Universitaires de France, 1955.

———. *Phenomenology: Its Genesis and Prospect.* New York: Harper & Row, 1965.

———, ed. *Edmund Husserl, Phenomenology and the Crisis of Philosophy.* New York: Harper & Row, 1965.

Levinas, Emmanuel. *La Théorie de l'intuition dans la phénoménologie de Husserl.* Paris: Alcan, 1930.

Lewis, C. I. *An Analysis of Knowledge and Valuation.* La Salle, Ill.: Open Court, 1946.

Locke, John. *An Essay Concerning Human Understanding.* New York: Dover Publications, 1959.

Malcolm, Norman. "Certainty and Empirical Statements." *Mind* LI (1942), 18–46.

———. "The Verification Argument." In *Philosophical Analysis,* edited by Max Black, pp. 244–98. Ithaca, N.Y.: Cornell University Press, 1950.

———. "On Knowledge and Belief." *Analysis* XIV (1954), 94–98.

Merleau-Ponty, Maurice. *Phenomenology of Perception.* London: Routledge and Kegan Paul, 1962.

———. *The Primacy of Perception.* Edited by James Edie. Evanston. Ill.: Northwestern University Press, 1964.

Patocka, Jan. "La Doctrine husserlienne de l'intuition eidetique et ses critiques récents." *Revue internationale de philosophie* LXXI–LXXII (1965), 17–33.

Pollock, John. "Criteria and Our Knowledge of the Material World." *Philosophical Review* LXXXVI, no. 1 (1967), 27–60.

Pos, H. J. "Valeur et limites de la phénoménologie." In *Problèmes actuels de la phénoménologie,* edited by H. L. van Breda. Paris: Desclée de Brouwer, 1952.

Quine, Willard V. *From a Logical Point of View.* Cambridge: Harvard University Press, 1953.

———. *The Ways of Paradox.* New York: Random House, 1968.

Ricoeur, Paul. "Étude sur les Méditations Cartésiennes de Husserl." *Revue philosophique de Louvain* LII (1954), 75–109.

Ryle, Gilbert. *The Concept of Mind.* New York: Barnes and Noble, 1949.

Sartre, Jean-Paul. *The Psychology of Imagination.* New York: Philosophical Library, 1948.

———. *Being and Nothingness.* New York: Philosophical Library, 1956.

Seebohm, Thomas. *Die Bedingungen der Möglichkeit der Transzendentalphilosophie.* Bonn: H. Bouvier, 1962.

Serrus, Charles. "L'Oeuvre philosophique de Edmund Husserl." *Études Philosophiques* IV (1930).

Shoemaker, Sydney, *Self-Knowledge and Self-Identity.* Ithaca, N.Y.: Cornell University Press, 1963.

Schutz, Alfred. "Type and *Eidos* in Husserl's Late Philosophy." *Philosophy and Phenomenological Research* XX (1959–60), 147–65.

Sokolowski, Robert. *The Formation of Husserl's Concept of Constitution.* The Hague: Martinus Nijhoff; New York: Humanities Press, 1964.

Spiegelberg, Herbert, "Phenomenology of Direct Evidence." *Philosophy and Phenomenological Research* II (1942), 427–56.

Stace, William. "Are All Empirical Statements Merely Hypotheses?" *Journal of Philosophy* XLIV (1947), 29–38.

Thévenaz, Pierre. "La Question du point du départ radical chez Descartes et Husserl." In *Problèmes actuels de la phénoménologie,* edited by H. L. van Breda. Paris: Desclée de Brouwer, 1952.

Todes, S. J., and Dreyfus, H. L. "The Three Worlds of Merleau-Ponty." *Philosophy and Phenomenological Research* XXII (1961–62).

Volkmann-Schluck, K. H. "Husserls Lehre von der Idealität der Bedeutung als Metaphysiches Problem." In *Phaenomenologica* II. The Hague: Martinus Nijhoff, 1959.

Wagner, Hans. "Kritische Betrachtungen zu Husserls Nachlass." *Philosophische Rundschau* I (1953–54).

Wahl, Jean. "Notes sur la première partie d'*Erfahrung und Urteil* de Husserl." *Revue de métaphysique et de morale* LVI (1951), 6–34.

Whitehead, Alfred N. *The Function of Reason.* Boston: Beacon Press, 1958.

Winthrop, Henry. "The Constitution of Error in the Phenomenological Reduction." *Philosophy and Phenomenological Research* IX (1948–49), 741–48.

Wittgenstein, Ludwig. *Philosophical Investigations.* New York: Macmillan, 1953.

Index